The Innovation Imperative in Health Care Organisations

NEW HORIZONS IN MANAGEMENT

Series Editor: Cary L. Cooper, CBE, *Distinguished Professor of Organizational Psychology and Health, Lancaster University, UK*

This important series makes a significant contribution to the development of management thought. This field has expanded dramatically in recent years and the series provides an invaluable forum for the publication of high quality work in management science, human resource management, organizational behaviour, marketing, management information systems, operations management, business ethics, strategic management and international management.

The main emphasis of the series is on the development and application of new original ideas. International in its approach, it will include some of the best theoretical and empirical work from both well-established researchers and the new generation of scholars.

Titles in the series include:

Handbook of Managerial Behavior and Occupational Health
Edited by Alexander-Stamatios G. Antoniou, Cary L. Cooper, George P. Chrousos, Charles D. Spielberger and Michael William Eysenck

Workplace Psychological Health
Current Research and Practice
Paula Brough, Michael O'Driscoll, Thomas Kalliath, Cary L. Cooper and Steven A. Y. Poelmans

Research Companion to Corruption in Organizations
Edited by Ronald J. Burke and Cary L. Cooper

Self-Management and Leadership Development
Edited by Ronald J. Burke and Mitchell G. Rothstein

Handbook of Employee Engagement
Perspectives, Issues, Research and Practice
Edited by Simon Albrecht

Human Resource Management in Small Business
Achieving Peak Performance
Edited by Cary L. Cooper and Ronald J. Burke

Research Handbook of Comparative Employment Relations
Edited by Michael Barry and Adrian Wilkinson

Psychological Ownership and the Organizational Context
Theory, Research Evidence, and Application
Jon L. Pierce and Iiro Jussila

Handbook of Stress in the Occupations
Edited by Janice Langan-Fox and Cary L. Cooper

The New Knowledge Workers
Dariusz Jemielniak

Narcissism in the Workplace
Research, Opinion and Practice
Andrew J. DuBrin

Gender and the Dysfunctional Workplace
Edited by Suzy Fox and Terri R. Lituchy

The Innovation Imperative in Health Care Organisations
Critical Role of Human Resource Management in the Cost, Quality and Productivity Equation
Edited by Peter Spurgeon, Ronald J. Burke and Cary L. Cooper

The Innovation Imperative in Health Care Organisations

Critical Role of Human Resource Management in the Cost, Quality and Productivity Equation

---

Edited by

Peter Spurgeon

Professor of Health Services Management, Medical School, University of Warwick, UK

Ronald J. Burke

Emeritus Professor of Organizational Studies, Schulich School of Business, York University, Toronto, Ontario, Canada

Cary L. Cooper CBE

Distinguished Professor of Organizational Psychology and Health, Lancaster University, UK

Edward Elgar

Cheltenham, UK • Northampton, MA, USA

Published by
Edward Elgar Publishing Limited
The Lypiatts
15 Lansdown Road
Cheltenham
Glos GL50 2JA
UK

Edward Elgar Publishing, Inc.
William Pratt House
9 Dewey Court
Northampton
Massachusetts 01060
USA

A catalogue record for this book
is available from the British Library

Library of Congress Control Number: 2012939096

MIX
Paper from
responsible sources
FSC® C018575
FSC
www.fsc.org

ISBN 978 1 84980 984 9

Typeset by Servis Filmsetting Ltd, Stockport, Cheshire
Printed and bound by MPG Books Group, UK

Contents

Contributors

John Appleby, The King's Fund, London, UK

Neal M. Ashkanasy, University of Queensland, Australia

Fred Barwell, Applied Research Ltd, UK

Helen Bevan, NHS Institute for Innovation and Improvement, UK

Matthew Cooke, University of Warwick, UK

Steve Cross, University of Warwick, UK

Cynthia D. Fisher, Bond University, Australia

Hugh Flanagan, ORCNI Ltd, UK

Amy L. Grove, University of Warwick, UK

Jean Hartley, University of Warwick, UK

Margaret M. Hopkins, University of Toledo, USA

Heather Laschinger, University of Western Ontario, Canada

Sandra G. Leggat, La Trobe University, Australia

Patti Mazelan, Applied Research Ltd, UK

James O. Meredith, University of Warwick, UK

Deborah A. O'Neil, Bowling Green State University, USA

John Øvretveit, Karolinska Institutet, Sweden

Astrid M. Richardsen, BI Norwegian Business School, Norway

March L. To, Hong Kong Baptist University

Editors' biographies

Peter Spurgeon

Peter Spurgeon worked in a number of universities and other sectors before joining the Health Services Management Centre, University of Birmingham, in 1984. He was Director of HSMC for a number of years, before joining Warwick University as Director of the Institute of Clinical Leadership. His main qualifications and membership are:

- B.Sc. Psychology, University of Southampton, 1968
- Ph.D, University of London, 1971
- Associate British Psychological Society
- Chartered Occupational Psychologist

Peter's main areas of interest include:

- medical leadership
- assessing managerial potential and performance
- organisational development and the management of change
- clinicians in management, organisational culture and risk management
- medical engagement

Peter has worked on specific assignments in Australia, Hong Kong, Italy, Greece, Mexico, Norway, Portugal and Zimbabwe. This work has involved advice to health ministers and policy makers about health service reform as well as the provision of managerial training programmes for senior executives. He holds the post of Adjunct Professor, Curtin University, Perth, Australia and at Bocconi University, Milan.

He has recently been Project Director of the Enhancing Engagement in Medical Leadership scheme on behalf of the NHS Institute for Innovation and Improvement and Academy of Medical Royal Colleges. He has also been instrumental in establishing the Faculty of Medical Leadership.

Ronald J. Burke

One of Canada's most prolific researchers, Professor Burke has focused on the relationship between the work environment and the individual's overall well-being, and over the past forty years has written articles for numerous academic and professional journals. In addition to his teaching and research activities, Professor Burke was the founding editor of the *Canadian Journal of Administrative Sciences*. He has served on the editorial board of two dozen journals and reviewed manuscripts for a dozen more journals. He has served as a member of two grants committees for the Social Sciences and Humanities Research Council of Canada, as Director of the Ph.D. program in the School of Business at York University, and as associate Dean Research, with the Schulich School of Business at York University. He has participated in research conferences in North and South America, the UK, Europe, Asia and Australia. He is a Fellow of the Canadian Psychological Association. Professor Burke previously held the Imperial Life Professorship in Organizational Behaviour and was a Senior Research Fellow at the National Centre for Management Research and Development, Ivey School of Business, The University of Western Ontario. As holder of this Professorship, he started the Women in Management Research Program at Ivey. Professor Burke earned a BA from the University of Manitoba and an MA and Ph.D. from the University of Michigan. After completing his Ph.D. in 1966 Professor Burke taught at the University of Minnesota, following which he joined the School of Business at York University. He has participated in over 300 management development programs as well as serving as a consultant on organizational effectiveness issues for private and public sector organizations. His views on management have also appeared in various media. An outstanding teacher, Professor Burke has frequently been nominated for MBA teaching awards, ranking first in 2001. Burke has published more than 500 journal articles and book chapters and presented more than 500 papers at academic conferences around the world. He has also edited or co-edited 39 books to date.

Cary L. Cooper

Cary L. Cooper is Distinguished Professor of Organizational Psychology and Health; Lancaster University Management School, UK. He is the author/editor of over 120 books (on occupational stress, women at work and industrial and organizational psychology), has written over 400 scholarly articles for academic journals, and is a frequent contributor to national newspapers, TV and radio. He is currently Founding Editor of the *Journal of Organizational Behavior* and Editor-in-Chief of the medical journal *Stress & Health.* He is a Fellow of the British Psychological Society, the Royal Society of Arts, the Royal Society of Medicine, the Royal Society of Public Health, and the British Academy of Management, and an Academician of the Academy of Social Sciences. Professor Cooper is past President of the British Academy of Management, a Companion of the Chartered Management Institute and one of the first UK based Fellows of the (American) Academy of Management (having also won the 1998 Distinguished Service Award for his contribution to management from the Academy of Management). In 2001, Cary was awarded a CBE in the Queen's Birthday Honours List for his contribution to occupational safety and health. He holds Honorary Doctorates from Aston University (DSc), Heriot-Watt University (DLitt), Middlesex University (Doc. Univ), Sheffield University (DSc) and Wolverhampton University (DBA). He was awarded an Honorary Fellowship of the Faculty of Occupational Medicine in 2005, an Honorary Fellowship of the Royal College of Physicians (Hon FRCP) in 2006, in 2007 a Life Time Achievement Award from the Division of Occupational Psychology of the British Psychological Society, in 2008 an Honorary Fellowship of the Royal College of Physicians of Ireland (College of Occupational Medicine), in 2010 an Honorary Fellowship of the European Academy of Occupational Health Psychology and an Honorary Fellowship of the British Psychological Society.

Acknowledgements

We believe that engaged women and men help to make organisations successful. We have previously examined ways of unleashing the talents of women and men in the private sector, the public sector, the non profit sector, and the small business sector. This collection extends our work to health care, a sector currently in the midst of wide-ranging change.

We thank our international contributors for their excellent chapters.

The staff at Edward Elgar has always been supportive and helpful.

My contributions were supported in part by York University.

Ronald Burke
Toronto, Canada

PART I

Overall context: quality, cost, productivity in health care organisations

1. Background and context

Ronald J. Burke, Peter Spurgeon and Cary L. Cooper

Health care typically comprises the largest single budget allocation for most countries. Furthermore the costs of providing good quality health care are predicted to increase substantially over the next decade. This pressure has been exacerbated by the global financial crisis and health care systems have come under intense pressure to lower (or at least contain) costs and to increase 'productivity'.

Managing health care is an international challenge (Letiche 2008; Institute for the Future 2005). Irrespective of the particular health system in each country, issues such as aging population, changing disease patterns, costly technologies and rising public expectations are common. To describe it as a crisis suggests it is emergent and specific, yet authors such as Sahney and Warden (1991) and Shortell (1992) were raising the same concerns some 20 years ago. Perhaps what is new today is that the crisis is more urgent and a response is needed.

A number of factors have come together to intensify this sense of crisis. It appears that the costs of health care systems are increasing at a rate faster than inflation so that when governments such as the UK coalition say that health payments are matching inflation it is relating only to the lower general inflation figure. The health service is in fact losing the proportionate difference – approximately 3 per cent per annum. At the same time concerns have been expressed about a general deterioration in the overall quality of care as well as patient safety issues in particular (Wachter 2008).

The process of change in health care organisations is relatively slow (Bohmer 2010). This has proved an area of particular frustration for governments as they observe individual, localised examples of good practice fail to spread across the system as they would hope. Health service staff would probably acknowledge a form of 'not invented here' syndrome and it is true that the dynamics of one setting rarely mirror that of another, but health systems simply must take up the challenge of enacting radical change and improvement much more quickly. The mechanisms for creating sustainable change are relatively well known. The list of good processes (below) is unlikely to prove contentious, to the extent that Currie et al. (2008) conclude that we can seem to go over the same ground, reporting similar conclusions but to little effect. For whatever reason health care systems just don't seem to be able to do what it is known they should do. Technical innovation alone is not enough. The process must be better managed.

Typical processes supporting sustainable change are:

- Senior leader commitment
- Clinical leadership
- Team based problem-solving
- Good information
- Ambitious targets
- Performance management
- Communication, communication, communication
- Alignment of organisation to new ways of working.
  NHS Institute for Innovation and Improvement (2010)

One aspect of better management relates to a concerted effort by health organisations to drive out waste and inefficiency. It is no coincidence that health care organisations across the world have adopted various versions of LEAN methodologies in order to try to tighten up simple aspects of product usage and expenditure. Alongside such initiatives goes the essential requirement to equip health care professionals with the leadership skills to push through critical changes. Lee (2010) in the USA and Spurgeon et al. (2011) in the UK advocate the need to ensure that doctors, in particular, encompass such skills in their training so that they, as a vital powerful professional group, can be at the forefront of creating the improvements.

THE IMPORTANCE OF HUMAN RESOURCE MANAGEMENT TO THE INNOVATIVE ORGANISATION

Health care is frequently described as a personal service and as such is highly dependent on its staff as a primary resource. Some 70 per cent of health organisation budgets are typically allocated to staff salaries. The high number of direct and indirect patient contacts delivered through this large staff pool means that the quality of the service is very vulnerable to deficiencies in attitudes and behaviours. Effective communication is therefore critical, not least in health system hotspots such as shift or interdisciplinary handovers.

Health care is a very complex business and many of the staff are highly skilled and well educated. Therefore systems that motivate and engage such staff will need to be designed at an appropriate level of sophistication. The many layers of the health care delivery system and multiple interactions make it a challenge for researchers to demonstrate directly how human resource management practice (West et al. 2006) and engagement (Spurgeon et al. 2011) relate to patient care. The paucity of this evidence may in part account for the relative slowness of health care organisations in utilising on a widespread scale leading-edge management practices and organisational processes. Human resource management can probably make a contribution to issues of cost and innovation at two levels

1. At an individual level through promoting greater engagement, commitment and subsequent productivity;
2. Better application of human resource management systems at all levels within the sector – educational, training and service organisation arrangements.

This text explores a number of examples of each of these levels, from authors around the world and in the context of different systems. Tensions within the relative cultures of clinical staff and managers in health care organisations are well documented (Mannion et al. 2005; Spurgeon et al. 2011). Medical staff in particular have been slow to rise to the challenge of developing the skills of effective leadership, preferring on the whole to rely on an assumed position of leadership based on often acknowledged outstanding technical skills. Gawande (2010) concludes that health care needs a new breed of physician leader.

Nursing is the largest single professional group in the health sector and there are disturbing indicators relating to this group, notably high levels of job dissatisfaction and intention to leave (Wall 2010), high levels of job stress (Harlos and Axelrod 2008) and the apparent link of these issues to the quality of patient care (Tseng et al. 2002). Recruitment in many developed countries is no longer easy, with a number of new work environments proving more attractive. The high levels of absenteeism within the nursing population also reduce the effective access to this key resource.

Finally health care provision today is firmly rooted in the concept of teamwork. However, putting people together in a series of sequential tasks does not necessarily constitute a team, nor do we typically make clear just what is required for appropriate teamwork behaviours.

STRUCTURE OF THE TEXT

It would seem that overall health care organisations have been more responsive to some specific problem-based issues such as quality and patient safety, than to the notion of human resource management. In part this represents the rather short-term problem solving orientation of health care, but also the rather diffused nature of human resource management, the difficulty of providing clear unambiguous evidence and frequently the relatively low status of HR in organisations.

This text is divided into three main parts. Part I attempts to provide an overview of the core issues relating to productivity (what is it in health care and how can it be measured: Chapter 2), quality in relation particularly to service cost (Chapter 3) and the notion of innovation as a potential but elusive contributor to improvement (Chapter 4).

Part II looks at the contribution of the human resource function (Chapters 5 and 6), and at a more specific individual behavioural level (Chapter 7). Finally Chapter 8 considers how management of the health care environment can create (or not) greater prosperity for change and innovation.

Parts III and IV provide a range of empirical examples of how better leadership and better management of staff respectively can contribute to improved organisational performance. The various strands from each section are brought together in the concluding chapter (17).

REFERENCES

Bohmer, R.M.J. (2010), 'Fixing health care on the front lines', *Harvard Business Review*, April, 62–69.

Currie, G., J. Waring and R. Finn (2008), 'The limits of knowledge management for public sector modernisation: the case of patient safety and quality', *Public Administration*, **86**, 363–383.

Gawande, A. (2010), 'Health care needs a new kind of hero', *Harvard Business Review*, April, 60–61.

Harlos, K. and L. Axelrod (2008), 'Work mistreatment and hospital administrative staff: policy implications for healthier workplaces', *Healthcare Policy*, **4**, 40–50.

Institute for the Future (2005), *Health and Health Care 2010: The Forecast, The Challenge*, San Francisco: Jossey-Bass.

Lee, T.H. (2010), 'Turning doctors into leaders', *Harvard Business Review*, April, 50–58.

Letiche, H.J. (2008), *Making Healthcare Care: Managing Via Simple Guiding Principles*, Charlotte, NC: Information Age Publishing Inc.

Mannion, R., H. Davies and M. Marshall (2005), 'Cultural characteristics of "high" and "low" performing hospitals', *Journal of Health and Organisation Management*, **19**, 431–439.

NHS Institute for Innovation and Improvement (2010), The NHS Sustainability Model, http://www.institute.nhs.uk/sustainability_model/introduction.html

Sahney, V. and G. Warden (1991), 'The quest for quality and productivity in health services', *Frontiers of Health Services Management*, **23**, 656–671.

Shortell, S.M. (1992), *Effective Hospital–Physician Relationships*, Ann Arbor, MI: Health Administration Press.

Spurgeon, P., J. Clark and C. Ham (2011), *Medical Leadership: From the Dark Side to Centre Stage*, Oxford: Radcliffe.

Tseng, H.M., S. Ketefian and R.W. Redman (2002), 'Relationship of nurses' assessment of organisational culture, job satisfaction and patient satisfaction with nursing care', *International Journal of Nursing Studies*, **39**, 79–84.

Wachter, R.M. (2008), *Understanding Patient Safety*, New York: McGraw-Hill.

Wall, S. (2010), 'Critical perspectives in the study of nursing work', *Journal of Health Organisation and Management*, **24**, 145–166.

West, M.A., J.P. Guthrie, J.F. Dawson, C.S. Borrill and M. Carter (2006), 'Reducing patient mortality in hospitals. The role of human resource management', *Journal of Organisational Behaviour*, **27**, 983–1002.

2. Productivity in health care

John Appleby

INTRODUCTION

It may seem surprising, but up to 1998 the entire value of the output created by government spending on the NHS was considered (by convention) to be the same value as the inputs that created these outputs. The volume of resources – capital and labour, plus goods and services – that went into the NHS was taken to be the volume of output created by that service. In such a world where outputs=inputs the ratio of the former to the latter – that is, productivity – would be forever stuck at unity regardless of any improvement in the way the NHS actually delivered its services.

The convention that outputs=inputs was neither a willful slight to the NHS concerning its capacity to change its productivity, nor a passive oversight; the same assumption was made across all government spending and activity, not just in the UK but in most other countries. Some countries assumed that government output grew at the average rate for all non-government output. Whatever the assumption, the problem had been a practical one: the difficulty in devising and measuring the output of much of what the government produced through activities and services it controlled or funded. Getting to grips with this measurement problem was important not just for the individual sectors of the public services but also for the economy as a whole. Government spending accounts for a large chunk of GDP and if the assumption that outputs=inputs was wrong (and that there was for example similar productivity growth in the public as private sectors) then the measure of overall GDP growth would be an underestimate.[1]

The lack of a proper measure of the output of the NHS (and, by implication, a proper measure of its productivity) for the purposes of the national accounts did not of course preclude such measures (or at least indicators) within the NHS. Since its inception the service had been assiduously collecting data on the number of patients it treated, attendances at outpatients departments, prescribed drugs and so on. To the extent that such measures could be considered outputs, they were at least *not* inputs. The NHS had also collected and reported on various measures which, while unlikely to be considered full measures of productivity, were at least indicative of the intensity of resource use – such as the number of patients treated per bed per year and the average length of stay of patients.

However, despite these local measures of output and productivity (such as they were), there existed no confident (and quantified) answer to legitimate questions about the overall productivity of the NHS, the extent to which it was improving the use of each taxpayers' pound each year, or the degree to which a particular organisational reform boosted value for money. Aside from trying to improve the accuracy of total GDP estimates, improving individual measures of government output would begin to help answer such financial and policy questions. And for the NHS, which from 2011 to 2015 faces its toughest financial settlement since 1948 yet is nevertheless exhorted to meet growing demands and to improve its quality of care, improving productivity is absolutely critical.

So, in just under a decade and a half, the NHS has moved from a service in which, by definition, it was impossible (statistically at least) to improve productivity, to one in which the 'Nicholson Challenge' as it was dubbed[2] became policy objective number one. The rest of this chapter examines this journey, starting with a simple definition of productivity, a description of some developments over the last decade in the way productivity is measured, how new data on patient reported outcome measures may help with the thorny issue of capturing the quality of the health service 'product', and finally the reality of the medium term imperative to improve NHS productivity as real funding flatlines post-2010 as a policy response to the global financial crisis.

WHAT IS PRODUCTIVITY?

Productivity is simply a measure of performance expressed as the ratio of outputs to inputs. How these are defined can vary; inputs could be measured in terms of the total costs or factors, or elements of the factors (such as labour) that are combined to produce an output. In turn, output could be measured in terms of the final product – a car – or elements of the final product – an engine.

As Figure 2.1 shows, outputs can be increased simply by increasing inputs (I^1 to I^2 increases outputs from O^1 to O^2). But improving productivity requires a larger increase in outputs for each given input (e.g. to O^3).

Although the terms productivity and efficiency are often used interchangeably, they refer to different (though related) concepts. While productivity is a ratio of outputs to inputs, efficiency is measured as the ratio of outputs with given inputs *relative to a maximum feasible output*

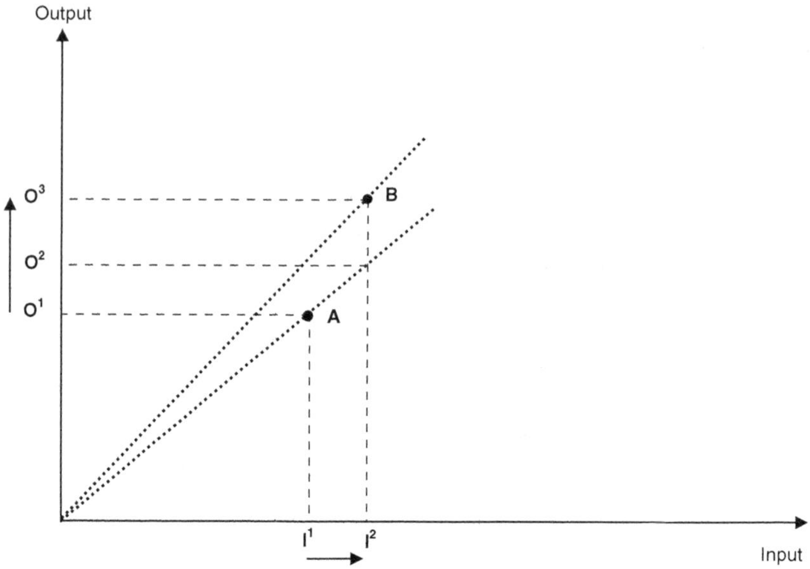

Figure 2.1 Productivity: the ratio of outputs to inputs

(given the inputs). The NHS could improve its productivity from one year to the next (as in Figure 2.1, by moving from A to B) whilst also becoming *less* efficient if what becomes feasible to produce with its given inputs increases – due, perhaps to technological or organisational changes – reflected in a shift upwards in the production function (P^1 to P^2) (see Figure 2.2). The new position, B, is further from the new production function curve (P^1) than A is from the old curve (P^2).

This simple definition of productivity can be extended to embrace outcomes – the value consumers derive from consumption of a product. It is in this sense that the quality of the output is defined. Productivity improvements may thus be a result not just of increased volumes of outputs relative to inputs, but of increased quality of outputs. The NHS may treat fewer patients each year, but improvements in survival rates (a possible measure of quality) could be such that productivity increases, for example.

PROGRESS IN MEASURING PRODUCTIVITY

While the arithmetic of productivity measurement may be straightforward, in practice there are considerable problems in constructing measures

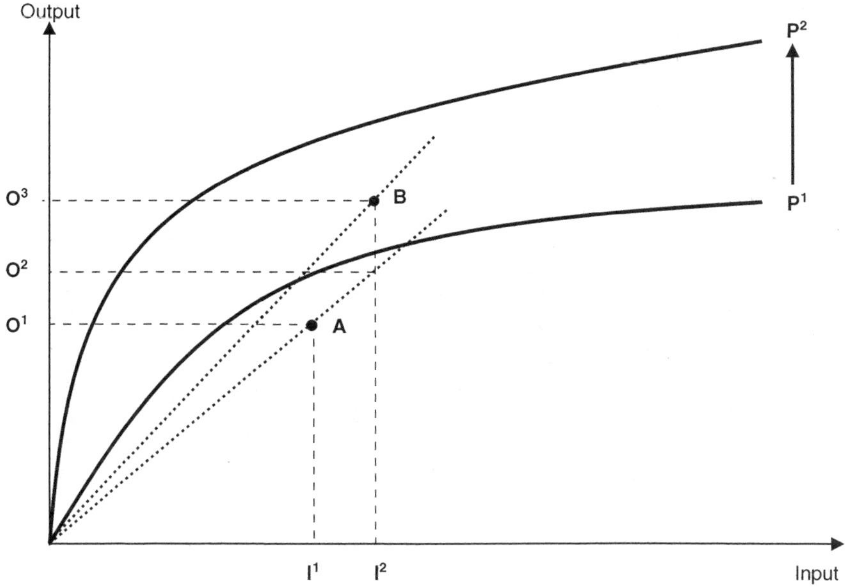

Figure 2.2 Productivity and technological advance

which accurately reflect the inputs used in health care and the outputs produced. However, the convention that outputs=inputs has undergone significant revision and over the last decade there have been useful improvements in the way NHS productivity is measured. A key development was the commissioning by the National Statistician of Professor Tony Atkinson's review of the measurement of government output and productivity for the national accounts. While the Atkinson review's scope was all government activity, a focus was on health due to its size and scale. It also focused more on ways to improve the measurement of output rather than input. Atkinson reported his findings in 2005.

Prior to Atkinson's review, the Office for National Statistics (ONS) produced a productivity measure for the NHS based on a measure of output which aggregated sixteen different types of NHS activity – inpatients, outpatients, accident and emergency activity etc. – to form a single measure. Different activities were weighted according to the proportion of the NHS budget devoted to that area to allow summation into an overall index. Problems with this measure included its lack of disaggregation (all inpatient activity – from a heart transplant to a hernia repair – was valued the same and hence the same weight in the overall output index), coverage (many services were not included due to lack of data), and, crucially, the

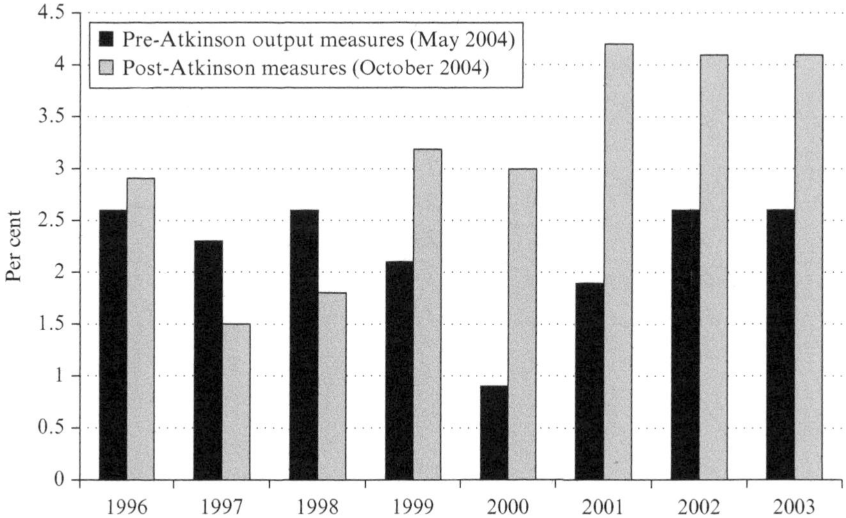

Source: Atkinson 2005.

Figure 2.3 Changing the way productivity is measured

lack of any measure or way to capture changes in the quality of the things the NHS produced.

As an interim measure, the Atkinson review team, the ONS and the Department of Health worked to improve the coverage and disaggregation of activity amongst other things. New estimates of NHS output were produced in 2004 which included, for example, a high degree of disaggregation for hospital activity – down to individual types of operations rather than just 'inpatients' or 'day cases' etc. (Pritchard 2004). The cost weights were also updated using NHS Reference Costs (cf. Department of Health 2011) and coverage of activity extended.

As Atkinson pointed out, changing the way that NHS output was measured could lead to either higher or lower values. As it happened, greater coverage and accuracy in measuring output tended to increase the value of the output index. As Figure 2.3 shows, between 1996 and 2003, the new (October 2004) measure managed to boost output in most years.

Atkinson's final recommendations covered four areas where output and productivity measurement could and should be improved:

1. Coverage: Geographic and service area (e.g. primary care and public health)

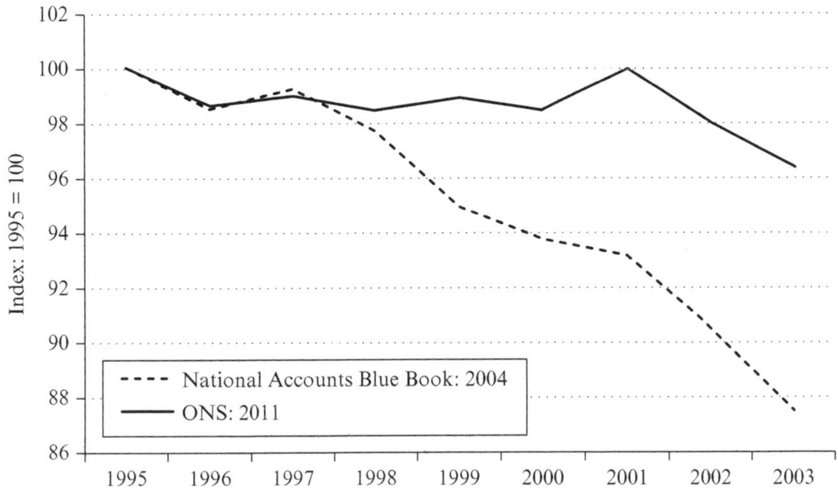

Source: Data: Peñaloza et al. 2011; Cullinane 2004.

Figure 2.4 Impact of changes to productivity measure for UK NHS: 2004 and 2011

2. Scope: Whole courses of treatment, technical change and substitution
3. Quality adjustment: Measure health outcomes, speed of access, patient experience
4. Technical aspects: Choice of deflators, measurement of inputs, triangulation.

In 2005, the Office of National Statistics set up the UK Centre for the Measurement of Government Activity (UKCeMGA) to develop and take forward the work arising from the recommendations in the Atkinson review. The impact of changes in all four areas is evident on the reported measure of NHS productivity. Compared with productivity noted in the National Accounts Blue Book for 2004 (Cullinane 2004), the measure published in 2011 (Peñaloza et al. 2011) (for the overlapping period 1995–2003) shows a marked improvement – although 'improvement' here is somewhat relative; rather than a cumulative reduction in productivity of around 12.5 per cent between 1995 and 2003, the reduction is now, on the basis of improved measures, just over 3 per cent (Figures 2.4 and 2.5).

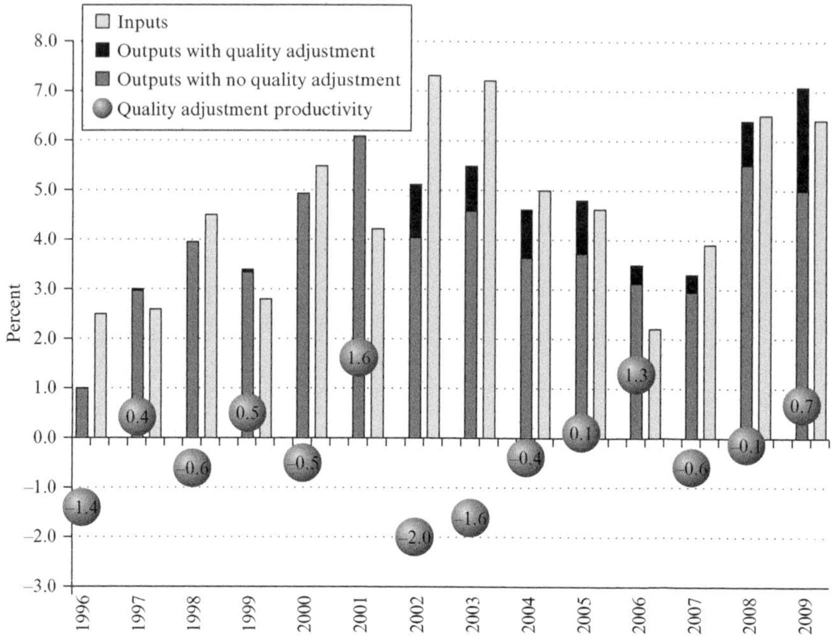

Source: Data: Peñaloza et al. 2011.

Figure 2.5 Impact of quality adjustment on productivity

Further Developments in Productivity Measurement: The Use of Patient Reported Outcome Measures (PROMs)

While considerable progress has been made in recent years in tackling some key recommendations from Atkinson's review – coverage of activities by health services has been extended significantly, for example – and though there are further steps that can be taken, there has been less progress in tackling the quality adjustment aspect of productivity measurement. Although indicative measures such as waiting times and patient satisfaction have been used to adjust crude outputs (and have tended to increase the output measure, as Figure 2.5 shows), further developments in accounting for the quality of the health service product may be afforded by new data collections; in particular, the collection of health-related quality of life information based on before and after operation patient-completed questionnaire instruments such as the EQ-5D to provide possible measures of quality that could be used to improve current measures of productivity.

The NHS in England was the first national health system to begin routine

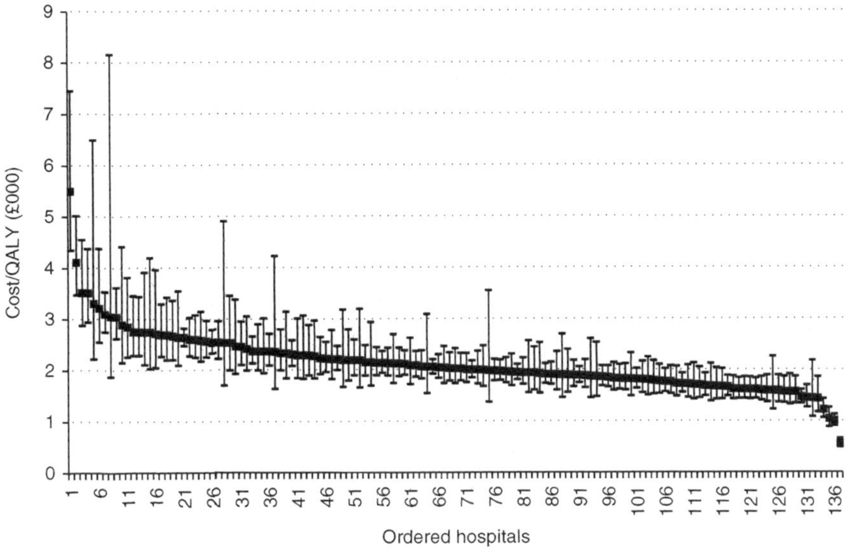

Source: Author's calculation.

Figure 2.6 Cost per QALY from hip operations: English NHS hospitals, 2009–10

collection of such data – patient reported outcome measures (PROMs) – in April 2009, for a small selection of surgical interventions – hip and knee replacements, varicose veins and hernias. Using general (EQ-5D) and disease-specific (e.g. the Oxford hip score) questionnaires, information on patients' own assessments of their health-related quality of life is starting to provide an important insight into the quality of health care from the patients' point of view – not just at a national level, but for individual hospitals and, as the data set grows, increasingly at the level of individual surgical teams and surgeons themselves.

Already PROMs data reveal variations between hospitals in health gain – albeit statistically insignificant from national average gains bar extremes of the distribution. However, the likelihood is that as the data set grows significant differences will emerge, suggesting that quality varies, and in turn suggesting the possibility of improvements in quality.

While it has been possible to, for example, calculate basic unit cost productivity measures such as the cost per hip operation using existing cost and activity data, PROMs allows more sophisticated ratios to be computed – such as cost per quality adjusted life years (QALYs). Figure 2.6 provides an illustration of this for hip replacements, using hospital-level EQ-5D data collected as part of the NHS PROMs exercise, individual hospital cost data for the hip procedures covered by PROMs and a simple set of assumptions about the average lifespan of a hip joint and patients' average change in health status over time following an operation (an assumption of general declining health).

The data reveal that the average cost of producing one QALY from a hip operation is around £2,000 - good value - but that there is fourfold variation across hospitals (driven almost entirely by variations in cost, not variation in quality as measured by QALYs produced). How the quality of hip operations (and not just their volume) per pound spent changes over time will provide a more valuable insight into health service productivity than has hitherto been possible.

THE NHS PRODUCTIVITY CHALLENGE

While PROMs have potential to grapple more effectively with the quality adjustment problem, for now their coverage includes only a very small subset of all NHS outputs. For the next few years the NHS faces an immediate and urgent challenge: to improve outputs at a time of no real growth in inputs.

As the stylised health care production relationship assumed in Figures 2.1 and 2.2 above suggests, a simple way to increase outputs (if not, necessarily, productivity) is to increase inputs. Indeed, as also noted above, this was in fact the convention for national accounting purposes. As it happens, it seems also to be the case in practice – at least on current measures of inputs and outputs. For years, as Figure 2.7 shows, the NHS has increased measured outputs at almost exactly the same rate of increase as its inputs. Productivity may not have improved (indeed it fell, on average, by 0.2 per cent per annum between 1995 and 2009 – the cumulative change implied by the annual productivity changes noted in Figure 2.5), but putting more resources in at least produced more out the other end.

But 'putting more in to get more out' dropped off the list of policy options following the global financial crisis in 2008/2009, the ensuing recession and the consequences of government policy to support the economy and deal with a growing burden of debt.

From the early outward signs of a collapse in the US sub-prime mortgage market in the spring of 2007, the global banking crisis unfolded. Financial institutions thought too big to fail, failed. On September 14th investors in Northern Rock withdrew over £1 billion in the biggest run on a bank in more than a century. In the autumn of 2007 more and more banks announced losses. In December the Bank of England cut a quarter

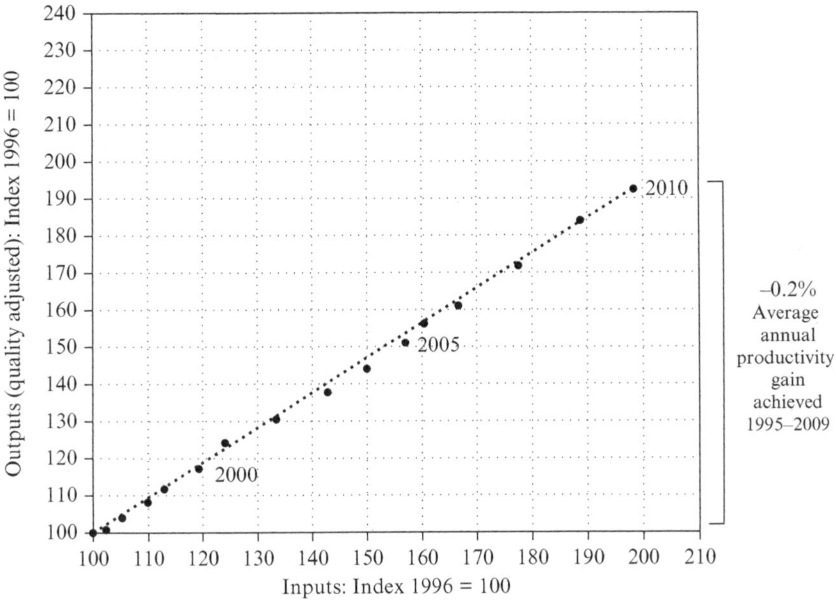

Note: 2010 figure assumed by author (long run – 1995–2009 – annual average change in inputs index (+5%) and outputs (+4.8%)).

Source: Data: Peñaloza et al. 2011.

Figure 2.7 UK NHS input and output indices: 1995–2010

of a per cent off interest rates – down to 5.5 per cent – as the scale of the economic impact started to become clear. This was followed a few months later by a £50 billion plan by the Bank to help banks facing a seizure in credit markets. By 2011, the cost of the financial support to banks and the world economy in general ran into trillions of pounds. The cost of support by the UK government was estimated at around £1.23 trillion – over 80 per cent of annual GDP. Meanwhile, at just 0.5 per cent, UK central bank interest rates hit their lowest level since 1694.

The economic impact of the crisis was revealed in 2008, when the ONS published the second quarter GDP figures. These showed the UK economy had contracted by 0.3 per cent. Five subsequent quarters were also negative and by quarter 3 of 2009 the UK economy had lost around 6 per cent of economic output. This loss will almost certainly be permanent as, while the UK economy will start to grow, it is unlikely to increase at a rate that would take it back to the trend it was on prior to 2007.

Financing the cost of supporting the banks and the economy as well as the growing gap between revenues and expenditure has meant a growing debt for the UK. Current policy to address this is essentially a combination of tax increases and cuts in public spending – in roughly 25:75 proportion. The government's 2010 spending review plans to reduce spending from its peak of 47.4 per cent of GDP in 2009/10 to 39.3 per cent in 2015/16 (Her Majesty's Treasury, 2010). This will be the most severe five-year period reduction in public spending since the Second World War (Brewer et al. 2011). For the NHS across the UK, it is likely (depending on inflation rates) that up to 2014/15 there will be small real reductions in funding – but not as great as in other parts of government due to various commitments to protect health spending (to varying degrees) across the four UK territories.

However, it is policy in England which has most clearly and directly anticipated the slowdown in funding growth, with a policy decision to improve productivity.

In his 2008/09 Annual Report published in May 2009, the English NHS Chief Executive Sir David Nicholson prepared the NHS to plan 'on the assumption that we will need to release unprecedented levels of efficiency savings between 2011 and 2014 – between £15 billion and £20 billion across the service over the three years' (Department of Health 2009). These figures were based on analysis by the Department of Health which assumed close to zero real growth from 2011/12 to 2013/14 in actual funding for the NHS and set this against spending that would be required to meet – as Sir David Nicholson reported to the House of Commons Health Select Committee (Health Select Committee, 2010) – demographic changes, upward trends in historic demand for care, additional costs of National Institute for Health and Clinical Excellence (NICE) guidance, changes in workforce and pay, and the costs of implementing government policy. It was the financial consequences of funding these pressures that produced the resultant 'gap' between actual and needed funding of between £15 and £20 billion by 2013/14.

Extended to 2014/15, Figure 2.8 places the NHS productivity challenge in historic context. With inputs essentially frozen in real terms, outputs need to increase to the value of around £20 billion over four years. Nicholson's use of the word unprecedented seems appropriate. The challenge equates to a need to increase productivity in the NHS by around 4.5 per cent each year for four consecutive years.

Other estimates support the general scale of the funding 'gap'. For example, an alternative assessment of the productivity challenge was produced in a joint analysis by the King's Fund and the Institute for Fiscal Studies (Appleby et al., 2009). While this reached similar conclusions in terms of the potential shortfall in NHS funding, a key difference with the

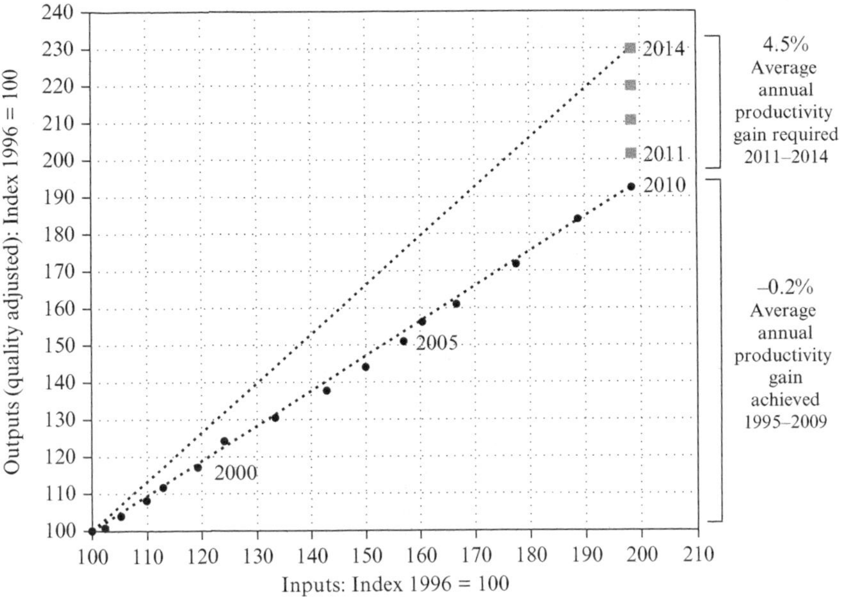

Note: 2010 figure assumed by author (long run – 1995–2009 – annual average change in inputs index (+5%) and outputs (+4.8%)).

Source: Data: Peñaloza et al. 2011.

Figure 2.8 The NHS productivity challenge

Department's analysis was the use of funding projections produced by Sir Derek Wanless's 2002 review of future NHS funding as a benchmark level of funding need (Wanless, 2002). These projections of NHS expenditure still stand as the most sophisticated attempt to date to estimate future heath care funding needs.

Wanless set out a number of potential funding scenarios for the NHS based on a large number of assumptions about demand, supply and costs of health care in the future. These ranged from changes in population and population structure to trends in smoking and obesity on the demand side, improvements in NHS productivity and improvements in service quality, reduced waiting, better use of ICT, improved infrastructure and so on. Using these assumptions, Wanless set out three funding scenarios for the NHS, depending on the amount of progress made: 'fully engaged', 'solid progress' and 'slow uptake'.

Using the Wanless solid progress scenario spending level as a benchmark,

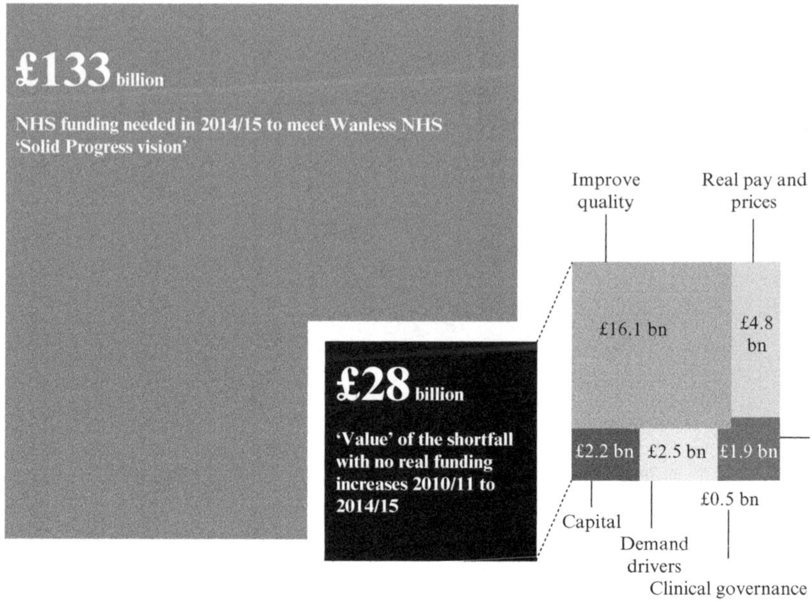

Figure 2.9 The productivity gap by 2014/15

and updating the 2009 King's Fund/IFS analysis to four years instead of three (to match the period covered by the 2010 Spending Review) the gap compared with no real increase in funding amounted to just under £28 billion by 2014/15. To appreciate the scale of the productivity challenge facing the NHS, Figure 2.9 shows – in proportion – the funding the NHS needs in 2014/15 (£133 billion), the cumulative shortfall (£28 billion) if there were no real increase in NHS funding or productivity for four years from 2011/12, and what this gap comprises.

The £28 billion gap is more than the £20 billion 'Nicholson challenge'. Both are of course only broad estimates arrived at in slightly different ways and under varying assumptions about, for example, future demand. But the latter also takes account of policy action on public sector wage growth – a real terms freeze for NHS employees which, under the Wanless-based analysis of real wage growth equates to a figure of around £4.8 billion. It also reflects a significant real cut in capital spending which, taken together, brings the assessments of the productivity gap to within touching distance of each other. Regardless of these estimates, the important point is the enormity of the figures, what really lies behind the monetary numbers and what it actually means to be more productive.

In a 1993 essay on the future of health economics research, Alan

Williams began by stating that the prime job of any health service was to be cost effective. While this may seem a rather reductionist view of the goals of health services, it in fact expresses the task facing the English NHS (one sharpened by its funding circumstances, but a task Williams was asserting as a continuous and ongoing enterprise regardless of the size or growth in budgets). Moreover, it raises fundamental questions about what it is health services are trying to do: what is the 'effect' in cost effectiveness? What is the 'product' in productivity? What is it we want more of per pound spent?

How a laudable national policy to tackle Williams's prime task is understood and plays out in practice at the front line, in hospital outpatient departments and in GP surgeries, will be imperfect. The danger is that what tends to count is what gets (easily) counted – cost – while what may be overlooked is the other side of the equation (or ratio) – the effect. Reducing costs, shaving back a bit on how long patients spend in hospital, switching to cheaper generic drugs, freezing vacant posts, postponing repairs to infrastructure – a list all too familiar to managers from previous efficiency drives – represent one aspect of the cost effectiveness task. But as Derek Wanless's approach to the question of how much we want to spend on health care revealed, reducing unit costs is just one part of the job. By far the larger part was what outcome was wanted. On this, Wanless's analysis was clear that health services needed to respond to changing demographics – changes in population size and structure, requiring increases in volumes of activity – but more importantly, improvements in the quality of care. In other words, the product was defined not just in terms of operations, or patients treated, but more broadly to include the quality of those activities and other aspects of health services that patients value, including elements of the process of care such as waiting times and access more generally.

CONCLUSION

From an assumption which by definition did not allow for the possibility of any change in productivity, new approaches and methodological developments aided by new data collection over the last decade have begun to more accurately capture how the NHS makes use of its resources to benefit patients. While the job of all health services, as Williams has noted, is to seek to be more cost effective (the price of not doing so measured in avoidable death, pain and ill health), current financial squeezes make this task even more urgent. In turn, this makes improving the way productivity is measured – in particular capturing improvements in quality – a priority.

NOTES

1. Roughly, every 1% increase in government productivity would raise overall GDP growth by 0.2%.
2. Coined by Stephen Dorrell MP (chair of the House of Commons Health Select Committee) in eponymous honour of the Chief Executive of the NHS in England, Sir David Nicholson, as shorthand for Department of Health policy to improve productivity in the NHS to the value of £20 billion between 2011 and 2015.

REFERENCES

Appleby, J., E. Crawford and C. Emmerson (2009), 'How cold will it be?: Prospects for NHS funding 2011 to 2017', London: The King's Fund. http://www.kingsfund.org.uk/publications/how_cold_will_it_be.html.

Atkinson, T. (2005), *Measurement of Government Output and Productivity for the National Accounts*, London: Palgrave Macmillan.

Brewer, M., C. Emmerson and H. Miller (eds) (2011), *The IFS Green Budget*, London: IFS. http://www.ifs.org.uk/publications/5460.

Cullinane, P. (ed.) (2004), *United Kingdom National Accounts: The Blue Book*, London: The Stationery Office.

Department of Health (2009), *The Year: NHS Chief Executive's Annual Report 2008/9*, London: Department of Health http://www.dh.gov.uk/prod_consum_dh/groups/dh_digitalassets/documents/digitalasset/dh_099700.pdf.

Department of Health (2011), *NHS Reference Costs 2009-2010*, London: Department of Health. http://www.dh.gov.uk/en/Publicationsandstatistics/Publications/PublicationsPolicyAndGuidance/DH_123459.

Health Select Committee (2010), *Second Report: Public Expenditure*, HC512. http://www.publications.parliament.uk/pa/cm201011/cmselect/cmhealth/512/51202.htm.

HM Treasury (2010), *Spending Review 2010*, Cmnd 7942, London: The Stationery Office. http://cdn.hm-treasury.gov.uk/sr2010_completereport.pdf.

Peñaloza, M.C., M. Hardie, R. Wild and K. Mills (2011), *Inputs and Productivity: Healthcare*, UK Centre for the Measurement of Government Activity Public Service Output.

Pritchard, A. (2004), 'Measuring government health services output in the UK national accounts: the new methodology and further analysis', *Economic Trends*, **613**, 69–81.

Wanless, D. (2002), *Securing Our Future Health: Taking a Long-term View*, Final report. London: HM Treasury. http://www.hm-treasury.gov.uk/consult_wanless_final.htm.

Williams, A. (1993), 'Priorities and research strategies in health economics for the 1990s', *Health Economics*, **2**, 295–302.

3. Raising quality and reducing costs – in one improvement?

John Øvretveit

INTRODUCTION

Cost saving may motivate health managers and policy-makers, but it is not top of the list for most people who work in health services. Important motivators for many are avoiding doing harm to patients, and the satisfaction of a job well done, which is recognised as such by patients, colleagues and management. Some personnel are motivated to learn about and use quality improvement methods and to take part in programmes to improve quality. In part this motivation comes from a recognition that the organisations and systems supporting their work often get in the way, or worse. Quality improvement methods help to reorganise work to serve patients better. For many personnel, being involved in a well-managed quality project can add to their work satisfaction and lead to new careers.

Human resource managers have a key role to play in making improvement more part of everyday work in health care and in enabling more health care staff to contribute. This chapter is not about how to do these things – which is well described elsewhere (Langley et al. 1996; NIII, 2006, 2010a, 2010b). Rather it is about selecting quality improvement changes that can also reduce waste and costs. The reason for this focus is that it is by choosing changes that are believed to improve the quality of patient care *and* reduce waste that the widespread support can be gained which is needed to carry through significant improvements. Such 'value improvements' unite management, clinical professionals and other health service staff and are more likely to be fully implemented (Øvretveit 2009b).

The purpose of this chapter is to describe the types of changes that are likely to be value improvements – to save money and improve quality – and provide research-informed recommendations about how to make the changes. The chapter first summarises some reports which have proposed making savings through improvement methods and strategies. It highlights their limitations and the criticisms likely to be made by clinicians and research-oriented managers scrutinising reports such as these, which often overstate the likely savings. The chapter then summarises two extensive reviews of the evidence, showing a number of factors which need to be considered when assessing whether savings reported in research could be made locally and what would need to be done to get similar results. Finally it provides the reader with an understanding of which improvements in which circumstances are likely both to save money and improve quality, and how to take such an initiative forward.

IMPROVEMENT SAVINGS – THE PROMISE

The challenges of reducing expenditure whilst protecting, and possibly improving, quality, are not something which will soon be over. There will be an increasing need to face these challenges, with both rising and changing demand, new, often more expensive treatments and health technologies, personnel shortages and demographic changes. A number of reports in 2010 provide lessons for coming years on the dangers of overpromising, on how budget constraints are normally responded to, and about what we need to do differently, locally and nationally. Later the chapter shows that improvement methods and strategies are a valuable tool, but first we consider some reports which have suggested they are perhaps the solution.

In many organisations in the NHS, the 'quality boom' of the years 2000–2009 led to real improvements in waiting times and clinical quality. In 2010, NHS managers responded to the budget crisis by a combination of 'easy' and indiscriminate across-the-board cuts. The regular targets were addressed: car park charges, color photocopying, early retirements, and then more substantially, agency staff and overtime, before cuts to permanent staffing levels and other changes which inevitably affect clinical services. There is a concern that the skills and capacity to make improvement changes, painstakingly built over the previous 10 years, were being lost. A number of reports have proposed a more strategic approach to reduce waste, inefficiency, and ineffective interventions (Appleby et al. 2010; McKinsey 2009; QIPP programme 2010; NIII 2010c). All cite areas where cost savings can be made at the same time as improving quality. Examples given in these reports include:

Improved commissioning

- Better priority setting for conditions and selection of patients for interventions
- Reducing unplanned admissions
- Promoting self care and case management

- Shift care to more cost-effective settings
- Better integration of care
- Better end of life care

Overall productivity savings

- Overall required productivity savings about 6% per year. Actual for last 15 years 0 or negative

Better organisational business processes

- 20% more space in acute trusts than required, costs £500m/yr
- Reduce support costs by sharing business services, 20–30% lower costs for same service
- Procurement – 100% variation between highest and lowest prices for common items
- Staff productivity – wide variation for consultants, GPs, community nurses
- Sickness absence – greater than 40%; reductions possible
- Skill mix – reduced costs with nurse substitution

Better clinical business processes

- Implementation of productive ward – £1300m
- Reduced length of stay – £1230m
- Reducing new to f/u ratios for outpatients – £249m
- Reduced DNA rates – £207m
- Reduced readmission rates – £108m

Improved quality of care

- Better management of leg ulcers, preventing readmission – £1050m
- Reducing HCAI – £1000m
- Reducing drug errors – £750m
- Implementing NICE guidelines – £600m
- Improved nutritional care – £130m
- Improving stroke pathway – £36m
- Reducing falls in hospitals – £15m
- Better management of diabetes patients when in hospital – £105m

These reports and more recent ones attract attention, but further scrutiny by a skeptical and research-oriented clinician or manager faced with an invitation to take part in one of the programmes would lead to a number of questions and criticisms of the evidence. This is unfortunate because there are improvements which have real potential.

RESEARCH EVIDENCE AND COST SAVINGS – THE BIG PICTURE

Two comprehensive reviews of empirical clinical and management research show that that there is great potential for savings and that changes can be made which improve quality (Øvretveit 2009a, 2010). But the evidence from these reviews suggests that realising the savings on the scale suggested in many reports is not possible in the short term, and shows that changes in financing and reform implementation will also be needed to bring about improvement. The evidence of these reviews supports some of the claims, but also leads to other conclusions about what is needed. An overview of the research gives the following picture.

There is no lack of evidence of waste, inefficiency and errors in health care, but the evidence of their costs is sparse, not strong, and mostly from the USA. There is far less evidence of the 'spend cost' of changes which are effective for reducing waste and improving quality – both a lesser amount of evidence and less strength of evidence of effectiveness of interventions and their costs. This does not mean that there are not changes which look promising for both improving quality and saving money, but it does mean that caution is needed about the certainty of findings reported from specific interventions, projects and programmes.

Even more caution is called for when extrapolating savings from specific projects to whole health systems or nations. The reports noted above assume that both the changes and the results achieved in experimental – or best-practice – projects can be reproduced on a large scale: very few are based on empirical evidence collected from many similar examples in different services. The examples cited often have the benefit of project resources, expertise and favourable conditions not available to typical services. Some of these 'context factors' are described as 'change capacity', 'receptiveness to change' and 'readiness for change' (Helfrich et al. 2009; Pettigrew et al. 1992; Weiner et al. 2008). In addition, savings are usually theoretical, rather than cash savings in end of the year budgets: the latter requires that saved time and materials are followed by a second 'cash change' to close beds, redeploy staff and/or reduce supplies ordered. The costs and challenges of these changes are often not considered, but are well known to managers. Implementation of changes to 'scale-up' to even 50 per cent of services is likely to cost more and take time, even if support is provided.

An analysis of the research also shows that savings may be made by different parties to those who spend on the improvement. Also, that short-term savings are rare and that savings often accrue only over a longer timescale. Further, whether savings are made depends on the financing system: many changes improve quality and reduce waste, but under most pay-for-item of service financing systems, a provider making these changes would lose money. In the USA changes are being made to measure and reward quality which are beginning to correct this, such as 'no-pay for never events' and some pay for performance schemes (Rosenthal et al. 2004; Øvretveit 2007). Here, there is as much interest in whether quality improvement will make money as will save money. New financing systems are also critical for the more transformational changes such as supporting self-care and reducing preventable admissions (Øvretveit 2010; Thornton and Sieff 2010). The implications are that providers, purchasers, regulators and others need to agree together how to invest in and reward changes which improve quality and save money.

Overall, there is little evidence of how much the 'spend cost' of quality improvements is, and the evidence is not strong of the cost to providers, but some savings have been reported. The stronger evidence is provided by the following studies:

- $0.7m annual savings from reducing deep surgical wound infection rates from 1.8 percent to 0.4 percent in a CQI project (Classen et al. 1992; James 1993);
- $0.47m annual savings from reducing practice variations in peripheral bypass surgery (Mayo Alumni 1995);
- $2.5m annual savings, or about 30 per cent of total patient care costs were reported as a result of one collaboration in ICUs (Clemmer and Spuhler 1998; Clemmer et al. 1999);
- $2.4m annual savings, from $20,000 reduced cost per case in an ICU using an improved multidisciplinary approach for caring for ventilator-dependent patients (Young et al. 1998);
- $0.06m first year, and $0.160 annual savings after reduced operating room cancellations and delays in one 650-bed Norwegian hospital (Øvretveit 2000);
- $0.01m to $0.6m annual savings in five different CQI projects in Sweden (Øvretveit and Granberg 2006);
- $3.3m annual savings in a US health insurer's administrative processes, due to process improvement (Miller 2005);
- $0.3m annual savings through earlier patient discharge, and delays in pathology specimen reception reduced from 13 mins to 1 min (Westwood and Silvester 2007).

Cases not reported in a scientifically refereed journal:

- $0.079m annual savings from process improvement to blood testing processes at Washington Hospital Centre (DC) Laboratory (case study by VMS 2004);
- $1.2m annual savings over two years through reducing hospital-acquired infections in the University of Pennsylvania medical centre (reported in Martin et al. 2009, Project lead: R. Shannon);
- $5.5m annual savings from reducing time patients in ICU were on ventilators (Intermountain health care, reported in Martin et al. 2009);
- $0.3m annual savings from reduced re-hospitalisations intervention in one Colorado health system.

EVIDENCE-BASED LOCAL STRATEGY TO SAVE THROUGH IMPROVEMENT

Local strategies can be more effective if they are based on good evidence of effectiveness of similar changes elsewhere. But other ingredients are needed to choose and carry forward a change which will successfully reduce costs and improve quality. The details of how to use quality methods and project management after a change is chosen are described in Langley et al. 1996, and NIII 2006, 2010a, b. Here, we consider the overall steps and the type of knowledge needed to carry out a successful value improvement.

How Can Providers Ensure Saving Through Quality Improvement?

The available evidence suggests that savings are possible through careful choice of change solutions, skilful implementation using quality methods and attention to the political and people aspects of change. The chance of success is higher if there are certain enabling conditions, such as financial incentives:

- choose improvements already proven to make services better for patients and reduce costs, especially in a similar service;
- where there is little research, use reported experiential evidence to guide action, but speak personally to the implementers and ask what helped and hindered – be positive-skeptical;
- make your own estimates of the current poor quality cost, the spend cost for a 50% solution, when the spend costs will start paying for themselves (time to pay-off) and the annual potential savings. Then track these costs. Research has shown this can be done well enough for practical purposes using routinely available data;

- adapt the change and manage implementation skillfully, especially the people aspect, using the methods and others' expertise and experience;
- measure and monitor progress and make corrections according to changing circumstances;
- join with others to change financial systems, and other external hindrances to help you invest in changes and build improvement capacity.

Part 1: Choosing a Cost-Saving Improvement

The first step involves gathering knowledge about, and ideally data on, the top five to ten safety and quality deficiencies in the service. Some information can come from formal or informal reports by personnel, some from patient complaints and satisfaction studies, and some from quality and safety indicator data collected by the service. The aim is to identify how many patients are affected by this problem and the severity of the problem, and to make the top 10 list.

The second step is to assess whether any of these safety and quality deficiencies are also likely to waste time and resources in the service, and estimate how much time and money they waste. This gives another top 10 list starting with the most costly.

A problem may be serious and affect many patients, and also very costly, but this does not mean it should be chosen as the subject of an improvement project or strategy. A third consideration has to be part of the choice equation: the effectiveness and cost of changes locally which could reduce this problem by 50 per cent. A third list is needed which shows possible evidence-based improvements from the research for the problem and the likely cost to make the improvement successfully – the latter requires a combination of what the research suggests and what resources people locally think may be needed.

When looking at the research and other reports such as those noted above, some of the considerations in choosing a proposed cost-saving improvement are:

- What is the strength of evidence about quality and financial outcomes?
- At the study site(s), what was the investment and expertise available to make the change, was this costed, and would this be available elsewhere?
- Were savings theoretical, in terms of staff time or materials, or as cash in end-of-year budgets? If the latter, what was the cost of any

second 'cash change' to realise the savings? Who made the savings and when?

- How much do the savings depend on the financing and regulation system: are investment resources available, what is the revenue payment system and do purchasers or regulators assess and reward quality or penalise for poor quality?

Part 2: Planning and Implementation

Finance for making an improvement change and finance to reward it are two 'environmental conditions' for saving from improving quality. But there are other conditions which are critical for effective implementation, and which affect the cost of implementing the change.

Before savings can be made, an effective change has to be carried out. Research has found that change to provider behaviour and organisation in health care is difficult. There are many internal and external constraints, and few enablers to implementing change. There is a limited 'change capacity' in the experience, skills, and systems of the average provider, and often not a 'change-ready' or 'receptive' culture.

There is some evidence that the specific constraints differ according to the type of improvement and type of provider organisation. The constraints to consistent hand hygiene to reduce infections are different to those for implementing a computer physician order entry system to reduce adverse drug events, or to redesign a pathway process for stroke patients. At a high level of abstraction, similar categories of constraints, such as lack of leadership or of resources, recur in the research reports. The challenges to making quality improvement in health care have been well documented and will not be repeated in detail here (IOM 2000; Berwick 1989, 1996; Øvretveit 1992, 2003, 2007).

It is only recently that more empirical research has become available about the context hindrances and helpers for effective improvement. The following summarises one study to show some of the evidence discovered in the search to answer this question. This is the review by Johnston et al. (2000) of research into clinical audit. This review found the barriers most often reported were fear of litigation, hierarchical and territorial suspicions, diminished clinical ownership, professional isolation, lack of resources, lack of expertise in project design and analysis, problems between groups and group members, lack of an overall plan for auditing, and 'organisational impediments'. The source of and solutions to the barriers are at different levels of the health system.

The current thinking, supported by some evidence, can be summarised as:

evidence of effective change + supportive environment

+ effective implementation = improvement

This means that effective improvement is achieved by choosing a change proven elsewhere and implementing it effectively in a supportive context. The challenges for an ordinary service in doing this can be summarised, from the research into different types of improvement, as the following:

Information

- a lack of local service information to identify and then prioritise quality problems (leading to choice of too-difficult problems, or ones not considered important by personnel/implementers, or not organisationally significant);
- lack of information about efficacy or local effectiveness of a solution to allow prioritisation of quality work (a service needs to choose a solution that can be effectively implemented locally, but good evidence is lacking to make this choice, and is 'crowded out' by publicity about atypical demonstration projects);
- a lack of quality comparison data or its use by patients or providers, or no negative consequences resulting from comparisons (e.g. through no choice of alternatives).

Uncertainty and skill deficiencies

- uncertainty, underestimation, or skepticism about the likely amount of time and effort required to implement and the likely results;
- lack of skills or time for improvement in an ordinary service or easy access to facilitation and support to make the change effectively;
- unfamiliarity with how to apply change or quality methods and lack of data or capacity to gather and analyse data.

Other urgent demands

- lack of time, skills and motivation to do all of the above, in the face of urgent other demands. Immediate patient needs trump long term systematic work which has uncertain results.

As regards 'improvement capacity' (a term rarely defined), a telephone survey by Walley et al. in 2006 of one senior manager in 19 trusts and 10 PCTs responsible for process improvement found capacity in acute trusts to be 'patchy, with some organisations having highly developed capability which is applied in many parts of the organisation, while others have very limited improvement skills and capacity.' They found 'only limited improvement capability in most PCTs' and that two Trusts stated that the costs of improvement could not be afforded. Other findings were,

- neither Acute trusts nor PCTs had 'clinical systems improvement culture or techniques embedded in their organisations';
- improvements were not linked to the organisation's strategy;
- 'command and control styles' hindered engagement of front line staff in service improvement;
- traditional training methods which were ineffective and did not use interactive learning.

Enabling Factors for Improvement

Many of the enabling factors found in research were the absence of the constraints and barriers noted above. We should not generalise from factors which enabled one type of improvement to others, but Johnston's study shows some that are frequently found for studies of many types of improvement. Johnston's review of studies of clinical audit methods found the main facilitating factors were modern medical records systems, effective training, dedicated staff, protected time, structured programmes, and a dialogue between purchasers and providers (Johnston et al. 2000). Similar in some respects, Walley et al. (2006) found the trusts most successful in improvement showed:

- senior management with awareness of the process and systems issues that they face;
- strong leadership able to implement difficult and sensitive change and harness staff-driven process improvement;
- a workforce receptive to new ideas, or not suffering 'change fatigue';
- strategies that have reconciled conflicting priorities and tensions between short- and long-term improvement pressures;
- a critical mass of people trained in the use of improvement tools and techniques.

One plausible enabling factor, but for which there is no evidence of effectiveness, is more research-based guidance to managers and implementers to choose, design and implement cost saving improvements. There is a reasonable amount of evidence about the rates and costs of poor quality, and this gives a good guide to the likely costs for an average provider. However there is less evidence of the effectiveness and spend costs of solutions, and some evidence that this is different for different providers. There is even less evidence to guide providers in how to adapt and implement improvements to ensure savings in their local service, and little experience-based support to advise.

The Boaden et al. (2008) review of QI approaches concludes that, 'While a number of lists of success factors have been produced, some of which are based on extensive empirical evidence, it is clear that the main issue is the way in which the improvement is implemented, rather than the nature of the improvement itself.'

CONCLUSIONS

Quality improvement methods have the potential to save money and reduce avoidable suffering for patients. Research shows the need for a questioning and considered approach when projecting savings shown in projects which may not have been scientifically evaluated. Only some changes show strong evidence in local sites or in many sites for quality improvement and cost savings. To ensure that efforts to improve quality and save money are effective, decision-makers would be advised to start with changes with the best evidence, and draw also on research into implementation and the supportive contexts needed for successful changes of these types (Grol et al. 2007). Promising improvements should not be ignored, but should be implemented using this knowledge and using evaluation approaches which also help implementation by providing timely feedback to implementers (Øvretveit 2002). The competences and knowledge in quality improvement built in the last 10 years will now be tested, and national initiatives and programmes are needed to mobilise this resource for the dual aim of improving quality and reducing waste. This dual aim is important to unite the different parties who will need to work hard and persistently to make the changes necessary to improve and transform health care and the NHS. However, the evidence points to the need for a considered, research-informed, targeted and strategic approach to change, which recognises the challenges in implementing proven or promising changes more widely.

REFERENCES

Appleby, J., C. Ham, C. Imison and M. Jennings (2010), *Improving NHS Productivity: More With the Same not More Of the Same*, London: Kings Fund.

Berwick, D.M. (1989), 'Continuous improvement as an ideal in health care', *New England Journal of Medicine*, **320** (1), 53–56.

Berwick, D.M. (1996), 'Improving healthcare', *British Medical Journal*, **312**, 605–18.

Boaden, R., G. Harvey, C. Moxham and N. Proudlove (2008), *Quality Improvement: Theory and Practice in Healthcare*, National Library for Health, NHS Institute for Innovation and Improvement, University of Warwick. www.institute.nhs.uk/qualityimprovement.

Classen, D.C., R.S. Evans, S.L. Pestotnik, S.D. Horn, R.L. Menlove and J.P. Burke (1992), 'The timing of prophylactic administration of antibiotics and the risk of surgical-wound infection', *New England Journal of Medicine*, **326**, 281–286.

Clemmer, Terry P., and Vicki J. Spuhler (1998) 'Developing and gaining acceptance for patient care protocols', *New Horizons*, **6** (1), 12–19 (Society of Critical Care Medicine).

Clemmer, Terry P., Vicki J. Spuhler, Thomas A. Oniki and Susan D. Horn (1999), 'Results of a collaborative quality improvement program on outcomes and costs in a tertiary critical care unit', *Crit Care Med*, **27** (9), 1768–1774.

Grol, R.P., M.C. Bosch, M.E. Hulscher, M.P. Eccles and M. Wensing (2007), 'Planning and studying improvement in patient care: the use of theoretical perspectives', *Milbank Q*, **85** (1), 93–138.

Helfrich, C., Y. Li, N. Sharp and A. Sales (2009), 'Organizational readiness to change assessment (ORCA): development of an instrument based on the Promoting Action on Research in Health Services (PARIHS) framework', *Implementation Science*, **4** (38), doi:10.1186/1748-5908-4-38.

IOM (2000), Committee on Quality of Health Care in America, 'Crossing the quality chasm: a new health system for the 21st century', Institute of Medicine, Washington, DC: National Academy Press.

James, B.C. (1993), 'Quality improvement in the hospital: managing clinical processes', *The Internist*, **34** (11), 13, 17.

Johnston, G. et al. (2000), 'Reviewing audit: barriers and facilitating factors for effective clinical audit', *Quality in Health Care*, **9**, 23–36.

Langley, G., K. Nolan, T. Nolan, C.L. Norman, and L.P. Provost (1996), *The Improvement Guide*, San Francisco: Jossey-Bass.

Martin, L.A., C.W. Neumann, J. Mountford, M. Bisognano and T.W. Nolan (2009), 'Increasing efficiency and enhancing value in health care: ways to achieve savings in operating costs per year', IHI Innovation Series white paper, Cambridge, MA: Institute for Healthcare Improvement. Available at: www.IHI.org

Mayo Alumni (1995), 'Can we be doing better', Fall, 7.

McKinsey & Company (2009), 'Achieving world class productivity in the NHS 2009/10–2013/14: detailing the size of the opportunity', online. Available at: www.dh.gov.uk/prod_consum_dh/groups/dh_digitalassets/documents/digitalasset/dh_116521.pdf (accessed 25 June 2010).

Miller, D. (ed.) (2005), *Going Lean in Healthcare*, in Institute for Healthcare Improvement (ed.), Innovation Series, Cambridge, MA: Institute for Healthcare Improvement.

NIII (2006), 'Delivering quality and value. Focus on: productivity and efficiency', NHS Institute for Innovation and Improvement. www.institute.nhs.uk.

NIII (2010a), 'The Productive Series', NHS Institute for Innovation and Improvement. Available at: www.institute.nhs.uk (accessed 21 May 2010).

NIII (2010b), 'Return on investment (ROI) calculator', National Institute for

Innovation and Improvement. http://www.institute.nhs.uk/quality_and_service_improvement_tools/quality_and_service_improvement_tools/Return_on_Investment_%28ROI%29_calculator.html (accessed 19 May 2010).

NIII (2010c), 'Focus on productivity and efficiency', NHS Institute for Innovation and Improvement. Available at: www.institute.nhs.uk (accessed 21 May 2010).

Øvretveit, J. (1992), *Health Service Quality*, Oxford: Blackwell Scientific.

Øvretveit, J. (2000), 'The economics of quality – a practical approach', *International Journal of Health Care Quality Assurance*, **13**, (5), 200–207.

Øvretveit, J. (2002), *Action Evaluation of Health Programmes and Change. A Handbook for a User Focused Approach*, Oxford: Radcliffe Medical Press.

Øvretveit, J. (2003), 'What is the best strategy for improving quality and safety of hospitals – a review and synthesis of the evidence', Copenhagen: WHO.

Øvretveit, J. (2007), 'Economics and effectiveness of interventions for improving quality and safety of health care – a review of research', available from Karolinska Institutet, Medical Management Centre, Stockholm.

Øvretveit, J. (2009a), 'Does improving quality save money? A review of evidence of which improvements to quality reduce costs for health service providers', London: The Health Foundation. http://www.health.org.uk/publications/research_reports/does_quality_save.html

Øvretveit, J. (2009b), *Leading Evidence Informed Value Improvement in Health Care*, Chichester, UK: Kingsham Press.

Øvretveit, J. (2010), 'Does improving care coordination save money: a review of research', London: The Health Foundation. www.health.org.uk.

Øvretveit, J. and C. Granberg (2006), 'Testing quality costing models: a report of the 16-month experience of 5 projects', available from Karolinska Institutet, Medical Management Centre, Stockholm.

Pettigrew, A., E. Ferlie and L. McKee (1992), 'Receptive and non-receptive contexts for change', Chapter 9 in A. Pettigrew, E. Ferlie and L. McKee, *Shaping Strategic Change: The Case of the National Health Service*, London: Sage, pp. 217–299.

QIPP (2010), 'The NHS Quality, Innovation, Productivity and Prevention Challenge: an introduction for clinicians from UK Department of Health', www.dh.gov.uk.

Rosenthal, M.B., R. Fernandopulle, H.R. Song and B. Landon (2004), 'Paying for quality: providers' incentives for quality improvement', *Health Affairs*, **23** (2), 127–141.

Thornton, S., and A. Sieff (2010), 'The patient will see you now', *Health Service Journal Supplement*, 24 June, 1.

VMS (2004), 'Hospital lab uses Six Sigma to reduce turnaround time and improve quality', ValuMetrix Services case study, Raritan, NJ: Ortho-Clinical Diagnostics, Inc. Available at: http://www.valumetrixservices.com/pdf/WHC_CaseStudy(final).pdf.

Walley, P., J. Rayment and M. Cooke (2006), 'Clinical systems improvement in NHS hospital trusts and their PCTs – a snapshot of current practice', University of Warwick/NIII.

Weiner, B.J., H. Amick and S.Y.D. Lee (2008), 'Review: conceptualization and measurement of organizational readiness for change. A review of the literature in health services research and other fields', *Medical Care Research and Review*, **65** (4), 379–436.

Westwood, N., and K. Silvester (2007), 'Eliminate NHS losses by adding Lean and some Six Sigma', *Operations Management*, **33** (5), 26–30.

Young, M.P., V.J. Gooder, M.H. Oltermann, C.B. Bohman, T.K. French and B.C. James (1998), 'The impact of a multidisciplinary approach on caring for ventilator-dependent patients', *International Journal for Quality in Health Care*, **10**, 15–26.

4. A trilogy for health care improvement: quality, productivity and innovation

Helen Bevan

In this chapter we examine critical issues of quality and productivity improvement through the lens of innovation. The aim is to get insight into the potential of innovation as a driver of change in the context of the quality and productivity challenges faced by England's National Health Service (NHS).

Whilst this chapter focuses on the specific English context, the leaders of health care organisations and systems across the world are grappling with the same issues: how to deliver effective, accessible health care when finances are constrained (Dare and Macaulay 2011). Whether the health care system is funded through direct tax or insurance schemes or private payers, health care leaders globally face the same triple challenges of an aging population, new technology and rising expectations of people who use services. Looking forward, this means that the need to think substantially differently and *innovate* in the way that we plan, commission, design and deliver health care services has never been greater than it is now wherever we are operating across the world.

WHY WE NEED INNOVATION FOR QUALITY AND PRODUCTIVITY IMPROVEMENT

There are multiple definitions of the term 'innovation' and variations as to what is and isn't included in the process of 'innovating' (Stone et al. 2008). For the purposes of this chapter we use the definition 'Doing things differently and doing different things' (quoted in Maher 2011). Innovation is a process that converts ideas and knowledge into benefits for people and organisations. Without innovation, the costs of public services such as health tend to rise more quickly than those for the rest of the economy (Mulgan and Albury 2003). At times when the existing patterns of health care spending in many health care systems are projected to exceed the available resources, health care leaders face clear choices: the first is to contain costs by cutting back on services or require often overstretched staff to work even harder. There is an alternative approach. It involves thinking differently, often in a radical manner, about the way that services can be delivered within available resources and taking action (innovating) to design and deliver services in different ways (Bessant et al. 2010).

In the context of England's National Health Service, there is also a more fundamental issue at play. British people appreciate and take for granted the availability of a comprehensive and accessible health system, free at the point of delivery. They regard the NHS as one of Britain's most precious 'national treasures' (Wind-Cowie and Gregory 2011). As David Nicholson, the chief executive of the NHS, has described the situation in a review of innovation within the health service:

> The NHS is a national success story. It is woven into the fabric of our society, and is a public expression of our social values. It is part and parcel of our national DNA. It touches all of us and all of us have a stake in its future. For more than 60 years the NHS has been there when we need it, nurturing and sustaining our health, caring for us in need, extending our lives. It remains true to its founding principles and to its unique system of primary care, but in other ways it has transformed itself through the strength of its research and the skill of its staff. (Department of Health 2011a, p. 4)

The challenging economic climate in which the NHS finds itself is not a short-term phenomenon: financial constraint is likely to remain a constant feature of the NHS for many years to come (Her Majesty's Treasury 2011). In the past, NHS services were expanded and improved as a result of additional resources being made available by the UK government (Appleby et al. 2009). This is unlikely to occur again in the near future given budgetary and policy constraints. As pressures on the health system increase, there is probably only one real choice in terms of retaining and expanding the comprehensive NHS services that the country has grown to expect. That is to redesign the way that people are supported in their health and health care. This is spelt out in the NHS review of innovation:

> It is widely accepted that more of the same will not do. More radical changes in the way services are delivered and how people work will be required. We need to plot a sustainable course for the future of the NHS. Innovation can help provide the route-map, improving quality at the same time as driving productivity and efficiency in a difficult financial environment. (Department of Health 2011a, p. 9)

In other words, we need to fundamentally rethink the relationship between quality, productivity and innovation.

THINKING DIFFERENTLY ABOUT QUALITY AND PRODUCTIVITY

Innovation, doing things differently, has a critical pre-requisite: *thinking differently* (Maher et al. 2007). Innovation is the outcome of a process of thinking more creatively, seeing potential for change and connections that were not apparent before (Serrat 2009). It was 'thinking differently' that led to the creation of the NHS more than 60 years ago. Since that time, people who have cared passionately for the ideals of the NHS have consistently seen the need to think differently to meet the challenges of an environment that is ever changing (Maher et al. 2007). And the current situation is no different.

This process of 'thinking differently' starts with our ability to free our minds to new possibilities (Maher 2009). So we should explore ways of challenging our mental model about the connection between quality and productivity. The seminal definition of NHS 'quality' comes from the report of the NHS Next Stage Review, led by Lord Ara Darzi, Minister of Health, published in 2008 (Darzi 2008). It describes quality as having three components: patient safety (quality care is safe and provided in a clean environment and minimises avoidable harm to patients), patient experience (which enhances compassion, dignity and respect) and effectiveness of care (measured by clinical outcomes, higher rates of survival and clinical improvement, patient reported outcome measures and lower complication rates). Moreover, Darzi specified that quality should not just be an aspiration but should become the central operating principle of the NHS. The *Next Stage Review* announced that the time had come to think differently; to 'move from an NHS that has rightly focused on increasing the quantity of care to one that focuses on improving the quality of care'.

Despite a change in government and new policy directions, this central focus on quality has remained at the core of the strategic decisions made about the NHS at the highest levels of government. In fact, the emphasis on quality as a driver of change has been expanded since Lord Darzi's comprehensive review. The most recent Operating Framework for the NHS specifies the need to move to a system in which 'quality and outcomes drive everything we do'. It describes a focus on 'clinical outcomes, including the reduction of health inequalities, to drive a change in culture, behaviour and the way we deliver clinical services' (Department of Health 2011b).

'Productivity' can be defined in standard economic terms as the ratio between the volume of resources (inputs) going into a system (in this case the NHS) and the quantity of health care provided (outputs), adjusted for relative costs and some aspects of quality (Comptroller and Auditor General's Report 2011). Data from the Office for National Statistics suggest that since 2000, whilst there has been a significant increase in investment in NHS services, NHS productivity has fallen year by year. Taxpayers have seen a better quality NHS as a result of this additional investment, for instance through reductions in hospital waiting times and improvements in care for people with cancer and heart disease. However, they have witnessed less overall outcome activity per taxpayer pound in return for the extra investment (House of Commons Committee of Public Accounts 2011).

This trend will need to be reversed and productivity will need to rise sharply if the NHS system is to deliver its goals within the financial resources that are likely to be available. Economic analysts suggest that a year-on-year NHS productivity increase of around 6 per cent will be required in coming years to meet the anticipated growth in demand, in line with present projections based on population and age profile data (Appleby et al. 2009). The level of likely year on year compound cost reduction is unprecedented in the experience of any health care system, anywhere in the world (as quoted by Stephen Dorrell, Chair of the Health Select Committee, 11 November 2010, Health Service Journal Summit). However, amidst this change to budgetary limitations, there is potential to create significant productivity gains across the NHS – if creative thinking and innovative strategies can be effectively employed.

Certain terms tend to be used interchangeably by NHS leaders. For example, we tend to refer to the phrases 'create value', 'improve efficiency' and 'reduce costs' on an equivalent basis. 'Value', another critical term, defines the relationship between costs and outcomes. So a 'high value' NHS intervention is one that delivers the most effective care within the least possible outlay of resources. For instance, by tackling variation in the way health care services are used across the country that cannot be explained by differences in patient illnesses or patient preferences, we maximise value and productivity by transferring resources (inputs) from lower value to higher value interventions (Department of Health 2011c). In terms of the relationship between productivity and efficiency, productivity is a specific measure of the efficiency of the NHS system in converting inputs (people, technology, materials etc.) into outputs and outcomes. Being productive is not necessarily about working harder, but about enabling the people and resources of the system to work more effectively, thereby improving the quality and value of services provided.

BOX 4.1 HOW MEASURES TO IMPROVE EFFICIENCY AND PRODUCTIVITY AND CREATE VALUE SUPPORT COST REDUCTION STRATEGIES IN PRACTICE

- By delivering the same or greater quantity and quality of service from less resource
- By delivering a greater quantity of service of the same or better quality from the same resource
- By delivering the same quantity but a better quality of service from the same resource

Source: adapted from NHS Scotland Efficiency and Productivity Programme (NHS Scotland 2009).

For the purposes of this chapter, we use the term 'productivity' to cover the range of activities employed to realise tangible efficiencies in delivery of care and enhance the value of care, as shown in Box 4.1.

An important aspect of 'thinking differently' about productivity is considering whether investment in innovation fits in the left hand part of the productivity ratio (volume of inputs) or the right hand side (quantity of outputs). There is a danger that when resources are severely constrained, leaders view resources for innovation as an 'input' that can be cut, so the result is less innovation. If we are to deliver the potential of innovation in the NHS, we need to view innovation activities firmly within the output part of the equation (CSC 2005), a means of achieving more value for each pound invested in the NHS.

So, how can we reframe the relationship between quality and productivity and how can actual gains be delivered? Generally within the NHS there is a perceived trade-off between quality and cost embedded in current models of thinking (Easton 2011a). Many NHS staff do not believe that it is possible to improve productivity by improving quality. In fact, deep within the culture of the NHS lies the frequently held belief that better quality costs more money. If we start from a viewpoint that the existing models of health care delivery are relatively fixed then the trade-off is viewed as inevitable (*Health Service Journal* 2011).

One of the major issues to date in this regard has been the lack of health care specific evidence about the relationship between productivity, cost and quality. There is surprisingly limited published material on the delivery of

NHS productivity programmes *per se* (Crump 2012). Øvretveit's review of the available literature on quality and cost in 2009 found a limited number of high quality published studies from which to draw conclusions. He suggests that a strategy of improving quality might have an important contribution to make to cost reduction but it has limitations (Øvretveit 2009). It is appropriate to enquire whether Øvretveit's conclusion reflects the fact that many of the studies that he analysed were published during a period of rapid growth in resources, during which time the primary goals were commonly improving quality and safety and freeing up capacity for alternative use rather than the release of cash (Crump and Adil 2009). In the past, our approach as leaders within major health care systems often has been, 'let's seek to improve quality and worry about the financial implications at a later date' – or, 'we need to reduce costs: we will try to take steps to avoid a negative effect on quality' (Nolan and Bisognano 2006). As a leadership community, we have not typically sought integrated goals for quality improvement and cost reduction nor specifically employed quality improvement techniques as a means of achieving cost reduction (Crump 2012).

However, in recent times, as health care leaders have risen to the economic challenges that confront them, we have begun to see emerging global evidence of a strong association between high quality health care processes, productive systems and lower costs, through innovative service redesign and an integrated approach to improvement. In addition, evidence is beginning to emerge that high quality processes can lead to fewer adverse events for patients, lower mortality and fewer hospital readmissions, all of which enhance productivity of a given health care system and reduce overall costs (Crump and Adil 2009).

The evidence for this approach is growing. England's NHS Institute for Innovation and Improvement (Crump 2012), CHKS in the wider UK (Robinson and Tyndale-Biscoe 2011) and the Commonwealth Fund in the USA (Commonwealth Fund 2011) have all examined the principles and practices of 'productive' health care organisations and systems, that is, those that are delivering higher quality services with lower resource usage. A transatlantic comparison of their conclusions suggests that, despite significant differences in funding and delivery systems, there are substantial parallels between them.

So, how are the leaders of these organisations thinking differently about quality and productivity and what innovative actions are they taking?

Paradoxically, the most important initial task in creating a successful quality and productivity improvement strategy does not appear to be identifying the size of the challenge or working out which areas of service delivery offer the greatest opportunities to enhance productivity (Nolan and Bisognano 2006). Rather, it is about linking the proposed improvement process to a shared aspiration for a hopeful future and the deeper values that lie at the motivational centre of people who work in health care. Accordingly, the research literature commonly reveals that in high performing health care organisations there is a focus on goals aimed at quality and access and/or population health, rather than efficiency per se. As the chief finance officer of one of the organisations featured in the Commonwealth Fund study described it: 'We don't have goals for efficiency. It's a by-product of our success in focusing on what's right for the patient and excellence in quality of care . . .. [It is] a trailing indicator' (Commonwealth Fund 2011, p. 6).

This phenomenon is closely linked with the use of clear, consistent and repeated communication and messaging that align values, beliefs and goals with day to day practice. Such an approach is supported by the wider literature on organisational values which tells us that making a profound connection with the highest of organisation wide values is a particularly effective method for building the kind of engaged and motivated workforce that is most likely to innovate (NHS Institute for Innovation and Improvement 2009a). It is about leaders who create a sense of 'us' (rather than 'us and them') for the entire employee community – based on shared values, experiences and aspirations (Bevan et al. 2011). And, research related to these issues provides compelling evidence that leadership investment on this front delivers tangible results. In the context of clinical engagement, there is a strong correlation between clinicians who are engaged and motivated and the production of high performance. This conclusion holds true in almost every primary dimension of performance, including quality, patient outcomes and mortality (NHS Institute for Innovation and Improvement 2009b).

Historically in health care, responsibility for delivering quality has been held by different people to those responsible for delivering financial balance, often driving in opposite directions (Easton 2011b). So, these 'high quality, high value' organisations stand apart in that senior leaders such as nursing, finance and medical directors are all active, visible champions of quality and cost reduction. They don't separate their goals and systems for delivering quality improvements from their goals and systems for delivering productivity and cost gains. They understand that it is the same waste, errors, duplication and harm that creates the quality problem that is also the source of waste in financial terms. Their strategies for delivering both quality and productivity improvement originate a common ideology which is rooted in systems thinking. They base their integrated approaches to quality and productivity improvement upon common characteristics such as: a drive for continuous improvement through tangible outcomes; data-based decision making; engaging everyone in the process of improvement; and focus on application of tools, techniques, and methods for innovation and improvement (Mohanty 1998). As a result, a focus on quality improvement creates corresponding positive effects upon productivity as well.

If we examine the wider literature on high performing organisations, we can see that globally, the most common characteristic of those health care systems that deliver outstanding performance in cost and quality is a systematic approach to capability building for improvement (Bevan et al. 2008. Change programmes in the NHS have often been top down, target driven national programmes or smaller scale pockets of service innovation delivering significant results but often with limited spread. The evidence suggests that much of the thinking about change and improvement that has served health care systems to date is probably insufficient for the change and reform that are needed to realise our ambitions for productivity gain.

OVERCOMING BARRIERS TO INNOVATION

Our existing mindsets or mental models create the biggest barriers to the radical changes required to deliver our quality and productivity goals. The reality is that, when we think about how to deliver quality and productivity improvements, it is difficult to envisage it in any other way to the way we know it already (Serrat 2009). As health care leaders, we tend to unconsciously adopt a 'first order' way of thinking about change in which we perceive change activities as doing more or less of what we do already, in the same mindset as at present (Bevan et al. 2011). As a result, existing organisational structures, methods for change and mindsets about change consistently slow, stall or stop radical innovations (Kenagy 2009a).

Cognitive science tells us that to some extent this is inevitable (de Bono 1992). As we learn the language of the world we live and work in, our minds tend to hold concepts that flow together in our thinking. Our thinking is highly constrained by our existing experiences and world views (Serrat 2009). The risk is that, because our prevalent way of thinking is first order, we try to 'wring out as much inefficiency as possible' from the existing system (*Health Service Journal* 2011) without fundamentally challenging the way that health care is delivered.

If we are going to sustain a universal health care system for future generations, we need to deliberately cultivate more 'second order change' thinking (Bevan et al. 2011), to help us fundamentally re-see, rethink and

BOX 4.2 SUGGESTED CHARACTERISTICS OF HEALTH CARE ORGANISATIONS THAT DELIVER HIGH QUALITY, HIGH VALUE CARE

- Creating a sense of 'higher purpose' that frames cost and quality improvement in the wider health care mission of the organisation
- Taking a holistic approach that integrates quality goals with efficiency goals
- Motivating, engaging and mobilising the workforce and leadership community for change
- Utilising evidence-based, structured approaches to innovation and improvement
- Building capacity and capability for change at scale
- Making effective use of measurement and data to drive improvement
- Standardising and simplifying processes, to reduce variation and waste
- Seeking solutions beyond organisational boundaries

Source: synthesised from Crump (2012), Robinson and Tyndale-Biscoe (2011) and Commonwealth Fund (2011).

redesign current arrangements. If we think in a second order way, we can consider how we develop services that meet people's needs more effectively yet deliver higher or similar quality at lower cost and meet the criteria in Box 4.2. First and second order approaches to delivering change are contrasted in Table 4.1.

Of course, in the NHS context, an effective quality and productivity improvement programme will be a mix of first and second order methods: seeking to deliver basic systems effectively and efficiently (first order) whilst at the same time, radically redesigning processes and structures of care (second order). However, we maximise our potential to deliver our cost improvement goals if we align our (second order) ambition for large scale change with a delivery strategy that is built on a second order ways of thinking innovatively.

Table 4.1 First order and second order thinking about quality and productivity improvement

Change thinking	First order	Second order
Underlying mental model (Maher et al. 2007)	Unaltered (More of, or less of . . . the same thing)	Altered (Stand back . . . reframe . . . see the big picture . . .)
Theme for quality and productivity	Tighter control and scrutiny; management grip	Call to action for radical system redesign
Innovation focus	• across the board budget reductions • cost improvement goals are separate from quality improvement goals and are of primary importance • make the current system 'leaner' and less wasteful • assess and understand performance • work harder • capture data	• unwarranted variation is driven out across the system • productivity and cost improvement goals are a subset of quality and patient goals • build meaning and understanding of the need for change, connected to higher purpose and NHS values • build commitment to take action across the organisation and the wider system • create the capacity and capability for change

A FRAMEWORK FOR INNOVATION

In addition to the lack of agreement about the definition of innovation (Stone et al. 2008), there are also many different types of innovation discussed in the literature and many different ways of talking about it. As a result, there is a lack of consistency across academic texts and commentaries on the topic (Williams 2011). Baker suggests a helpful typology of innovation which includes three main types of innovation (process, service and strategy) each of which can vary in the speed and pervasiveness of change (incremental to radical) and impact (sustaining versus discontinuous) (Baker 2002).

Health and social care specific examples of the three types of innovation are shown in Table 4.2. The examples show that process and service innovation can also vary from incremental to radical and from sustaining

Table 4.2 Examples of process, service and strategic innovation

Process innovation	Service innovation	Strategic innovation
• Redesigning the appointment process in the GP surgery • Reinventing the triage process in Accident and Emergency • Making it easier for patients to order repeat prescriptions • Redesigning the job application process within recruitment and selection • Introducing a rapid turnaround 'one stop shop' for outpatient testing	• Creating new specialist services in the community, e.g., intravenous therapy, deep vein thrombosis, complex wound clinics • Introducing hyperacute stroke services across the city • Creating a 'virtual' induction for all newly appointed clinical staff • Radical redesign of the clinical pathway for people who break their hips • Introducing 'virtual wards' for intensive support outside of hospital	• Transforming the paradigm of urgent and emergency care across the community • Designing radical new integrated models of health and social care for people with long term conditions • Shifting power: patients, families and communities as co-creators and producers of health (Doherty and Mendenhall 2006) • Building new approaches to large scale change based on mobilising principles from social movements and community organising (Bevan et al. 2011)

to discontinuous. By its very nature, strategy innovation will be at the radical, discontinuous end of the innovation spectrum. There are also connections between the types of innovation, i.e., strategy innovation may lead to process and/or service innovations.

Process innovations are those that involve reducing or eliminating unwarranted variation and/or activities that do not add value from an existing process. They tend to be narrower in scope than service innovations, focusing on a discrete part of, or contribution to, a wider service, typically without changing the nature of the overall service or patient pathway. Generally, they are less complex and quicker to implement than the other types of innovation but offer less potential to deliver significant outcomes in terms of quality and productivity improvements. Process innovations are the most common type of innovation in health care.

Service innovations seek to improve (incrementally) or transform (radically) an offering for an entire service or pathway of care typically covering multiple processes. Service innovation brings more risk than process innovation since it is more complex and the innovation is more likely to cross existing departmental or organisational boundaries. However, the quality and productivity gains of service innovation are typically more significant than those of process innovation. Strategies for service innovation that are relevant to improving productivity and quality in health care include (Parker 2006):

- Integration: creating more effective relationships between the contributions to the health and social care system which result in seamless, integrated care
- Substitution: providing higher value, lower cost care for patients or service users through:

  location substitution: substituting high tech clinical environments for community based settings
  skills substitution: enhancing the skills of specific groups of staff to undertake roles previously undertaken by those with a higher skill level, for instance enabling nurses to prescribe drugs, a role that was previously only carried out by doctors
  technological substitution: maximising the use of new technologies in the service. A specific type of technological substitution is channel shift (Cabinet Office 2009) by which organisations seek to encourage their service users or patients to access or interact with services via channels other than those to which they are accustomed. A typical channel shift is moving from face to face or phone interaction to self-service online.
  clinical substitution: moving from a medical care model to community care or family or self care model
  organisational substitution: looking at a wider range of providers to those who have traditionally delivered NHS care, for instance voluntary and community groups and social enterprises.

- Segmentation: grouping patients by their specific requirements and designing discrete services around that group of patients in ways that enable them to get the service they want and need at the time they need and want it.
- Simplification: counterbalancing the risk of creating extra structures and extra complexity, ensuring that every step in the care process adds value for patients and minimising the potential for additional costs as a result of the innovation. An importance aspect is *reverse innovation* (Department of Health 2011a) – decommissioning an activity that is shown to have no added value or that has been replaced by something new or better.

Service innovations in health care may involve any combination of these strategies. Sometimes, a service innovation does not involve a wide enough range of strategies. For instance, a commonly reported scenario is one where a service innovation is introduced with the intention to substitute a hospital based service with a more cost effective community based service. However, the change is not followed up with simplification: the hospital service continues to operate in parallel, so the service ends up being 'doubled up', in multiple locations (Parker 2006). This makes an important point about the relationship between innovation and productivity. Innovation per se does not necessarily lead to enhanced productivity. It only enhances productivity if it is implemented and diffused in a way that leads to more effective outcomes from the resources invested. If innovation is not managed effectively it can end up costing more (CSC 2005).

Strategy innovation is about thinking in an entirely new way about the basis on which the organisation, system or industry operates. As Gary Hamel who pioneered the concept concludes: 'the question today is not whether you can reengineer your processes; the question is whether you can reinvent the entire industry model' (Hamel 1998). Most organisational innovation is at process and service level, but these innovations may lack the pervasiveness to deliver change at the scale or pace required. Strategy innovation is relevant when the financial and technological challenges that are faced can't be met without abandoning the prevailing management model and rethinking the system (Barsh 2008).

NHS leaders may need to fundamentally reframe their thinking about the relationship between cost and quality and the activities that their organisations need to undertake to deliver the value that service users need within the resources available (strategy innovation). However, innovation that originates within existing organisations may not be radical enough to deliver sufficient change in the required timescale. Hence, Christensen and colleagues promote the need for radical, innovation-driven change to organisations and industries through disruptive innovation; changes that 'disrupt' long-established practices in organisations, industries or areas of business (see Christensen et al. 2000); Christensen et al. 2009. A disruptive innovation is one that typically originates from 'left field' (NHS Confederation 2008), from innovators who probably come from outside of the existing system. Their innovations reinvent or introduce products and services in ways that the existing system and existing customers do not expect. Over time, these disruptive innovations redefine the nature of value within the system. They create new markets and demands for services and go on to displace previous ways of organising things.

Technological innovation often provides the foundation for disruptive

BOX 4.3 EXAMPLES OF EXISTING AND POTENTIAL DISRUPTIVE INNOVATION IN HEALTH CARE

- 'theranostics' (a fusion of diagnostics, genetic testing and personalised therapies)
- regenerative medicine using stem cell techniques
- out-of-hospital diagnostic testing
- telehealth and telecare
- patient ownership of their own health and their own health records
- new methods of risk profiling for a range of diseases
- new methods of delivery for medicines and other treatments including nanodevices and engineered viruses

Source: NHS Confederation 2008; Christensen et al. 2000, 2009; Department of Health 2011a.

innovation (Christensen et al. 2000; Christensen et al. 2009). By contrast to disruptive innovation, a *sustaining innovation* seeks to improve the performance of existing services and ways of working along the dimensions that existing service users, payers and commissioners value (Christensen et al. 2000; Christensen et al. 2009). A sustaining innovation could be, for instance, a radical service innovation or an incremental process innovation.

Examples of current and potential disruptive innovations in health care are shown in Box 4.3. A specific example is telehealth which is about using technology to deliver health and social care at a distance. Telehealth has the potential to deliver significant benefits in both quality and productivity: a 15 per cent reduction in patient visits to the emergency department, a 20 per cent reduction in emergency admissions, an eight per cent reduction in costs and a 45 per cent reduction in mortality rates (Department of Health 2011d). The NHS innovation review concludes that the NHS has the potential to adopt these technologies on a scale that would put it at the forefront of the management of chronic diseases globally (Department of Health 2011a).

A specific issue to consider in reviewing the list of potential disruptive innovations is whether the wider availability of new technologies (and the rising user expectations that come with them) might have unintended consequences. Rather than significantly reducing costs, they might create challenges for cost control (NHS Confederation 2008) if the supply of new treatments and technologies induces demand. In addition, if the large scale gains of disruptive innovation are to be achieved disruptive thinking will also be needed in the way that new innovations are rolled out across the NHS. The slow, incremental way that change has typically happened to date will be insufficient (Department of Health 2011a). In reality, the future health care system is likely to need both sustaining and disruptive innovation to deliver its quality and productivity challenges. If we just concentrate on large dramatic changes there is a risk that we will miss the incremental impact of multiple small changes (NHS Confederation 2008).

What is the distinction between strategy innovation as proposed by Hamel and disruptive innovation as described by Christensen? Both concepts are at the radical end of innovation. If the quality and cost imperatives necessary to secure the future for the NHS are to be delivered, both strategy and disruptive innovation are likely to be characteristics of that process.

Strategy innovation is about leaders implementing innovations as a result of changing their paradigm of thinking about their organisation or system and its wider context. It is about changing the 'design of the playing field and rules of the game' (Gersick 1991). Disruptive innovation, by contrast, is about specific innovations that appear in a system, typically from outside of the existing system, that fundamentally challenge the status quo and force the existing system to change its game. Disruptive innovation presents an opportunity for leaders in the existing system to rethink many of the existing assumptions about health and health care delivery. As a result, it can help create the conditions where leaders recognise that, in order to respond or compete, they need to change the nature of their business or the way that they think about it – its processes, where it happens, and what its goals are (strategy innovation).

WHO DELIVERS INNOVATION?

Having considered the typology of innovations, what can we conclude about where innovations come from? Do the most effective health care innovations come from inside or outside the system? The available evidence challenges the myth that innovation comes largely from policy makers or very senior leaders. A study across Commonwealth countries found that 82 per cent of public sector innovations come from staff at multiple levels of the system (Borins 2002). The most frequent initiators of public management innovations were 'local heroes', visionary middle-level and front-line public servants who took risks to innovate despite disincentives in the system that discouraged them from doing so. Hamel (1998) suggests that this is to a large extent inevitable. In senior leadership teams there is often an absence of the diverse points of view that stimulate innovative practice, and existing leaders often have a significant emotional investment in the status quo. In these circumstances it may be easier for leaders to maintain or improve existing processes than to ask difficult questions about what change might be really needed. It may also be easier to use traditional logic to promote the benefits of a modification to the existing system than to prove that something innovate and new will pay off (Kerr 1975).

Christensen and colleagues suggest that, since the problem that health systems face is a disruptive one and since those working within the system are constrained by existing thinking and practice, transformational disruptive innovations are likely to come from outside of the existing system or organisation. They also argue that disruptive innovations like, for instance, telehealth, should not be introduced into existing organisations operating to prevailing business models. They believe that this will never result in transformation of how the organisation operates because the existing system will just absorb the innovation to sustain the way it currently operates. Instead, 'disruptive start-up organisations', separate from the main business, should be established (Christensen et al. 2011). However, other commentators argue that whilst the ideas of innovation thinkers like Christensen are important in helping leaders of industries determine whether an idea has 'disruptive' potential, they don't help leaders to be more creative or help solve the problems that innovators will face when their concepts are put into operation (CSC 2005).

Kenagy, who was a collaborator with Christensen in his early work on disruptive innovation in health care (Christensen et al. 2000), now takes a different view to Christensen. Kenagy believes that the most effective innovations will come from inside, not outside, the system, as a result of a systematic and 'adaptive' approach to innovation design that involves the entire workforce in change (Kenagy 2009b). In fact, in the foreword to Kenagy's book, Christensen concedes that there are 'two critical pathways for improving the quality and reducing the cost of health care'. The first is Christensen's own concept of disruptive innovation. The second is Kenagy's kind of innovative design approach that gives existing organisations 'far greater flexibility in adapting to the demands of the market than I had ever thought achievable'.

To meet the quality and productivity challenges facing the NHS, we need a multiplicity of sources of innovation. New ways of delivering services will not just come from inside the organisation (Steen 2009). Paradoxically, evidence suggests that transformational ideas are much more likely to become widely accepted if they start from the organisational legacy and are what people are used to (Srivastava and Fry 1992). That's not surprising given that our existing mental models are so powerful. So, in framing quality and productivity improvement, we need a really clever balance between transformational proposals and grounding and building on the current reality. We need to 'think differently' about how to do this.

A specific leadership challenge in helping others to 'think differently' in challenging times is that, in situations of economic constraint and uncertainty, people's propensity to think creatively and build innovation into their working practices wanes significantly. Uncertainty about the future causes people to emotionally disengage from their work. Communication and collaboration declines as does people's sense of freedom and autonomy (Breen 2004). Fear, including fear of the unknown, has a stronger dampening effect on productivity than almost any other emotion. It sucks creativity out of organisations (Bevan 2011). Studies show that leaders have a disproportionately large effect on the cultures of their organisations or systems, creating the conditions that help or hinder innovation (Maher 2010). Leaders are 'signal generators' whose words and behaviours are constantly being scrutinised and interpreted. There is an 'amplification effect' which means that the signals sent through our leadership actions resonate throughout the whole organisation (Bevan et al. 2011). An NHS-wide survey of the styles of top leaders showed that, whilst leaders were effective at leading from the front and delivering challenging goals, they might not be so effective at motivating and energising the workforce for the long term or building the trusting relationships across organisational boundaries needed for the breadth of change that the NHS faces (Drew and Bevan 2011). In a national NHS survey, two thirds of NHS respondents reported that they were not adequately supported by their senior leaders in their activities in support of innovation and improvement (*NHS Innovation and Improvement Survey* 2009).

The factors that contribute to a culture for innovation are well documented (Maher et al. 2010). These include: *risk taking*, creating a climate that enables people to feel psychologically safe in trying out new ways of working; *rewards*, rituals and symbols that recognise innovative behaviour and which are mostly non financial; *relationships*, enabling people with a variety of experiences and perspectives to innovate together; and *sharing knowledge* as the fuel of innovation. By explicitly focusing on these factors, leaders can avoid fear-based approaches and tap into the potential of people to contribute, to be creative and to be motivated internally. Creating the right conditions can result in higher innovation, motivation and productivity (Bason 2010). This is an underpinning theme of the 'high value, high quality organisations' featured earlier in the chapter (Crump 2012; Robinson and Tyndale-Biscoe 2011; Commonwealth Fund 2011).

A SYSTEMATIC APPROACH TO INNOVATION

There is a growing recognition that radical innovation does not just happen on its own. Most NHS change has typically happened incrementally, small gains at a time, even when bigger improvements are being sought. There is nothing wrong with incremental change, in fact, we should always review and celebrate all attempts at making a difference, regardless of the results because they show that people are more likely to attempt further innovation in the future (Maher et al. 2008). However, there are steps that we can take to change the largely incremental approach to innovation (Bessant et al. 2010).

The global experience of organisations that have been most successful in harnessing innovation for better outcomes points to one consistent message: innovation is a structured and disciplined process, the product of the deliberate use of practical tools (Maher et al. 2008). This systematic approach to innovation is increasingly being adopted by health care and other public service organisations (Murray et al. 2009).

In the literature there are a variety of innovation process models for leaders to follow involving multiple steps or stages towards innovation. There is similarity in the content and underpinning philosophies of the models. However, they differ in where the innovation process starts (i.e., whether or not 'thinking differently' is seen as part of, or a step prior to, the innovation process), the breadth of innovation covered and where the model ends (does it stop at the end of the ideas assessment phase, does it cover diffusion of the idea or the broader systematic changes needed to embed the change in the wider system?). Whilst the literature suggests that using an innovation process model can make a difference to innovation outcomes (Murray et al. 2009), the evidence base does not extend to an assessment of different innovation process models or an evaluation of whether any one model is more effective than another in a specific context. Therefore, in determining which one to use, it is a question of which one is the best 'fit' to the context of the innovation.

The NHS Institute for Innovation and Improvement (Maher et al. 2008) has specifically designed a five stage process to enable NHS frontline staff and leaders to assess and stimulate service innovations for quality and productivity improvement. The process starts by assessing the idea to see how much of a difference it might make across multiple dimensions of performance. Does it really represent a source of quality and cost improvement? The next step considers context: how new or innovative is the idea compared to what is going on elsewhere in the organisation, the wider health and social care system or internationally? The third step is to assess how big a process change it really is. How does it compare to the usual or past approach in that specific context? Does it really represent radical rethinking of the way that services are delivered or change takes place? The fourth stage tries to stretch thinking to see whether more innovative aspects can be added that will make an even bigger difference or come up with alternative proposals to deliver the solution that is sought. The final step is to develop a summary statement that sets out an assessment of the innovativeness of the idea compared to the typical practice in the comparison context.

Steen (2009) suggests a three step model. It starts with an 'ideas generation' stage whereby ideas are collected, a 'conversion' stage where proposals are selected, developed and tested and a 'spread' stage where ideas are widely diffused. NESTA (Murray et al. 2009) offers a broader six stage model that starts with factors that *prompt and inspire* innovation as well as diagnosis. The second stage is *proposals and ideas*: setting out methods for ideas generation. The third stage, *prototyping and pilots*, is followed by *sustaining:* at this stage the idea becomes established practice. The fifth stage, *scaling and diffusion*, is followed by *systematic change*, which is about putting the factors in place in the wider environment that make the innovation viable at scale in the future.

At the end of the day, innovation in the current NHS context has to deliver more than small scale, discrete changes. It needs to be replicable in order to be replicated across multiple teams and settings (Department of Health 2011a). Utilising a structured innovation methodology helps us to apply existing ideas or services in new contexts as much as it helps us to create services that are based on completely new ideas.

In addition to a growing body of evidence about the process of innovation, there is also a growing movement of radical thinking about the methods to utilise within that process. Particularly in a health care context, this refers to the use of powerful methods adapted from the design industry that engage patients, families, service users and communities as active co-creators at every stage in the innovation process (Bessant and Maher 2009).

CONCLUSIONS

Innovation is a vital part of the leader's toolkit if we are to deliver our quality and productivity goals and secure the future of our comprehensive, universal health care system offering the best value and high quality care for all.

In order to do things differently we need to think differently, seeing quality and productivity as integrated goals and understanding that actions that seek to improve value and reduce waste and unwarranted variation can also lead to high quality care. Innovation is everyone's business, from members of front line clinical teams leading process and service innovations to entire communities engaged in large scale strategy innovation. The most innovative organisations know that innovation is a systematic process, the product of the intentional use of practical tools. It is hard to imagine that, say, financial control could naturally emerge without deliberate systems and structures to manage it. So, why might we think that innovation might happen on its own just by having the right culture, bringing in more creative thinkers or funding more innovation initiatives (Maher et al. 2010)? There is much that leaders can do to create the conditions where innovation can flourish, building trust, motivation and productivity and a sense of optimism about innovating towards a hopeful future.

The history of innovation suggests that, in times when things are uncertain and unstable, the most innovative organisations often have the greatest advantage (Kenagy 2009b). And the prize is significant. As the NHS Innovation Review concludes:

> We [the NHS] have the potential to create the best health system in the world, enhancing the quality of life for people with long term conditions, preventing people from dying prematurely, helping people recover from ill health and ensuring that patients have a positive experience of care. (Department of Health 2011a, p. 5)

The circumstances of scarce resources create the situation where we need to think about and deliver services in fundamentally different ways. They help create an environment where the biggest breakthrough innovations can happen. We have the potential to do what might have previously seemed impossible.

REFERENCES

Appleby, J., R. Crawford and C. Emmerson (2009), *How Cold Will It Be? Prospects for NHS Funding 2011–17*, The Kings Fund. http://www.nhshistory.net/howcoldwillitbe.pdf.

Baker, K. (2002), 'Innovation', retrieved from http://www.au.af.mil/au/awc/awcgate/doe/benchmark/ch14.pdf

Barsh, J. (2008), 'Innovative management: a conversation with Gary Hamel and Lowell Bryan', *McKinsey Quarterly*, 1.

Bason, C. (2010), *Leading Public Sector Innovation – Co-creating for a Better Society*, Policy Press.

Bessant, J., and L. Maher (2009), 'Developing radical service innovations in healthcare – the role of design methods', *International Journal of Innovation Management*, **13** (4) (Dec), 555–568.

Bessant, J., T. Hughes and S. Richards (2010), *Beyond Light Bulbs and Pipelines: Leading and Nurturing Innovation in the Public Sector*, National School of Government.

Bevan, H. (2011), 'Who's afraid of the big bad wolf?', *Health Service Journal*, 13 January. http://www.hsj.co.uk/comment/opinion/helen-bevan-whos-afraid-of-the-big-bad-wolf/5023625.article.

Bevan, H., C. Ham and P. Plsek (2008), *The Next Leg of the Journey: How Do We Make High Quality Care for All a Reality?*, NHS Institute for Innovation and Improvement.

Bevan H., P. Plsek and L. Winstanley (2011), *Leading Large Scale Change: A Practical Guide*, NHS Institute for Innovation and Improvement.

Borins, S. (2002), 'The challenge of innovating in government', Chapter 3 in M. Abramson and I. Littman (eds), *Innovation,* Rowman & Littlefield.

Breen, B. (2004), 'The six myths of creativity', *Fast Company*, 1 December. http://www.fastcompany.com/magazine/89/creativity.html?page=0%2C1

Cabinet Office (2009), *Channel Strategy Guidance.* http://webarchive.nationalarchives.gov.uk/+/http://www.cabinetoffice.gov.uk/media/261368/channel_strategy_modules.pdf.

Christensen, C., R. Bohmer and J. Kenagy (2000), 'Will disruptive innovation cure health care?', *Harvard Business Review,* September–October.

Christensen, C., J. Grossman and J. Hwang (2009), *The Innovator's Prescription: A Disruptive Solution For Healthcare*, McGraw Hill.

Christensen, C., M. Horn, L. Caldera and L. Soares (2011), *Disrupting College: How Disruptive Innovation Can Deliver Quality and Affordability to Postsecondary Education*, Center for American Progress, Innosight Institute. http://www.americanprogress.org/issues/2011/02/disrupting_college.html.

Commonwealth Fund (2011), *Achieving Efficiency: Lessons from Four Top-Performing Hospitals.*

Comptroller and Auditor General's Report (2011), *Management of NHS Hospital Productivity*, HC (2010–2011) paragraph 1.7.

CSC (2005), *What Innovation Is*, Computer Sciences Corporation. www.innovationtools.com/pdf/innovation_update_2005.pdf.

Crump, B. (2012), *Delivering Quality and Cost Plans: How Can We Improve the Odds?*, NHS Institute for Innovation and Improvement. Paper in production.

Crump, B., and M. Adil (2009), 'Can quality and productivity improve in a financially poorer NHS?', *BMJ*, 21 November, **339**, 1175–7.

Dare F., and J. Macaulay (2011), *The Health of Nations Perspective from Global Leaders Reveal Untapped Opportunities*, Cisco. http://www.cisco.com/web/about/ac79/docs/hc/Health_of_Nations_ExecSumm.pdf.

Darzi, A., Baron of Denham (2008), *High Quality Care For All: NHS Next Stage Review final report*, June 2008, Department of Health. www.dh.gov.uk/en/Publicationsandstatistics/Publications/PublicationsPolicyAndGuidance/DH_085825.

de Bono, E. (1992), *Serious Creativity*, Harper-Collins.

Department of Health (2011a), *Innovation, Health and Wealth: Accelerating Adoption and Diffusion in the NHS.* http://www.dh.gov.uk/en/Publicationsandstatistics/Publications/PublicationsPolicyAndGuidance/DH_131299.

Department of Health (2011b), *The Operating Framework for the NHS in England 2012/13*, p. 11. http://www.dh.gov.uk/prod_consum_dh/groups/dh_digitalassets/documents/digitalasset/dh_131428.pdf.

Department of Health (2011c), *NHS Atlas of Variation in Health Care*. https://docs.google.com/viewer?a=v&pid=explorer&chrome=true&srcid=0B8ePB71diJorY2FmYzhhZjAtM2Y5Yi00MzI2LWI1MmItZDcwNjBiNTQzNzEw&hl=en_US.

Department of Health (2011d), *Whole System Demonstrator Programme, Headline Findings* http://www.dh.gov.uk/prod_consum_dh/groups/dh_digitalassets/documents/digitalasset/dh_131689.pdf.

Doherty, W., and T. Mendenhall (2006), 'Citizen health care: a model for engaging patients, families, and communities as co producers of health', *Families, Systems, & Health*, **24**, (3), 251–263.

Drew J., and H. Bevan (2011), 'Trust me, I'm a leader: creating a climate for higher performance', *Health Service Journal*, 29 November. http://www.hsj.co.uk/resource-centre/best-practice/organisational-development-resources/trust-me-im-a-leader-creating-a-climate-for-higher-performance/5037975.article.

Easton, J. (2011a), 'A future driven by innovation', presentation at NHS Innovation Expo, 10 March.

Easton, J. (2011b), 'Delivering quality in tough times', presentation to the South West LHIN Quality symposium, 28 April. www.youtube.com/watch?v=AuAsV9o0UWs.

Gersick, C.J.G. (1991), 'Revolutionary change theories: a multilevel exploration of the punctuated equilibrium paradigm', *Academy of Management Review*, **16** (1), 10–36.

Hamel, G. (1998), 'Opinion: strategy innovation and the quest for value', *Sloan Management Review*, Winter, p. 7.

Health Service Journal (2011), 'HSJ interview: Clayton M. Christensen, author of The Innovator's Prescription', *Health Service Journal*, 3 November.

Her Majesty's Treasury (2011), The Chancellor's Autumn Statement. http://cdn.hm-treasury.gov.uk/autumn_statement.pdf.

House of Commons Committee of Public Accounts (2011), *Management of NHS Hospital Productivity: 26th Report of the Session 2010–11.*

Kenagy, J. (2009a), 'We won't take control of healthcare by rearranging the deck chairs on the Titanic', *FYA*, **8**, (13), 6 July.

Kenagy, J. (2009b), *Designed to Adapt: Leading Health Care in Challenging Times*, Second River Healthcare Press.

Kerr, S. (1975), 'On the folly of rewarding A while hoping for B', *Academy of Management Journal*, **18**, 769–783.

Maher, L. (2009), 'A bright future', *Health Director*, July.

Maher, L. (2010), 'Creating the culture for innovation', *Health Service Review*, May.

Maher, L. (2011), 'Innovation, efficiency and productivity in health services', *World Medical Journal*, **57** (June), 116.

Maher, L., P. Plsek, S. Garrett and H. Bevan (2007), *Thinking Differently*, NHS Institute for Innovation and Improvement. http://www.institute.nhs.uk/building_capability/new_model_for_transforming_the_nhs/thinking_differently_guide.html.

Maher, L., P. Plsek and H. Bevan (2008), *Making a Bigger Difference: A Guide for NHS Front Line Staff on Assessing and Stimulating Service Innovation*, NHS Institute for Innovation and Improvement. www.institute.nhs.uk/making-a-bigger-difference.

Maher, L., P. Plsek, J. Price and M. Mugglestone (2010), *Creating the Culture for*

Innovation: A Practical Guide for Leaders, NHS Institute for Innovation and Improvement.
Mohanty, R. (1998), 'Understanding the integrated linkage: quality and productivity', *Total Quality Management*, **9** (8).
Mulgan, G., and D. Albury (2003), *Innovation in the Public Sector,* Strategy Unit, Cabinet Office paper. See http://www.idea.gov.uk/idk/aio/1118552.
Murray R., J. Caulier-Grice and G. Mulgan (2009), *Open Book of Social Innovation*, Young Foundation and NESTA. www.nesta.org.uk/library/documents/Social_Innovator_020310.pdf.
NHS Confederation (2008), *Disruptive Innovation: What Does it Mean for the NHS?* Futures debate, Paper 5, September.
NHS Innovation and Improvement Survey (2009), NHS Institute for Innovation and Improvement. http://www.institute.nhs.uk/images//stories/Building_Capability/Innovation/UK_NHS_Survey_March10.pdf.
NHS Institute for Innovation and Improvement (2009a), *Living our Local Values: The Value of Values.*
NHS Institute for Innovation and Improvement (2009b), *The Link Between Medical Engagement and Performance.* http://www.institute.nhs.uk/building_capability/enhancing_engagement/medical_engagement_and_organisational_performance.html.
NHS Scotland (2009), *Efficiency and Productivity Programme: Delivery Framework.* http://www.scotland.gov.uk/Publications/2009/06/22125603/3.
Nolan, T., and M. Bisognano (2006), 'Finding the balance between quality and cost', *Healthcare Financial Management* (USA), April, 67–72.
Øvretveit, J. (2009), *Does Improving Quality Save Money?,* London: Health Foundation. http://www.health.org.uk/public/cms/75/76/313/572/Does%20improving%20quality%20save%20money.pdf?realName=1d2aAZ.pdf.
Parker, H. (2006), *Making the Shift: A Review of NHS Experience*, Health Services Management Centre and NHS Institute for Innovation and Improvement. http://www.bhamlive3.bham.ac.uk/Documents/college-social-sciences/social-policy/HSMC/publications/2006/Making-the-Shift.pdf.
Robinson, R., and J. Tyndale-Biscoe (2011), *What Makes a Top Hospital?* CHKS.
Serrat, O. (2009), *Harnessing Creativity and Innovation in the Workplace*, Knowledge Solutions. http://www.adb.org/documents/information/knowledge-solutions/harnessing-creativity-and-innovation-in-the-workplace.pdf.
Srivastava, S., and R. Fry (1992), *Executive and Organizational Continuity: Managing the Paradoxes of Stability and Change*, Jossey-Bass.
Steen, J. (2009), *The Three Stages of Innovation Strategy.* http://www.slideshare.net/timkastelle/the-three-stages-of-innovation-strategy-2304224.
Stone, A., S. Rose and B. Lal (2008), *Measuring Innovation and Intangibles: A Business Perspective*, Science and Technology Policy Institute. http://www.athenaalliance.org/pdf/MeasuringInnovationandIntangibles-STPI-BEA.pdf.
Williams, L. (2011), *Organizational Readiness for Innovation in Healthcare: Some Lessons from the Recent Literature*, Health Services Management Centre, University of Birmingham.
Wind-Cowie, M., and T. Gregory (2011), *A Place for Pride*, Demos. http://www.demos.co.uk/publications/aplaceforpride.

PART II

Human resource management

5. The contribution of 'best-practice' HR management to better organisational performance

Sandra G. Leggat

INTRODUCTION

Health care is all about people – the people who receive the care and the people who provide the care. While there is plenty of complex technology in health care, most delivery comprises a relationship between a health professional and a patient. The performance of health systems and health care organisations is dependent upon the performance of their health workers (Dussault, 1999). Yet, when there are failures in health care systems poor people management is often found to be a contributing factor.

Studies of high-performing organisations in private sector industries have consistently pointed to a positive relationship between human resource management (HRM) and organisational performance (Delaney and Huselid, 1996; Guthrie, 2001; Youndt et al., 1996; Barraud-Didier and Guerrero, 2002). This research suggests that bundles of HRM systems and practices that are aligned to the particular needs of an organisation contribute to better organisational performance (MacDuffie, 1995). There is increasing evidence that this relationship is also present in public health care (Harmon et al., 2003; Aiken et al., 1994; West et al., 2006; Harley et al., 2007; Laschinger et al., 2001; Leggat et al., 2010).

The aim of this chapter is to convince the reader of the necessity of good people management in health care organisations; that better organisational performance, including better quality of care delivery, is conditional upon 'best practice' HRM. The chapter begins with an overview of the evidence for best practice HRM and the state of the research in health care. I then explore the unique aspects of health care organisations that impact organisational performance and discuss why best practice HRM is essential.

THE EVIDENCE FOR BEST PRACTICE HRM

The evidence continues to grow that effective management of the people who work in the organisation, that is, the human resources (HR), is positively related to organisational performance (Delaney and Huselid, 1996; MacDuffie, 1995; Batt, 1999; Batt, 2002; Youndt et al., 1996; Snell and Youndt, 1995). Richardson and Thompson summarised the relationship through a systematic review, finding 'positive statistical relationships between the greater adoption of HR practices and business performance' (Richardson and Thompson, 1999, p. xi). In a large number of studies bundles of HRM practices have been defined as high performance work systems (HPWS), although they may also be referred to as high commitment workplaces (Takeuchi et al., 2003), high-involvement work systems (Guthrie, 2001), high performance work environment (Scotti et al., 2007) and strategic HRM (Huselid et al., 1997). The components of HPWS have been described as 'a group of separate, but interconnected human resource practises that together recruit, select, develop, motivate and retain employees' (Zacharatos et al., 2005, p. 79). The underlying premise of HPWS is that management can create the conditions in workplaces that motivate employees to achieve the goals of the organisation (Whitener, 2001). HPWS practices are presumed to affect performance by enhancing employees' knowledge, skills, abilities and commitment and by providing them with the information and discretion necessary to capitalise on these skills and commitment in completing their jobs (Preuss, 2003; Guthrie, 2001; Huselid, 1995). That is, employees are empowered to achieve organisational goals through effective human resource management that fosters increased information flows and devolution of decision making power, leading to greater productivity (Zacharatos et al., 2005).

It is not entirely clear what the essential components of the HPWS bundle are, as there have been a range of variables included in the HPWS studies (Godard, 2004; Becker and Gerhart, 1996), but generally they comprise practices that would be considered representative of good HRM, such as workforce planning, teamwork, and employee participation (Huselid et al., 1997). Zacharatos et al. (2005) developed a comprehensive index, including: security, selective hiring, contingent reward, extensive training, teams and decentralised decision making, reduced status distinctions, information sharing, transformational leadership, high-quality work (defined as appropriate workload, role clarity, and employee control) and measurement of management practices as representative of HPWS. The research is clear that while there are links recorded between individual HR practices and organisational performance, stronger effects can be achieved through the 'package' of HPWS (Combs et al., 2006).

As is the case with much field research in organisations and management, the majority of the studies from which the evidence is drawn are cross-sectional correlations and there is some concern that insufficient longitudinal studies have been completed to confirm the effects (Boselie et al., 2005). However, pragmatists would suggest that this is the best evidence available and should be used while awaiting further study.

Most HRM-performance studies have been in manufacturing, which is a different industry from health care (Preuss, 2003). A meta-analysis suggested that service-based industries did not demonstrate the same strength in effect of HPWS as that achieved in manufacturing (Combs et al., 2006). In particular, in public health care systems organisational performance is more difficult to define and measure than the shareholder value and financial returns used in the manufacturing studies (Buchan, 2004). Unlike other industries health care operates with:

- complex decision-making negotiated between the patient and health care professional, in which errors in decision-making may result in death or injury,
- external pressures, with confusing combinations of public and private administration, financing and delivery, and
- organisational goals which are often ambiguous and potentially conflicting (Leatt and Porter, 2003).

Buchan (2004) adds that the diverse health professional workforce, more loyal to their professions and patients than to their employing organisations and represented by powerful professional associations or trade unions, distinguishes health care from other industries. All of this suggests that studies from other industries may not be generalisable to health care, and evidence of an HRM-organisational performance link must be found in public health systems.

HEALTH CARE RESEARCH ON BEST PRACTICE HRM AND ORGANISATIONAL PERFORMANCE

Organisational Performance in Health Care

As a public good, the performance goals for health care are often varied and can be conflicting. These organisations are held accountable for service delivery, teaching and research, and within government policy and funding constraints, aim to achieve access, quality and financial targets. Unlike other industries, financial performance on its own is not an appropriate performance measure (Leggat et al., 1998) and many studies in health care focus on quality of care either instead of or in addition to financial measures of performance. Quality of care has been measured as patient mortality, reduction in adverse events (most commonly, impact on medication errors), specific clinical outcomes and patient satisfaction. Although there are fewer studies than in other industries, health care researchers around the world have been demonstrating the link between HRM and organisational performance, including quality of care.

It is difficult in organisational research to establish causality, as it is often impossible to isolate the interventions from environmental and organisational factors that confound results. As a consequence, intermediate HRM outcomes, such as job satisfaction and staff retention, which are postulated to have a relationship with organisational performance (Paauwe and Richardson, 1997) are often used. Psychological constructs such as engagement, commitment and satisfaction, and employee behaviours, such as absenteeism and turnover, have been studied as intermediate indicators. The relationships between HRM and intermediate outcomes have received empirical support (Bartram et al., 2007; Patrick and Laschinger, 2006; Zacharatos et al., 2005), as have the relationships between the intermediate outcomes and organisational performance (see for example, Harter et al., 2002, for a meta-analysis of these relationships).

Magnet Hospital Studies

The earliest work in this area relates to the studies of magnet hospitals, which examined the characteristics of American hospitals that attracted nurses (McClure et al., 1983). Studies on magnet hospitals have consistently shown that effective HRM is related to positive organisational and patient outcomes, such as lower mortality rate (Aiken et al., 1994). The magnet studies identified that factors such as autonomy, control over resources, relationships with doctors, emotional exhaustion and decision-making correlated with intermediate measures of nurse satisfaction and terminal measures of quality of care (Kramer and Schmalenberg, 2004; Rafferty et al., 2001; Upenieks, 2003; Laschinger et al., 2001). Importantly, while the initial studies took place in the largely private American system, magnet results have been shown in public health care systems in other countries as well (Armstrong and Laschinger, 2006).

Studies of Aspects of HRM

Health care studies have demonstrated relationships between a variety of human resource management practices and assorted intermediate and terminal performance outcomes. These relationships exist in developed countries, such as the United States (US), the United Kingdom (UK), Canada, Australia and throughout Europe, and more recently similar results have been suggested for developing countries (Agarwal et al., 2011; Jahangir and Shokrpur, 2009). These HRM-performance studies have focused on all health professional employees, as well as on specific groups, such as nurses (the largest human resource component). The research among nurses is consistent with the magnet studies. Links have been found between HRM of nurses and intermediate measures such as job satisfaction (Jahangir and Shokrpur, 2009) and intent to leave (Estryn-Behar et al., 2007). There is also a relationship with the patient care nurses deliver. For example, non-supportive nursing environments and poor team relationships contributed to nurses' decision to leave, and this turnover was related to increases in medical errors (O'Brien-Pallas et al., 2008). Importantly, the nursing studies and the studies of other health professionals return similar results (Holtom and O'Neill, 2004).

Teamwork is a recurring HRM construct in studies with all types of health professionals, with consistent results of a positive relationship between perceptions of effective teamwork and quality of patient care (Davies et al., 2007; Adinolfi, 2003). A large study of 500 teams in primary care, community mental health, hospital and breast cancer care completed in the UK (Borrill et al., 2000) reported a significant negative relationship between the percentage of staff working in teams and patient mortality. Research in 61 English hospitals suggested strong negative associations between the perceptions of HR practices of teamwork, training and performance appraisal and patient mortality (West et al., 2002), and more recently a study of nearly 1500 clinicians found that effective teamwork was associated with greater job and patient satisfaction (Chang et al., 2009). Employee participation has been coupled with teamwork, with an American Veterans Affairs study identifying that patients who were treated by teams where the members reported higher levels of participation displayed greater improvement in activities of daily living as compared with teams with lower reported levels of participation (Alexander et al., 2005).

Other aspects of HRM, such as education and training, have a positive relationship with client satisfaction in Dutch homes for elderly care (Ott and van Dijk, 2005) and a negative relationship with patient mortality in UK hospitals (West, 2001).

High Performance Work Systems

While these studies have tested components of HPWS, there are the consistent findings that systems of HPWS have stronger effects than individual HRM components (Combs et al., 2006; Dyer and Reeves, 1995). There is mounting evidence of positive links between HPWS and health care organisational performance (Harris et al., 2007), including perceived quality of care (Young et al., 2009; Leggat et al., 2010; Bartram et al., 2007), client and staff satisfaction and operating efficiency (Rondeau and Wagar, 2001), and negative links with medical errors (Gowen et al., 2005). Preuss (2003) found a similar positive relationship between HPWS and organisational performance in health care that was mediated by information quality.

This brief summary outlines the increasing evidence of an empirical link between best practice HRM and organisational performance in health care.

WHY BEST PRACTICE HRM IS ESSENTIAL IN HEALTH CARE ORGANISATIONS

Given the fact that health care is a labour intensive industry (Dubois et al., 2006), coupled with the evidence for best practice HRM, one would expect this industry would excel in HRM. Yet there is little evidence for effective HRM in health systems around the world (Bartram et al., 2007; Leggat et al., 2005; Leggat et al., 2006; Saltman and Figueras, 1997; Rigoli and Dussault, 2003; Franco et al., 2002; Stanton et al., 2010; Bach, 2000; Agarwal et al., 2011; Khatri et al., 2006). There have been considerable worldwide concerns about health system performance in patient safety and quality (HMSO, 2001; McLean and Walsh, 2003; World Health Organization, 2001; Committee on Quality of Healthcare in America, 2001; Baker and Flintoff, 2004; Duckett, 2003), with evidence that hospitals have not been successful in achieving acknowledged best practice (Dwyer and Leggat, 2002; OECD, 2004; Braithwaite and Hindle, 1999; Ibrahim and Majoor, 2002). The enquiries and reports on significant system failures identify lack of management as a contributing factor (Dunbar et al., 2007 HMSO, 2001; Garling, 2008; Davies, 2005), with researchers concluding that it is unlikely that improvements in quality of care will be made without addressing existing limitations in HRM (Leggat et al., 2008; Committee on Quality of Healthcare in America, 2001; Leggat et al., 2011b).

The research suggests that HPWS benefit organisations by impacting three areas: (1) the work organisation, (2) the management of the production (or service delivery) processes, and (3) employee relations (Belanger et al., 2002). Each of these aspects makes a contribution to organisational performance, and best practice HRM is essential to reap the benefits in these areas.

Work Organisation

The health care workforce is characterised by well-educated, well-meaning professionals who are largely socialised and rewarded for independent work (Horsburgh et al., 2006). Health professions are bound more by requirements of external regulatory agencies than by internal organisational expectations of performance (Deber et al., 2004; Degeling et al., 1998). Instead of an interdisciplinary care delivery model, hospital organisation and hierarchy reinforces parallel care processes that only occasionally intersect (Leggat, 2008; Glouberman and Mintzberg, 2001), with impermeable cultural boundaries among health professionals (Degeling et al., 2001). It is well documented that health professions have differing views on the evidence for effective practice (Degeling et al., 1998), and the education, training and work practices of our health workers provide limited opportunities for the multidisciplinary evidence sharing and debate necessary to achieve consensus on the organisation of the work (Dopson et al., 2002). HPWS influence organisational performance through productivity gains that build on the knowledge that workers amass over time (Felstead and Gallie, 2002; Butler et al., 2004), and therefore best practice HRM is essential to counteract the strong division of labour that limits effective health care delivery.

Wilson (1989) identified four organisational types, based on clarity of outputs and outcomes: craft, production, procedural, and coping. Public health care organisations largely display complex, unobservable outputs and outcomes suggesting that these organisations are classified as 'coping' organisations. Outputs refer to the activities of the organisational workforce, and in craft production the work of health professionals tends to be complex and difficult to supervise. Patient outcomes may be observable, but are complex, as individual patient, and societal and environmental factors influence the outcomes. In Wilson's model coping organisations cannot be effectively managed through production or procedural mechanisms based on scientific management. Many of the quality and safety improvement solutions proposed, such as specialisation and standardisation, are based on principles of mass production, which Wilson suggests are the wrong approach for coping organisations. Coping organisations require effective HRM (Wilson, 1989).

Management of the Service Delivery Processes

Health care tends to be craft-based production – a trained health care professional provides his or her craft for individual patients, with little need for management. But as health care moved from service delivery primarily in the community (that is, in your home or the doctor's surgery) to institutions such as hospitals, aspects of mass production were introduced. The organisation and operation of the hospital illustrates the difficulties transferring craft production to a setting that requires teamwork, coordination and integrated production. Hospitals display a fundamental inconsistency in that they are organised in formal managerial and clinical hierarchies which are based on scientific management principles, yet they try to maintain professional autonomy for clinicians (Leggat and Dwyer, 2005). In addition, externally imposed standards of practice, which are outside managerial control, impose resource requirements. It has been recognised that recent advice to improve the quality and safety of patient care increases this tension between work design that ensures responsibility and accountability, while at the same time promoting autonomy (Matthews and Pronovost, 2008).

This has resulted in an emphasis on managing (through the hierarchies) those aspects of operations that don't interfere with the craft production relationship between clinician and patient. This was demonstrated by a review of management decisions in the UK National Health Service (NHS) which found little managerial control over medicine (Harrison and Lim, 2003), and by Australian studies where managers reported they spent less time and effort on clinical management (Braithwaite, 2004; Braithwaite et al., 2007). Clinician managers view 'management' as second rate to their clinical profession (McConnell, 2002) and few have had education or training in management (Leggat et al., 2011a). Yet, it is no longer just the management researchers recommending increasing focus on best practice HRM. For example patient safety researchers, such as Gowen et al. (2005) found significant relationships between clinical errors and HRM through a survey of over 500 American hospitals. Shaw (2006) summarised the elements of a clinical performance management system of: job description, work program, operational rules, selection and appointment procedures, contracts, appraisal and peer review, and continuing professional development. This list comprises standard HRM functions, and with the addition of security, teamwork and participation, would be similar to the HPWS components identified by Zacharatos et al. (2005). Mannion et al. (2005) identified HRM as a distinguishing factor between high and low performing UK trusts, and Griffiths et al. (2008) reported a link with infection control. There is growing recognition of the importance of HRM in improving clinical outcomes, with more hospitals linking responsibility for patient safety and quality with HRM at the senior management level.

Employee Relations

In many countries, the broader industrial relations framework presents as an enabler or barrier to HRM implementation. It has been suggested that HPWS implementation is more successful in jurisdictions with a supportive industrial relations framework (Hillard and McIntyre, 1998), and a few studies have even found stronger effects of HPWS among unionised employees (Harley et al., 2007; Berg and Frost, 2005). But the health professional unions and professional associations, who represent current practitioners, largely support the status quo in health system organisation and health care delivery (Kachur and Krajic, 2006). In effect, health care workers, who are largely professionally registered and focused on independence of practice, are likely to be opposed to HRM practices that require them to change their mode of practice to achieve interdisciplinary patient-centred care. A strong HRM response is needed to compel these health professionals to work collaboratively to achieve better patient care.

The importance of middle managers in achieving best practice HRM is widely recognised (Stanton et al., 2010; Bowen and Ostroff, 2004) and in other industries it is the middle managers who enact best practice HRM. In health care, however, the middle managers lack the resources to manage their staff effectively (McConville and Holden, 1999), with a range of studies highlighting the inconsistencies in HRM practices among hospital units (Veld et al., 2010; Young et al., 2009; Stanton et al., 2010). This has led to consistent recommendations for health care middle managers to be supported to implement best practice HRM on a planned and systematic basis (McConville and Holden, 1999; Stanton et al., 2010).

CONCLUSIONS

There is mounting evidence that best practice HRM in health care is associated with better performance on relevant intermediate and terminal measures of organisational performance. Importantly, there appears to be a strong association between HRM and the quality of patient care that is delivered. There is also extensive evidence that health systems do not display best practice HRM and do not achieve best practice health care delivery. As compared to other industries, public health care systems comprise inefficient work organisation, restrictive craft production, and a workforce that is largely satisfied with these arrangements. It is clear that health care organisations require strong HRM systems, consistently applied by managers, to compel their workforce to work together to realise the necessary improvements in quality of care and patient safety that have been difficult to achieve.

REFERENCES

Adinolfi, P. (2003), 'Total quality management in public health care: a study of Italian and Irish hospitals', *Total Quality Management*, **14,** 141–150.

Agarwal, A., S. Garg and U. Pareek (2011), 'Strengthening human resources practices in healthcare in India, the road ahead', *Journal, Indian Academy of Clinical Medicine*, **12,** 38–43.

Aiken, L.H., A. Smith and E.T. Lake (1994), 'Lower Medicare mortality among a set of hospitals known for good nursing care', *Medical Care*, **32**, 771–87.

Alexander, J.A., R. Lichtenstein, K. Jinnett, R. Wells, J. Zazzali, and D. Liu (2005), 'Cross-functional team processes and patient functional improvement', *Health Services Research*, **40**, 1335–1356.

Armstrong, K.J., and H.K.S. Laschinger (2006), 'Structural empowerment, magnet hospital characteristics, and patient safety culture', *Journal of Nursing Care Quality*, **20**, 124–32.

Bach, S. (2000), 'Health sector reform and human resource management: Britain in comparative perspective', *International Journal of Human Resource Management*, **11**, 925–42.

Baker, G.R., and V. Flintoff (2004), 'The Canadian Adverse Events Study: the incidence of adverse events among hospital patients in Canada', *Canadian Medical Association Journal*, **170**, 1678–86.

Barraud-Didier, V., and S. Guerrero (2002), 'Impact of social innovations on French companies' performance', *Measuring Business Excellence*, **6**, 42–48.

Bartram, T., P. Stanton, S.G. Leggat, G. Casimir and B. Fraser (2007), 'Lost in translation: making the link between HRM and performance in healthcare', *Human Resource Management Journal*, **17**, 21–41.

Batt, R. (1999), 'Work organisation, technology, and performance in customer service and sales', *Industrial and Labor Relations Review*, **52**, 539–64.

Batt, R. (2002), 'Managing customer services: human resource practices, turnover, and sales growth', *Academy of Management Journal*, **45**, 587–98.

Becker, B.E., and B. Gerhart (1996), 'The impact of human resource management on organisational performance: progress and prospects', *Academy of Management Journal*, **39**, 779–801.

Belanger, P., A. Giles and G. Murray (2002), 'Workplace innovation and the role of institutions', in G. Murray, J. Belanger, A. Giles, and P. Lapointe (eds), *Work and Employment Relations in the High Performance Workplace*, London: Continuum.

Berg, P., and A. Frost (2005), 'Dignity at work for low wage, low skill service workers', *Industrial Relations,* **60**, 657–82.

Borrill, C., M. West, D. Shapiro and A. Rees (2000), 'Team working and effectiveness in the NHS', *British Journal of Healthcare Management*, **6** (8), 364–371.

Boselie, P., G. Dietz and C. Boon (2005), 'Commonalities and contradictions in HRM and performance research', *Human Resource Management Journal*, **15**, 67–94.

Bowen, D.E., and C. Ostroff (2004), 'Understanding HRM-firm performance

linkages: the role of the "strength" of the HRM system', *Academy of Management Review*, **29**, 203–221.
Braithwaite, J. (2004), 'An empirically-based model for clinician-managers' behavioural routines', *Journal of Health Organisation and Management Decision*, **18**, 240–61.
Braithwaite, J., and D. Hindle (1999), 'Research and the acute care hospital of the future', *Medical Journal of Australia*, **170**, 292–3.
Braithwaite, J., S. Luft, W. Bender, J. Canne, J.I. Westbrook, M.T. Westbrook, N.A. Mallock, R. Iedema, D. Hindle and T. Jochelson (2007), 'The hierarchy of work pursuits of public health managers', *Health Services Management Research*, **20**, 71–83.
Buchan, J. (2004), 'What difference does ("good") HRM make?', *Human Resources for Health*, **2**, 1–7.
Butler, P., A. Felstead, D. Ashton, A. Fuller, T. Lee, L. Unwin and S. Walters (2004), 'High performance management: a literature review', in C.F.L.M. Studies (ed.), *Learning as Work Research Paper*, Leicester: University of Leicester.
Chang, W.Y., J.C. Ma, H.T. Chiu, K.C. Lon and P.H. Lee (2009), 'Job satisfaction and perceptions of quality of patient care, collaboration and teamwork in acute care hospitals', *Journal of Advanced Nursing*, **65**, 1946–55.
Combs, J., Y. Liu, A. Hall and D. Ketchen (2006), 'How much do high-performance work practices matter? A meta-analysis of their effects on organisational performance', *Personnel Psychology*, **59**, 501–28.
Committee on Quality of Healthcare in America (2001), *Crossing the Quality Chasm. A New Health System for the 21st Century*, Washington, DC: National Academy Press.
Davies, G. (2005), 'Queensland Public Hospitals Commission of Inquiry Report', Brisbane: Government of Queensland.
Davies, H.T.O., R. Mannion, A.E. Powell and M.N. Marshall (2007), 'Exploring the relationship between senior management team culture and hospital performance', *Health Care Research Review*, **64**, 46–65.
Deber, R., A. Topp and D. Zakas (2004), 'Private delivery and public goals: mechanisms for ensuring that hospitals meet public objectives', Background Paper prepared for the World Bank.
Degeling, P., J. Kennedy and M. Hill (1998), 'Do professional subcultures set the limits of hospital reform?', *Clinician in Management*, **7**, 89–98.
Degeling, P., J. Kennedy and M. Hill (2001), 'Mediating the cultural boundaries between medicine, nursing and management – the central challenge in hospital reform', *Health Services Management Research*, **14**, 36–48.
Delaney, J.T., and M.A. Huselid (1996), 'The impact of human resource management practices on perceptions of organisational performance', *Academy of Management Journal*, **39,** 949–969.
Dopson, S., L. Fitzgerald, E.B. Ferlie, J. Gabbay, L. Locock and H.C.M. Review (2002), 'No magic targets! Changing clinical practice to become more evidence based', **27**, 35–47.
Dubois, C.-A., E. Nolte and M. Mckee (2006), 'Human resources for health in Europe', in C.-A. Dubois, M. Mckee and E. Nolte (eds), *Human Resources for Health in Europe*, Open University Press.
Duckett, S.J. (2003), 'Commentary on the King Edward Inquiry: every defect a treasure', *Australian Health Review*, **26**, 24–5.
Dunbar, J.A., P. Reddy, B. Beresford, W.P. Ramsey and R.S.A. Lord (2007), 'In

the wake of hospital inquiries: impact on staff and safety', *Medical Journal of Australia*, **186**, 80–3.

Dussault, G. (1999), 'Human resources development: the challenge of health sector reform', Prepared for the Latin American and the Caribbean Department, Human Development Division, New York: World Bank.

Dwyer, J., and S.G. Leggat (2002), 'Innovation in hospital care', *Australian Health Review*, **25**, 19–31.

Dyer, L., and T. Reeves (1995), 'Human resource strategies and firm performance: what do we know and where do we need to go?', *International Journal of HRM*, **6**, 656–70.

Estryn-Behar, M., B.I.J.M. Van Der Heijden, H. Oginska, D. Camerino, O. Le Nezet, P.M. Conway, C. Fry and H.-M. Hasselhorn (2007), 'The impact of social work environment, teamwork characteristices, burnout and personal factors upon intent to leave among European nurses', *Medical Care*, **45**, 939–950.

Felstead, A., and D. Gallie (2002), 'For better or worse? Non-standard jobs and high involvement work systems', SKOPE Research Paper, Warwick: University of Warwick.

Franco, L.M., S. Bennett and R. Kanfer (2002), 'Health sector reform and public sector health worker motivation: a conceptual framework', *Social Science and Medicine*, **54**, 1255–66.

Garling, P. (2008), 'Final report of the Special Commission of Inquiry: Acute Care Services in NSW Public Hospitals', Sydney: NSW Government.

Glouberman, S., and H. Mintzberg (2001), 'Managing the care of health and the cure of disease – Part 1: Differentiation', *Health Care Management Review*, **21**, 56–69.

Godard, J. (2004), 'A critical assessment of the high-performance paradigm', *British Journal of Industrial Relations*, **42**, 349–78.

Gowen, C.R., K.L. Mcfadden and W.J. Tallon (2005), 'On the centrality of strategic human resource management for healthcare quality results and competitive advantage', *Journal of Management Development*, **25**, 806–26.

Griffiths, P., A. Renz and A.M. Rafferty (2008), 'The impact of organisation and management factors on infection control in hospitals: a scoping review', London: Kings College.

Guthrie, J.P. (2001), 'High-involvement work practices, turnover, and productivity: evidence from New Zealand', *Academy of Management Journal*, **44**, 180–190.

Harley, B., B.C. Allen and L.D. Sargent (2007), 'High performance work systems and employee experience of work in the service sector: the case of aged care', *British Journal of Industrial Relations*, **45**, 607–33.

Harmon, J., D.J. Scotti, D. Behson, G. Farias, R. Petzel, J.H. Neuman and L. Keashly (2003), 'Effects of high-involvement work systems on employee satisfaction and service costs in veterans' healthcare', *Journal of Healthcare Management*, **48**, 1–14.

Harris, C., P. Cortvriend and P. Hyde (2007), 'Human resource management and performance in healthcare organisations', *Journal of Health Organisation and Management*, **21**, 448–459.

Harrison, S., and J.N.W. Lim (2003), 'The frontier of control: doctors and managers in the NHS 1966 to 1997', *Clinical Governance: An International Journal*, **8**, 13–18.

Harter, J.K., F.L. Schmidt and T.L. Hayes (2002), 'Business-unit-level relationship between employee satisfaction, employee engagement, and business outcomes: a meta-analysis', *Journal of Applied Psychology*, **87**, 268–79.

Hillard, M., and R. Mcintyre (1998), 'The ambiguous promise of high performance work organisation', *Review of Radical Political Economics*, **30**, 25–33.

HMSO (2001), 'Public inquiry into children's heart surgery at the Bristol Royal Infirmary 1984–1985. Learning from Bristol', London: Her Majesty's Stationery Office.

Holtom, B.C., and B.S. O'Neill (2004), 'Job embeddedness: a theoretical foundation for developing a comprehensive nurse retention plan', *Journal of Nursing Administration*, **34**, 216–227.

Horsburgh, M., R. Perkins, B. Coyle and P. Degeling (2006), 'The professional subcultures of students entering medicine, nursing and pharmacy programmes', *Journal of Interprofessional Care*, **20**, 425–31.

Huselid, M. (1995), 'The impact of human resource management practices on turnover, productivity and corporate financial performance', *Academy of Management Journal*, **38**, 635–72.

Huselid, M., S. Jackson and R. Schuler (1997), 'Technical and strategic HRM effectiveness as determinants of financial performance', *Academy of Management Journal*, **40**, 171–88.

Ibrahim, J., and J. Majoor (2002), 'Corruption in the health care system: the circumstantial evidence', *Australian Health Review*, **25**, 20–6.

Jahangir, F., and N. Shokrpur (2009), 'Three components of organisational commitment and job satisfaction of hospital nurses in Iran', *Health Care Manager*, **28**, 375–80.

Kachur, E.K., and K. Krajic (2006), 'Structures and trends in health professional education in Europe', in C.-A. Dubois, M. Mckee and E. Nolte (eds), *Human Resources for Health in Europe*, Maidenhead, England: Open University Press.

Khatri, N., J. Wells, J. Mckune and M. Brewer (2006), 'Strategic human resource management issues in hospitals: a study of a university and a community hospital', *Hospital Topics*, **84**, 9–20.

Kramer, M., and C. Schmalenberg (2004), 'Essentials of a magnetic work environment: part 1', *Nursing*, **34**, 50–54.

Laschinger, H.K.S., J. Shamian and D. Thomson (2001), 'Impact of magnet hospital characteristics on nurses' perceptions of hospital burnout, quality of care and work satisfaction', *Nursing Economics*, **19**, 209–219.

Leatt, P., and J. Porter (2003), 'Where are the healthcare leaders? The need for investment in leadership development', *Healthcare Papers*, **4**, 14–31.

Leggat, S.G. (2008), 'Operations management: the search for value in healthcare organisation and performance', Chapter 2 in R. Sorenson and R. Iedema (eds), *Managing Clinical Processes in Health Services*, Sydney: Mosby Elsevier.

Leggat, S.G., and J. Dwyer (2005), 'Improving hospital performance: culture change is not the answer', *Healthcare Quarterly*, **8**, 60–6.

Leggat, S.G., L. Narine, L. Lemieux-Charles, J. Barnsley, G.R. Baker, C. Sicotte, F. Champagne and H. Boilodeau (1998), 'A review of organisational performance assessment in health care', *Health Services Management Research*, **11**, 3–23.

Leggat, S.G., T. Bartram and P. Stanton (2005), 'Performance monitoring in the Victorian health care system: an exploratory study', *Australian Health Review*, **29**, 17–24.

Leggat, S.G., T. Bartram and P. Stanton (2006), 'People management in Victorian

Community Health Services: an exploratory study', *Australian Journal of Primary Health*, **12**, 59–65.
Leggat, S.G., T. Bartram and P. Stanton (2008), 'Exploring the lack of progress in improving patient safety in Australian hospitals', *Health Services Management Research*, **21**, 32–39.
Leggat, S.G., T. Bartram, G. Casimir and P. Stanton (2010), 'Nurse perceptions of the quality of patient care: confirming the importance of empowerment and job satisfaction', *Health Care Management Review*, **35**.
Leggat, S.G., C. Balding and J. Anderson (2011a), 'Empowering health-care managers in Australia: an action learning approach', *Health Services Management Research*.
Leggat, S.G., T. Bartram and P. Stanton (2011b), 'High performance work systems: the gap between policy and practice in health care reform', *Journal of Health Organisation and Management*, **25** (3), 281–297.
MacDuffie, J.P. (1995), 'Human resource bundles and manufacturing performance', *Industrial and Labor Relations Review*, **48**, 197–215.
Mannion, R., H.T.O. Davies and M.N. Marshall (2005), 'Cultural characteristics of "high" and "low" performing hospitals', *Journal of Health Organisation and Management*, **19**, 431–39.
Matthews, S.C., and P.J. Pronovost (2008), 'Physician autonomy and informed decision making. Finding the balance for patient safety and quality', *Journal of the American Medical Association*, **300**, 2913–15.
McClure, M., M. Poulin and M. Sovie (1983), 'Magnet hospitals: attraction, retention of professional nurses', Kansas City: American Nurses Association.
McConnell, C.R. (2002), 'The health care professional as a manager: finding the critical balance in a dual role', *Health Care Manager*, **20**, 1–10.
McConville, T., and L. Holden (1999), 'The filling in the sandwich: HRM and middle managers in the health sector', *Personnel Review*, **28**, 406–24.
McLean, J., and M. Walsh (2003), 'Lessons into the inquiry into obstetrics and gynaecology services at King Edward Memorial Hospital 1990–2000', *Australian Health Review*, **26**, 12–23.
O'Brien-Pallas, L.O., G. Tomblin-Murphy, J. Shamian, X.M. Li, G. Kephart, H.K.S. Laschinger and Y. Liu (2008), 'Research synthesis report. The nursing labour market in Canada: an occupational sector study', Toronto: Nursing Health Services Research Unit, University of Toronto.
OECD (2004), 'Towards high-performing health systems', Paris: OECD.
Ott, M., and H. Van Dijk (2005), 'Effects of HRM on client satisfaction in nursing and care for the elderly', *Employee Relations*, **27**, 413–24.
Paauwe, J., and R. Richardson (1997), 'Introduction', special issue on HRM and performance, *International Journal of Human Resource Management*, **8**, 257–62.
Patrick, A., and H.K.S. Laschinger (2006), 'The effect of structural empowerment and perceived organisational support on middle level nurse managers' role satisfaction', *Journal of Nursing Management*, **14**, 13–22.
Preuss, G.A. (2003), 'High performance work systems and organisational outcomes: the mediating role of information quality', *Industrial and Labor Relations Review*, **56**, 590–605.
Rafferty, A.M., J. Ball and L.H. Aiken (2001), 'Are teamwork and professional autonomy compatible, and do they result in improved hospital care?', *Quality in Health Care*, **10**, ii32–37.
Richardson, R., and H. Thompson (1999), 'The impact of people management

practises on business performance: a literature review', London Institute of Personnel and Development.

Rigoli, F., and G. Dussault (2003), 'The interface between health sector reform and human resources in health', *Human Resources for Health*, **1**, 9.

Rondeau, K., and T. Wagar (2001), 'Impact of human resource management practice on nursing home performance', *Health Services Management Research*, **14**, 192–202.

Saltman, R., and J. Figueras (1997), 'European health care reform. Analysis of current strategies', in Europe, WHOROF (ed.), WHO regional publications. European series no. 72, Copenhagen.

Scotti, D.J., J. Harmon and S.J. Behson (2007), 'Links among high-performance work environment, service quality and customer satisfaction: an extension to the healthcare sector', *Journal of Healthcare Management*, **52**, 109–125.

Shaw, C. (2006), 'Managing the performance of health professionals', in C.-A. Dubois, M. Mckee and E. Nolte (eds), *Human Resources for Health in Europe*, Maidenhead, England: Open University Press.

Snell, S.A., and M.A. Youndt (1995), 'Human resource management and firm performance: testing a contingency model of executive controls', *Journal of Management*, **21**, 711–737.

Stanton, P., S. Young, T. Bartram and S.G. Leggat (2010), 'Singing the same song: translating HRM messages across managerial hierarchies', *International Journal of Human Resource Management*, **21**, (4).

Takeuchi, N., M. Wakabayashi and Z. Chen (2003), 'The strategic HRM configuration for competitive advantage: evidence from Japanese firms in China and Taiwan', *Asia Pacific Journal of Management*, **20**, 447–80.

Upenieks, V.V. (2003), 'The interrelationship of organisational characteristics of magnet hospitals, nursing leadership and nursing job satisfaction', *Health Care Manager*, **22**, 83–98.

Veld, M., J. Paauwe and P. Boselie (2010), 'HRM and strategic climates in hospitals: does the message come across at the ward level?', *Human Resource Management Journal*, **20**, 339–56.

West, E. (2001), 'Management matters: the link between hospital organisation and quality of patient care', *Quality in Health Care*, **10**, 40–48.

West, M.A., C. Borrill, J.F. Dawson, J. Scully, M. Carter, S. Anelay, M.G. Patterson and J. Waring (2002), 'The link between the management of employees and patient mortality in acute hospitals', *International Journal of Human Resource Management*, **13**, 1299–1310.

West, M.A., J.P. Guthrie, J.F. Dawson, C.S. Borrill and M. Carter (2006), 'Reducing patient mortality in hospitals: the role of human resource management', *Journal of Organisational Behaviour*, **27**, 983–1002.

Whitener, E.M. (2001), 'Do "high commitment" human resource practices affect employee commitment? A cross-level analysis using hierarchical linear modeling', *Journal of Management*, **27**, 515–35.

Wilson, J.Q. (1989), *Bureaucracy: What Government Agencies Do and Why They Do It*, New York: Basic Books.

World Health Organization (2001), 'Quality of care: patient safety', Report by the Secretariat. World Health Organization.

Youndt, M.A., S.A. Snell, J.W. Dean and D.P. Lepak (1996), 'Human resources management, manufacturing strategy, and firm performance', *Academy of Management Journal*, **39,** 836–866.

Young, S., T. Bartram, P. Stanton and S. Leggat (2009), 'High performance work systems and employee well-being: a two stage study of a rural Australian hospital', *Journal of Health Organisation and Management*, **24**, 182–99.

Zacharatos, A., J. Barling and R. Iverson (2005), 'High-performance work systems and occupational safety', *Journal of Applied Psychology*, **90**, 77–93.

6. Fostering creativity in health care: health care workers as agents of creativity

March L. To, Neal M. Ashkanasy and Cynthia D. Fisher

FOSTERING CREATIVITY IN HEALTH CARE: HEALTH CARE WORKERS AS AGENTS OF CREATIVITY

Consistent with the rapidly changing nature of modern health care, both in the UK (Greener, 2009) and the US (Wallace and Schneller, 2008), there is an emerging imperative for creative thinking in health care management. In this respect, West and Richter (2008) discuss how managers of today's organisations need to foster a climate of creativity, where positive outcomes for patients are a function of innovative thinking, instead of a reliance on traditional approaches that may not always be best for patient outcomes. Thus, health care workers at all levels have a part to play in creativity by taking the initiative. Particularly important are frontline workers' reflection and self-initiative. Howkins and Thornton (2002), for example, observe that, 'Creativity in healthcare means adopting and implementing new ways of thinking in order to change the way nurses work' (p. 3). At the same time, creativity in healthcare has to take account of the need to manage error, although, as Keith and Frese (2011) have pointed out, creativity and error management are not necessarily antithetical. For example 'quick stick' ECG leads (see Lateef et al., 2008, for one example) were invented by nurses frustrated at delays in responding to patients' complaints of chest pain. A traditional 12-lead ECG setup requires careful site preparation to work reliably, but a downside is that the patient's chest pain would often disappear before ECG leads could be attached. Quick stick leads overcome this problem, and serve to illustrate how creative ideas and error management can go hand-in-hand when employees are given the opportunity to be inventive.

In this chapter, we focus specifically on personal and contextual facilitators of creative behavior, and on creating an optimal match between the two. Consistent with other writers in the creativity literature (Amabile, 1983, 1996; George and Zhou, 2002, 2007; Oldham and Cummings, 1996), we define creativity as the generation or production of ideas or solutions that are both novel and potentially useful. In this respect, ideas are novel if they are unique relative to ideas currently available in the organisation. In particular, and as Shalley et al. (2004) note, novel ideas are considered creative if they have new potential for direct or indirect value to the organisation or its clients, in either the short run or long run. Creativity can range from solutions for incremental adaptation to radical breakthroughs in the delivery of services, and can be produced by organisational members in any job at any level (George, 2007; Shalley and Gilson 2004; Madjar et al., 2002).

The structure of our chapter is as follows. First, we review findings that have emerged from research on the organisational contexts that enhance or restrict the likelihood of creative idea generation across the board. We next provide a more nuanced consideration of how contexts may interact with individual characteristics to enhance or restrict creativity, such that the optimal environment for enhancing creativity may vary as a function of individual traits and goals. Finally, we draw implications for managing the health care workforce toward greater creative achievements.

FACILITATORS AND INHIBITORS OF CREATIVITY

The Social Environment

A social environment at work comprises influential others including supervisors and peers. Researchers (Shalley et al., 2004; To et al., 2012; Zhou and Shalley, 2003) suggests that supervisors and co-workers play a key role in creativity. Shalley et al. (2004) suggest in particular that supportive leadership styles promote intrinsic motivation and creativity, whereas those that are controlling in nature tend to diminish intrinsic motivation and creativity (see also Deci and Ryan, 1985). George and Zhou (2007) highlight three particular ways that supportive supervisors can encourage creativity, these being developmental feedback, interactional justice, and trust. According to these authors, developmental feedback promotes a focus on improvement; interactional justice ensures that subordinates will be treated with respect even if their ideas end up unsuccessful; and trust assures subordinates that their efforts, attempts, and risk taking are worthwhile because supervisors have the expertise and professionalism to follow through on creative ideas. Frese et al. (1999) found that the more supervisors encouraged employees, the more creative ideas they submitted to the organisation's suggestion program. In contrast, controlling supervisors who closely monitor subordinate behavior, make decisions without subordinate participation, and demand adherence to strict rules and guidelines, are likely to decrease subordinates' creativity. In support of this view, George and Zhou (2001) found that close monitoring was detrimental to employee creativity.

Despite these main effects, Shalley et al. (2004) suggest that the influence of supervisory support on creativity may be moderated by individual differences. This view is supported by recent research evidence that supervisory support does not always have a main effect on subordinates' creativity (e.g., Baer and Oldham, 2006; George and Zhou, 2001; To et al., 2012; Zhou, 2003). Supervisory support may not be equally effective in cueing creativity for all types of subordinates. While some individuals may rely more on supportive leaders for encouragement to be creative, others may continue to offer creative ideas even when supervisory support for creativity is low.

Apart from the supervisor, co-workers are also important in generating a facilitating environment for creativity. Coworkers contribute to the formation of team norms and practices that may facilitate or inhibit creativity (Shalley et al., 2004; Zhou and Shalley, 2003). Shalley et al. (2004) point out that employees should be more creative when their co-workers are nurturing and supportive, whereas non-supportive, competitive co-workers should undermine intrinsic motivation and therefore creativity. However, Shalley et al. (2004) also review evidence that provides mixed support for these arguments. For example, Amabile et al. (1996) and Zhou and George (2001) found that individuals were more creative when their co-workers were supportive and encouraging. In contrast, Shalley and Oldham (1997) found that individuals in competition with others produced more creative ideas than those who were not in competition with their colleagues. It appears that a social environment featuring high support from supervisors and co-workers (versus competition) may not be universally effective in encouraging creativity.

Reward Systems

One might expect that rewards for creativity would increase creative attempts (see Shalley and Gilson, 2004), although this is not uniformly true. Rewards can be extrinsic or intrinsic. Further, rewards may be seen as controlling or alternatively as conveying valuable and empowering information about competence (Deci and Ryan, 1985). We know that intrinsic motivation is a key factor in promoting creativity, and occurs when individuals feel high personal control (autonomy) as well as high competence. Because rewards, if extrinsic and heavy-handed, may reduce autonomy, there is some possibility that their use may backfire. Amabile et al. (1990) have suggested that the expectation of receiving extrinsic rewards may not foster creativity because creativity is prompted by internal drives which are undermined by strong extrinsic rewards. Amabile (1996) argues that such contingent rewards may serve to control individuals' behavior and therefore reduce intrinsic motivation and creativity. On the other hand, Eisenberger and Armeli (1997) argued that rewards can also convey important information about competence, as well as recognition. This informational component of rewards may actually increase intrinsic motivation and ultimately creativity (Eisenberger and Armeli, 1997). Shalley and Gilson (2004) point out that if rewards are distributed in informational ways, and given in recognition of competence, creative attempts and accomplishments, then extrinsic rewards should promote rather than prevent creativity. Whether rewards are seen as controlling or as informational may come down to an individual perception, suggesting that reward systems have different effects on different people (Zhou and Shalley, 2003).

The Work Itself

As mentioned above, autonomy is important to intrinsic motivation, so the freedom of choice of work methods and activities is expected to facilitate creativity (Liu et al., 2011). Recent research evidence shows that autonomy is fundamental to creativity (Liu et al., 2011). People who have control over job activities show more initiative (Ohly and Fritz, 2010; To and Fisher, 2011). Perception of control is also associated with felt responsibility and ownership (Parker et al., 2006), which may lead to appraisal of a situation as a challenge rather than a threat and focus attention on potential gains from creative efforts (Lazarus and Folkman, 1984).

Nevertheless, a small but emerging body of research by researchers such as Fisher and To (2011) and Rodell and Judge (2009) suggests that challenge stressors (e.g., responsibility, complexity, or autonomy) may not have uniformly positive effects. While challenge stressors present the opportunity for personal growth, they also imply a greater amount of effort, higher accountability, and the risk of failure (Fisher and To, 2011). Rodell and Judge (2009) found that, while challenge stressors had a positive effect on initiative-taking such as citizenship behavior, these stressors also indirectly increased counterproductive behaviors through negative affect. In other words, to some individuals, demanding or autonomous tasks may be seen as threats or burdens rather than as positive challenges (Fisher and To, 2011). In sum, while research tends to suggest an overall facilitating role of autonomy on creativity, it is unlikely that all types of employees respond equally positively to autonomy. The potential negative effect may be stronger for individuals who feel responsible for decisions that may lead to serious consequences. In the following sections, we look more closely at the role of person-environment fit in fostering creativity.

THE ROLE OF PERSON-ENVIRONMENT FIT IN FOSTERING CREATIVITY

Thus far, we have discussed what is known about creating environments conducive to creativity. Ultimately, however, creative behavior comes down to the individual, and individuals are not all alike. The occurrence of creativity in health care relies on workers' initiative in seeking out better solutions or improvements in the daily delivery of health care. Moreover, triggering that initiative may depend on achieving an optimal match of employee traits with the most compatible environment for that particular employee. Creativity researchers have long maintained that creativity is a product of individual factors, contextual influences, and the interaction of the two (Shalley et al., 2000; Shalley et al., 2004; Woodman et al., 1993). A growing body of research on person-environment fit (P-E fit) further emphasises the important role of congruence between individuals and environments in fostering creativity (Choi, 2004; Raja and Johns, 2010; Livingstone et al., 1997).

Trait Activation Theory

We argue that trait activation theory may offer a useful lens to understand how environments and traits interact to influence behavior. Trait activation theory holds that personality traits are not uniformly activated and displayed in all situations. Instead, traits represent latent potential or predispositions, which are displayed as trait-expressive behaviors only when triggered by trait-relevant situations (Tett and Burnett, 2003; Tett and Guterman, 2000). In a direct test of the trait activation contention, Tett and Guterman (2000) found that correlations between self-reported trait measures and corresponding behavioral intentions were stronger in situations offering relevant cues for trait expression. Understanding what triggers trait expression requires consideration of relevant situational features.

In the workplace, trait-relevant cues can stem from sources such as the job itself, social norms or practices, and/or the organisational context (Tett and Burnett, 2003). Employees gain intrinsic rewards through trait expression *per se*, where an individual's expression of her or his personality is seen to be inherently desirable (Tett and Burnett, 2003). Also, workers can obtain extrinsic rewards when trait expressions are recognised and valued positively by others (Tett and Burnett, 2003). In sum, trait activation is the process by which individuals express their traits most strongly when presented with trait-relevant situational cues (Tett and Burnett, 2003; Tett and Gutermann, 2000).

Trait activation and creativity

The idea that organisational contexts need to allow the manifestation of individuals' propensity to be creative has some empirical support from organisational research. For instance, George and Zhou (2001) argued that, although high levels of openness to experience predispose individuals to be creative in general, this predisposition may not always manifest as creativity. This is because organisations sometimes present employees with strong situations that shape or constrain their behavior. In order for employees high on openness to exhibit creative performance, organisational contexts need to encourage and allow their trait expression. George and Zhou (2001) found evidence to support their idea that individuals with high openness to experience perform more creatively when they receive positive supervisor feedback and have flexibility in their work roles. Similarly, Zhou and Oldham (2001) theorised and found that individuals with more creative personalities exhibit the highest level of creative performance when they expect the opportunity to assess their own work. Such an opportunity implies autonomy rather than external control, and allows for competence information to be obtained, thus supporting the intrinsic motivation necessary for creativity.

Raja and Johns (2010) hypothesised and found that people high on neuroticism performed less creatively when job scope was high. High scope jobs require greater self-confidence, initiative, uncertainty tolerance, and accountability (Oldham and Hackman, 1980). Raja and Johns (2010) suggest that these job characteristics offer trait-relevant cues to neurotic individuals. Specifically, they argue that 'a high scope job could be seen as an excessive burden, resulting in the worsening of P-E fit, which in turn will magnify the negative effects of neuroticism on creativity' (p. 988). Their results showed that neuroticism was more strongly negatively related to creativity when job scope was high.

The dispositional variables that we will focus on in this chapter are trait goal orientations. We will describe three goal orientation constructs and the respective trait-relevant contexts that we believe may activate each goal orientation and thereby influence creativity. Based on trait activation theory, we develop a model of the interactive effects of goal orientations

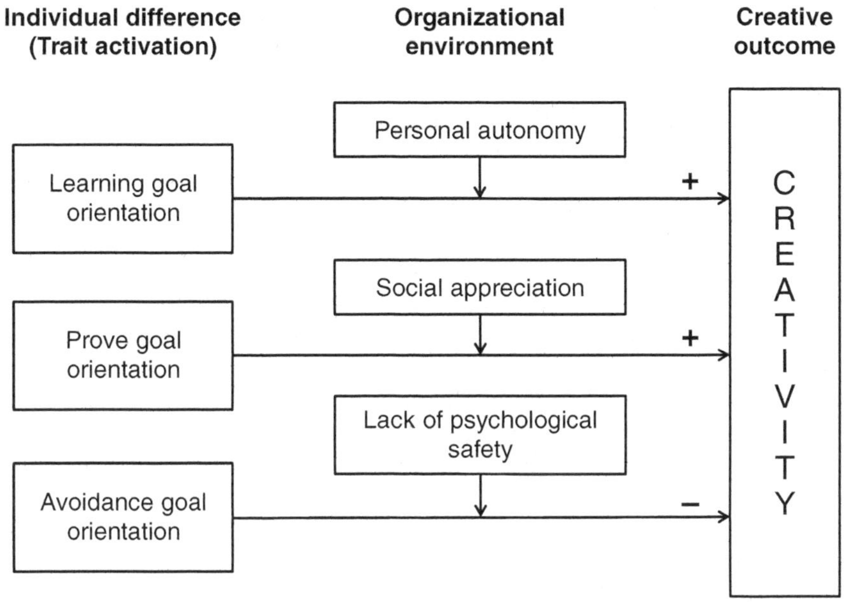

Figure 6.1 Creativity as a product of trait activation and organisational environment

and organisational environments as they may affect health care workers' creativity (Figure 6.1).

Goal orientation, trait activation, and creativity

Gong et al. (2009) demonstrate that dispositional goal orientation has important consequences for creativity (see also Janssen and Van Yperen, 2004). Researchers such as Hirst et al. (2011), To (2011), and To and Fisher (2011) showed that contextual influences not only facilitate but also inhibit the creative expression of dispositional goal orientation. Hirst et al. (2011) call for future research to identify 'specific trait-context combinations that are relevant to creativity.' In the following paragraphs, we define goal orientation constructs and discuss how goal orientation may be expressed in response to trait-relevant contexts to influence creativity in health care.

Goal orientation

Dweck and her colleagues (Dweck and Leggett, 1988; Elliot and Dweck, 1988) define goal orientation as two major classes of goal pursuit in achievement situations: (1) learning goal orientation is to develop competence through expanding individual abilities by mastering challenging situations; and (2) performance goal orientation is to validate competence by seeking favorable judgments or avoiding negative judgments from others.

Learning goal orientation and performance goal orientation are associated with different personal attributions of competence (Dweck and Leggett, 1988; Elliot and Dweck, 1988; VandeWalle et al., 2001). Learning goal orientation is associated with an incremental theory, where ability is seen as a malleable attribute that can be developed; whereas performance goal orientation is associated with an entity theory, where ability is seen as a fixed, innate attribute that is difficult to change (Dweck and Leggett, 1988). Since ability is perceived as malleable, individuals with a learning orientation tend to believe that effort is a means to enhance task performance and is a determinant of success. In contrast, individuals with a performance orientation tend to believe that successful performance is primarily attributable to high innate abilities, not effort. For these individuals, unsuccessful performances are seen as threatening and lasting indictments of their ability.

The early goal orientation literature suggested that learning goal orientation was more beneficial than performance goal orientation for performance on a wide range of tasks (e.g. Ford et al., 1998; Phillips and Gully, 1997; VandeWalle et al., 2001). More recent research, however, suggests that such a conclusion may be premature because a performance goal orientation, which focuses attention on obtaining favorable judgment from others, may also facilitate job performance (Porath and Bateman, 2006). To clarify the predictive effects of performance goal orientation, Elliot and his associates (e.g., Elliot and McGregor, 2001; Elliot and Church, 1997) further bifurcated performance goal orientation into prove goal orientation and avoid goal orientation (cf. VandeWalle, 1997).

According to VandeWalle (1997, p. 1000), performance-prove orientation is 'a focus on demonstrating one's competence and the gaining of favorable judgment from others' and a performance-avoid orientation is 'a focus on avoiding negation of one's competence and the avoiding of negative judgment from others.' Research evidence suggests that a performance-prove orientation (from here on: prove goal orientation) can also be associated with superior performances (e.g., Barron and Harackiewicz, 2000; Elliot and Church, 1997). Individuals with a performance-avoid orientation (from here on: avoidance goal orientation) may be more likely to develop withdrawal behavior if encountering or anticipating setbacks and difficulties in performance (Barron and Harackiewicz, 2000; Elliot and McGregor, 2001).

Goal orientation has often been conceptualised and measured as a dispositional trait (see DeShon and Gillespie, 2005; Payne et al., 2007 for reviews).The question of whether goal orientation expresses itself in consistent patterns of functioning across situations remains unclear, however. Some researchers view goal orientation as a situation-specific state based on the task or context at hand or as an experimentally induced state (see DeShon and Gillespie, 2005; and Payne et al., 2007 for reviews). Other researchers consider goal orientation stable within domains (e.g., VandeWalle, 1997). DeShon and Gillespie (2005) hold that transient accessibility of goal orientations can be a result of environmental cuing of specific goals. These authors argue further that goal orientations that are frequently simulated become highly accessible and therefore are chronically ready to be activated. In their examination of the stability of goal orientation, Button et al. (1996, p. 28) viewed goal orientation as a 'somewhat individual difference construct that can be influenced by situational characteristics.' In short, while trait goal orientation predisposes individuals to adopt certain response patterns, contextual factors may cause them to adopt a different or less characteristic response pattern (Button et al., 1996).

In the following sections, and drawing in particular on the work of Hirst et al. (2011), we propose three specific environmental features relevant to the creative expression of different goal orientations by health care employees. The three types of environment we discuss are: (1) autonomous, (2) socially appreciative, and (3) lacking in psychological safety. Specifically, we propose that these environments interact with goal orientation to predict creativity.

Autonomous Context and Creative Expression of Learning Goal Orientation

Dispositional goal orientation research has suggested that trait learning goal orientation facilitates creativity (Hirst et al., 2009; Gong et al., 2009; Janssen and Van Yperen, 2004). Learning goal orientation focuses attention on developing competence by acquiring new knowledge and skills and directs attention to the value of the activity itself (Elliot and Harackiewicz, 1994; Harackiewicz et al., 2002; Pekrun et al., 2006). Individuals high on learning goal orientation tend to persist in the face of obstacles, view negative feedback as useful information for improvement, and desire to work on challenging tasks (e.g., Button et al., 1996; Cron et al., 2005; VandeWalle, 1997).

Creativity often requires the development and generation of something new for which the requisite task activities have yet to be mastered (Hirst et al., 2009; Janssen and Van Yperen, 2004). Efforts to develop new and useful solutions may expose individuals to difficult tasks, setbacks, or failures. In this case, a strong learning goal orientation can assist in coping with the challenges and obstacles of creative process engagement in an effective way. Moreover, learning goal orientation focuses attention on the elaboration and development of new knowledge and deep processing strategies leading to effectiveness in complex and unfamiliar tasks (Janssen and Van Yperen, 2004; Steele-Johnson et al., 2000). In sum, the mastery propensity residing in trait learning goal orientation can facilitate the adoption of favorable patterns in response to opportunities to be creative.

Based on the idea that individuals find expression of their own personality to be inherently pleasurable, Tett and Burnett (2003) argue that employees gain intrinsic rewards through trait expression *per se*. Learning goal oriented individuals focus attention on ongoing competence development through effort. We therefore argue that learning goal orientation is likely to be expressed in response to the cues that the job environment permits discretion and autonomy for mastery (To and Fisher, 2011). Recent research evidence has offered indirect support for this contention. For instance, Hirst et al. (2011) found that learning goal orientation is positively related to creativity when centralisation is low, but not when centralisation is high. Decentralised decision-making conveys an invitation to voice and to share one's viewpoint, and thus empowers employees to grapple with non-routine challenges and problems. Hirst et al. (2011) suggest that low centralisation brings out the mastery inclination of individuals high on learning goal orientation, and that this manifests as creativity. In contrast, high centralisation that reduces opportunities to explore removes the creative benefit of a learning goal orientation, which is driven by intrinsic task motivation or engagement with challenging work.

We propose therefore that an autonomous context activates learning goal orientation in those who are so disposed, and motivates them to attempt to be creative. An autonomous context, where work paths and outcomes are contingent upon one's own decisions and effort, is likely to align with and to activate the mastery propensity (To, 2011; To and Fisher, 2011). Our first proposition is:

Proposition 1: Autonomous contexts activate learning goal oriented workers' mastery propensity that manifests as enhanced creativity.

Social Appreciation and Creative Expression Of Prove Goal Orientation

Tett and Burnett (2003) argue that personality traits can also be expressed in response to social cues (e.g., team norm, supervisors' expectation, etc.). Workers gain extrinsic reward when trait expressions are recognised and valued positively by others (Tett and Burnett, 2003). Following this reasoning, we argue that social appreciation is at the core of expression of prove goal orientation, and can serve to foster creativity.

Earlier research suggested a negative influence of trait prove goal orientation on innovative behavior. Janssen and Van Yperen (2004) suggest that prove-oriented individuals tend to define job success primarily in terms of demonstration of competence. In itself, trait prove goal orientation may lead individuals to avoid efforts to be creative because the associated risk of failure would demonstrate incompetence rather than producing the public success that these individuals pursue. More recently, however, Hirst et al. (2009) have emphasised situational influences on the relationship between performance goal orientation and creativity. Individuals with a strong performance goal orientation rely on situational cues to determine which behaviors are appropriate to display in order to maximise extrinsic reward and minimise punishment (Hirst et al., 2009). Hirst and his associates hypothesised and found that prove goal orientation was positively related to creativity only when team learning behavior was high. Team learning behavior was defined as reflective decision making, asking questions, seeking feedback, and openly discussing errors. The authors explain that team learning behavior serves as a source of social validation or extrinsic reward for creative risk-taking. When team norms communicate that learning and creativity are arenas in which to demonstrate ability, high prove individuals will be motivated to engage in these activities in order to obtain social appreciation (Hirst et al., 2009). However, when learning is not advocated in a team, prove goal oriented individuals will perceive they are unlikely to be recognised for devoting effort toward learning and creative activities, and will be less likely to do so.

Another contextual feature that may activate the creative propensity residing in prove goal oriented individuals is supervisory support (To et al., 2012). Supervisory support for creativity not only provides subordinates with encouragement and assistance to engage in the creative processes, but also conveys expectations that creativity is expected and valued (Madjar et al., 2002; Tierney and Farmer, 2004). Contrary to earlier thinking, however, recent research evidence does not show a significant across-the-board relationship between supervisory support for creativity and subordinates' creativity (e.g., Baer and Oldham, 2006; George and Zhou, 2001; Zhou, 2003). This suggests that supervisory support may not be equally effective in cueing creativity among all subordinates. Shalley and Gilson (2004) suggest that the relationship may be moderated by individual differences. High learning goal orientation people might not rely on supportive cues from supervisors as much as high prove goal people do. VandeWalle et al. (2000, p. 998) suggested that 'the adaptive response pattern, optimism, and hope of learning-goal-oriented individuals helps them to remain resilient when they face the unfavorable situation of a low consideration supervisor.' Perhaps supervisory support for creativity is more effective in promoting creativity in subordinates who are particularly concerned about being seen as competent performers, such as prove goal oriented individuals.

We suggest that when supervisors show strong preferences and support for creativity, prove-oriented individuals will be motivated to engage more in creativity to demonstrate ability or outperform their peers in terms of creativity (To, 2011). In contrast, when creativity is not advocated or appreciated, high prove goal oriented individuals may choose to rehearse familiar tasks to increase efficiency, or enact proven and established task strategies to ensure successful performance, rather than risk attempts to be creative (To, 2011; see also Janssen and Van Yperen, 2004). In sum, the central idea is that the potential for social appreciation of creativity is likely to cue prove goal individuals to engage more in creative activities. This task engagement (for the purpose of obtaining favorable judgments from others) is in turn a trait expression of prove goal orientation. Thus:

Proposition 2: Social appreciation for creativity activates prove goal oriented workers' 'achievement-by-outperforming' propensity that manifests as creativity.

(Lack of) Psychological Safety and Expression of Avoidance Goal Orientation

Trait avoidance goal orientation focuses on avoiding negative judgments from others, which implies a tendency to avoid challenges that carry the risk of mistakes (Hirst et al., 2009; VandeWalle, 1997). High avoidance goal individuals are more likely to withdraw after encountering setbacks and negative feedback (Barron and Harackiewicz, 2000; VandeWalle, 1997). Attempts to be creative expose individuals to the possibility of failures and errors, which are likely to be perceived as a warning of low ability by those high on avoidance goal orientation. Reasonably, expression of avoidance goal orientation is likely to reduce creative efforts (Hirst et al., 2009).

According to trait activation theory, traits can be activated by social cues that arise in working with others. A key social context that is relevant to avoidance goal orientation activation is psychological safety. Low psychological safety reflects a sense of insecurity for interpersonal risk taking in a work unit (Edmondson, 1999). Organisational routines are developed to maintain predictability, yet creativity can be seen as raising levels of uncertainty and challenging the status quo (George, 2007). Also, being creative is very often associated with risk of failure and mistakes. Thus, creativity may be greatly reduced if a context signals high interpersonal risk for unsuccessful creative attempts (George, 2007). This effect should be especially strong for avoidance goal oriented individuals who want to avoid mistakes or avoid negative judgments from others. Perhaps individuals who focus on task mastery rather than judgments from others may be less vulnerable to a context featuring low psychological safety. Consistent with this view, Hirst et al. (2009) suggest that high avoidance oriented people would be more likely to shy away from creativity when the team context does little to encourage learning. This is because the psychological risks associated with creativity attempts would be higher when team learning behavior is low (Hirst et al., 2009).

In sum, we propose that a work environment which is potentially psychologically risky will activate trait avoidance goal orientation in those who are high on this trait. It will reinforce avoidance-oriented people's concern about negative reactions or judgments and the potential for embarrassment, rejection, or loss of self-esteem. To avoid looking bad, these individuals may choose to play it safe by avoiding the risk inherent in creative attempts (Hirst et al., 2009). Therefore:

Proposition 3: Low psychological safety activates avoidance goal oriented workers' prevention propensity that manifests as reduced creativity.

IMPLICATIONS FOR MANAGING THE HEALTH CARE WORKFORCE

We began by reviewing contextual factors that may be associated with greater employee creativity on average. These included the social contexts of supervisor and team support for creativity, rewards, and the design of work to permit autonomy. These contextual features might present reasonable targets for inventions to enhance overall creativity in health care organisations. However, as the remainder of the chapter showed, the effect of any given context on individual creativity may depend on the employee's goal orientation, and whether the particular context triggers trait-relevant behavior (To, 2011). We argued that the propensity of individuals within each goal orientation to engage in (or not to engage in) creativity depends on the organisational environment (Figure 6.1). Thus, an organisational environment of personal autonomy would be likely to encourage learning goal orientation individuals to be creative; an environment of social appreciation and team learning would be likely to encourage prove goal orientation individuals to be creative; and an organisational environment that lacks psychological safety would be likely to inhibit prove goal employees from creative behavior.

Given that a population of employees is likely to include individuals who span all three goal orientations, the lesson for health care managers is clear. This is that a climate that combines personal autonomy, social appreciation for creativity from supervisors and teams, and psychological safety is likely to be most conducive to fostering overall creativity. So the question that emerges here is how and whether climates like this can be developed in health care organisations. The answer is, of course, affirmative, and, if findings reported by Zammuto et al. (2000) are to be believed, such climates are not as rare as some would lead us to believe. Zammuto and his colleagues looked at health care institutions in the USA and categorised them, based on the Quinn and Rohrbaugh (1983) competing values framework, into four quadrants: (1) Human Relations (flexible/internal), Open Systems (flexible/external), Internal Process (control/internal), and Rational Goal (control/external). The open systems category entails a proactive outlook and internal processes characterised by higher levels of trust, morale, and leader credibility, and lower levels of conflict and resistance to change. The result is an ideological emphasis on innovation and change. This seems to be a good match for the recommendations flowing from our consideration of the contexts supporting individual level creativity as well. Zammuto and his colleagues cite a study by Shortell et al. (1995), in which hospitals that most successfully implemented an innovation requiring workforce participation in creativity (total quality management) were found to display open systems values.

In conclusion, we argue that creativity is most likely to emerge in health care organisations that fall into the open systems quadrant of the Quinn and Rohrbaugh (1983) competing values framework. Such an organisational environment facilitates the level of personal autonomy learning goal orientation individuals need to enable them to explore new ideas; the level of social support needed by prove goal individuals to feel comfortable in acting creatively; and the level of psychological safety that avoidance goal individuals need to risk behaving creatively. The underlying proposition of this chapter is therefore that creative ideas (such as quick stick ECG leads) are most likely to occur when health care employees work in an environment where the organisational setting caters for their learning goal preferences and proclivities.

REFERENCES

Amabile, T.M. (1983), 'The social psychology of creativity: a componential conceptualization', *Journal of Personality and Social Psychology*, **45**, 357–376.

Amabile, T.M. (1996), *Creativity in Context: Update to the Social Psychology of Creativity*, Boulder, CO: Westview Press.

Amabile, T.M., P. Goldfarb and S.C. Brackfield (1990), 'Social influences on creativity: evaluation, coaction, and surveillance', *Creativity Research Journal*, **3**, 6–21.

Amabile, T.M., R. Conti, H. Coon, J. Lazenby and M. Herron (1996), 'Assessing the work environment for creativity', *Academy of Management Journal*, **39**, 1154–1184.

Baer, M., and G.R. Oldham (2006), 'The curvilinear relation between experienced creative time pressure and creativity: moderating effects of openness to experience and support for creativity', *Journal of Applied Psychology*, **4**, 963–970.

Barron, K.E., and J.M. Harackiewicz (2000), 'Achievement goals and optimal motivation: a multiple goals approach', in C. Sansone and J.M. Harackiewicz (eds), *Intrinsic and Extrinsic Motivation: The Search for Optimal Motivation and Performance*, San Diego, CA: Academic Press, pp. 229–254.

Button, S.B., J.E. Mathieu and D.M. Zajac (1996), 'Goal orientation in organizational research: a conceptual and empirical foundation', *Organizational Behavior and Human Decision Processes*, **67**, 26–48.

Choi, J.N. (2004), 'Person-environment fit and creative behavior: differential impacts of supplies-values and demand-ability versions of fit', *Human Relations*, **57**, 531–552.

Cron, W.L., J.J.W. Slocum, D. VandeWalle and Q. Fu (2005), 'The role of goal orientation on negative emotions and goal setting when initial performance falls short of one's performance goal', *Human Performance*, **18**, 55–80.

Deci, E.L., and R.M. Ryan (1985), *Intrinsic Motivation and Self-Determination in a Work Organization*, New York: Plenum.

DeShon, R.P., and J.Z. Gillespie (2005), 'A motivated action theory account of goal orientation', *Journal of Applied Psychology*, **90**, 1096–1127.

Dweck, C.S., and E. Leggett (1988), 'A social-cognitive approach to motivation and personality', *Psychological Review*, **95**, 256–273.

Edmondson, A. (1999), 'Psychological safety and learning behavior', *Administrative Science Quarterly*, **44**, 350–383.

Eisenberger, R., and S. Armeli (1997), 'Can salient reward increase creative performance without reducing intrinsic creative interest?', *Journal of Personality and Social Psychology*, **72**, 652–663.

Elliot, A.J., and M.A. Church (1997), 'A hierarchical model of approach and avoidance achievement motivation', *Journal of Personality and Social Psychology*, **72**, 218–232.

Elliot, A.J., and C.S. Dweck (1988), 'Goals: An approach to motivation and achievement', *Journal of Personality and Social Psychology*, **54**, 5–12.

Elliot, A.J., and J.M. Harackiewicz (1994), 'Goal setting, achievement orientation, and intrinsic motivation: a mediational analysis', *Journal of Personality and Social Psychology*, **66**, 968–980.

Elliot, A.J., and H.A. McGregor (2001), 'A 2 x 2 achievement goal framework', *Journal of Personality and Social Psychology*, **80**, 501–519.

Fisher, C.D., and L.M. To (2011), 'Micro job design: affective reactions to real-time task characteristics', Paper presented at the 9th Industrial and Organisational Psychology Conference, Brisbane, Australia.

Ford, J.K., E.M. Smith, D.A.Weissbein, S.M. Gully and E. Salas (1998), 'Relationship of goal orientation, metacognitive activity, and practice strategies with learning outcomes and transfer', *Journal of Applied Psychology*, **83**, 218–233.

Frese, M., E. Teng and C.J. Wijnen (1999), 'Helping to improve suggestion systems: predictors of making suggestions in companies', *Journal of Organizational Behavior*, **20**, 1139–1155.

George, J.M. (2007), 'Creativity in organizations', *Academy of Management Annals*, **1**, 439–477.

George, J.M., and J. Zhou (2001), 'When openness to experience and conscientiousness are related to creative behavior: an interactional approach', *Journal of Applied Psychology*, **86**, 513–524.

George, J.M., and J. Zhou (2002), 'Understanding when bad moods foster creativity and good ones don't: the role of context and clarity and feeling', *Journal of Applied Psychology*, **87**, 687–697.

George, J.M., and J. Zhou (2007), 'Dual tuning in a supportive context: joint contribution of positive mood, negative mood, and supervisory behaviors to employee creativity', *Academy of Management Journal*, **50**, 605–622.

Gong, Y., J.C. Huang and J.L. Farh (2009), 'Employee learning orientation, transformational leadership, and employee creativity: the mediating role of employee creative self-efficacy', *Academy of Management Journal*, **52**, 765–778.

Greener, I. (2009), *Healthcare in the UK: Understanding Continuity and Change*, Bristol, UK: Policy Press.

Harackiewicz, J.M., K.E. Barron, J.M. Tauer and A.J. Elliot (2002), 'Predicting success in college: a longitudinal study of achievement goals and ability measures as predictors of interest and performance from freshman year through graduation', *Journal of Educational Psychology*, **94**, 562–575.

Hirst, G., D. van Knippenberg and J. Zhou (2009), 'A cross-level perspective on employee creativity: goal orientation, team learning behavior and individual creativity', *Academy of Management Journal*, **52**, 280–293.

Hirst, G., D. van Knippenberg, C.-H. Chen and C. Sacramento (2011), 'How does bureaucracy impact on individual creativity? A cross-level investigation of team contextual influences on goal orientation-creativity relationships', *Academy of Management Journal*, **54**, 624–641.

Howkins, E., and C. Thornton (2002), 'Creativity in healthcare', in E. Howkins and C. Thornton (eds), *Managing and Leading Innovation in Healthcare*, New York: Baillière Tindall.

Janssen, O., and N.W. Van Yperen (2004), 'Employees' goal orientations, the quality of leader-member exchange, and the outcome of job performance and job satisfaction', *Academy of Management Journal*, **47**, 368–384.

Keith, N., and M. Frese (2011), 'Enhancing firm performance and innovativeness through error management culture', in N.M. Ashkanasy, C.E.P. Wilderom and M.F. Peterson (eds), *The Handbook of Organizational Culture and Climate, Second Edition*, Thousand Oaks, CA: Sage, pp. 137–157.

Lateef, F., A. Annathurai and T.T. Loh (2008), 'The V-Quick patch versus the standard 12-lead ECG system: time is the essence', *International Journal of Emergency Medicine*, **1**, 43–48.

Lazarus, R.S., and S. Folkman (1984), *Stress, Appraisal, and Coping*, New York: Springer.
Liu, D., X.-P. Chen and X. Yao (2011), 'From autonomy to creativity: a multilevel investigation of the mediating role of harmonious passion', *Journal of Applied Psychology*, **96**, 294–309.
Livingstone, L., D. Nelson and S. Barr (1997), 'Person-environment fit and creativity: an examination of supply-value and demand-ability versions of fit', *Journal of Management*, **23**, 119–146.
Madjar, N., G. Oldham and M. Pratt (2002), 'There's no place like home? The contributions of work and non-work sources of creativity support to employees' creative performance', *Academy of Management Journal*, **45**, 757–767.
Ohly, S., and C. Fritz (2010), 'Work characteristics, challenge appraisal, creativity, and proactive behavior: a multi-level study', *Journal of Organizational Behavior*, **31**, 543–565.
Oldham, G.R., and A. Cummings (1996), 'Employee creativity: personal and contextual factors at work', *Academy of Management Journal*, **39**, 607–634.
Oldham, G.R., and J.R. Hackman (1980), 'Work design in organizational context', in B.M. Staw and L.L. Cummings (eds), *Research in Organizational Behavior* (Vol. 2). Greenwich, CT: JAI Press.
Parker, S.K., N. Turner and H.M. Williams (2006), 'Modeling the antecedents of proactive behavior at work', *Journal of Applied Psychology*, **91**, 636–652.
Payne, S.C., S.S. Youngcourt and J.M. Beaubien (2007), 'A meta-analytic examination of the goal orientation nomological net', *Journal of Applied Psychology*, **92**, 128–150.
Pekrun, R., A.J. Elliot and M.A. Maier (2006), 'Achievement goals and discrete achievement emotions: a theoretical model and prospective test', *Journal of Educational Psychology*, **98**, 583–597.
Phillips, J.M., and S.M. Gully (1997), 'Role of goal orientation, ability, need for achievement, and locus of control in the self-efficacy and goal-setting process', *Journal of Applied Psychology*, **82**, 792–802.
Porath, C.L., and T.S. Bateman (2006), 'Self-regulation: from goal orientation to job performance', *Journal of Applied Psychology*, **91**, 185–192.
Quinn, R.E., and J. Rohrbaugh (1983), 'A spatial model of effectiveness criteria: toward a competing values approach to organizational analysis', *Management Science*, **29**, 363–377.
Raja, U., and G. Johns (2010), 'The joint effects of personality and job scope on in-role performance, citizenship behaviors, and creativity', *Human Relations*, **63**, 981–1005.
Rodell, J.B., and T.A. Judge (2009), 'Can "good" stressors spark "bad" behaviors? The mediating role of emotions in links of challenge and hindrance stressors with citizenship and counterproductive behaviors', *Journal of Applied Psychology*, **94**, 1438–1451.
Shalley, C.E., and L.L. Gilson (2004), 'What leaders need to know: a review of social and contextual factors that can foster or hinder creativity', *The Leadership Quarterly*, **15**, 33–53.
Shalley, C.E., and G.R. Oldham (1997), 'Competition and creative performance: effects of competitor presence and visibility', *Creativity Research Journal*, **10**, 337–345.
Shalley, C.E., L.L. Gilson and T.C. Blum (2000), 'Matching creativity requirement

and the work environment : effects on satisfaction and intentions to leave', *Academy of Management Journal*, **43**, 215–223.
Shalley, C.E., J. Zhou and G.R. Oldham (2004), 'The effects of personal and contextual characteristics on creativity: where should we go from here?', *Journal of Management*, **30**, 933–958.
Shortell, S.M., J.L. O'Brien, J.M. Carman, R.W. Foster, E.F.X. Hughes, H. Boerstler and E.J. O'Connor (1995), 'Assessing the impact of continuous quality improvement/total quality management: concept versus implementation', *Health Services Research*, **30**, 377–401.
Steele-Johnson, D., R.S. Beauregard, P.B. Hoover and A.M. Schmidt (2000), 'Goal orientation and task demand effects on motivation, affect, and performance', *Journal of Applied Psychology*, **85**, 724–738.
Tett, R.P., and D.D. Burnett (2003), 'A personality trait-based interactionist model of job performance', *Journal of Applied Psychology*, **88**, 500–517.
Tett, R.P., and H.A. Guterman (2000), 'Situation trait relevance, trait expression, and cross-situational consistency: testing a principle of trait activation', *Journal of Research in Personality*, **34**, 397–423.
Tierney, P., and S.M. Farmer (2004), 'The Pygmalion process and employee creativity', *Journal of Management*, **20**, 413–432.
To, M.L. (2011), 'Within-person relationships between mood and creativity: the moderating roles of trait goal orientation and trait-relevant context', unpublished dissertation.
To, M.L., and C.D. Fisher (2011), 'When does negative mood boost creativity? A trait activation perspective', Paper presented at the Annual Meeting of the Academy of Management, San Antonio.
To, M.L., C.D. Fisher, N.M. Ashkanasy and P.A. Rowe (2012), 'Within-person relationships between mood and creativity', *Journal of Applied Psychology*, **97**, 599–612.
VandeWalle, D. (1997), 'Development and validation of a work domain goal orientation instrument', *Educational and Psychological Measurement*, **57**, 995–1015.
VandeWalle, D., S. Ganesan, G.N. Challagalla and S.P. Brown (2000), 'An integrated model of feedback-seeking behavior: disposition, context, and cognition', *Journal of Applied Psychology*, **85**, 996–1003.
VandeWalle, D., W.L. Cron and J.W. Slocum (2001), 'The role of goal orientation following performance feedback', *Journal of Applied Psychology*, **86**, 629–640.
Wallace, M., and E. Schneller (2008), 'Orchestrating emergent change: the "hospitalist movement" in US healthcare, *Public Administration*, **86**, 761–778.
West, M.A., and A.W. Richter (2008), 'Climates and cultures for innovation and creativity at work', in J. Zhou and C.E. Shalley (eds), *Handbook of Organizational Creativity*, New York: Taylor and Francis Group, pp. 3–31.
Woodman, R.W., J.E. Sawyer and R.W. Griffin (1993), 'Toward a theory of organizational creativity', *Academy of Management Review*, **18**, 293–321.
Zammuto, R.F., B. Gifford and E.A. Goodman (2000), 'Managerial ideologies, organization culture, and the outcomes of innovation: a competing values perspective', in N.M. Ashkanasy, C. Wilderom, and M. Peterson (eds), *Handbook of Organizational Culture and Climate*, Thousand Oaks, CA: Sage, pp. 263–280.
Zhou, J. (2003), 'When the presence of creative coworkers is related to creativity: role of supervisor close monitoring, developmental feedback, and creative personality', *Journal of Applied Psychology*, **88**, 413–422.

Zhou, J., and J.M. George (2001), 'When job dissatisfaction leads to creativity: encouraging the expression of voice', *Academy of Management Journal*, **44**, 682–696.

Zhou, J., and G.R. Oldham (2001), 'Enhancing creative performance: effects of expected developmental assessment strategies and creative personality', *Journal of Creative Behavior*, **35**, 151–167.

Zhou, J., and C.E. Shalley (2003), 'Research in employee creativity: a critical review and directions for future research', *Research in Personnel and Human Resources Management*, **22**,165–217.

7. Hospital restructuring and downsizing: déjà vu all over again[1]

Ronald J. Burke

Health care organisations underwent dramatic restructuring during the mid-1990s in several countries and appear to be on the threshold of another wave of downsizing and restructuring. These processes resulted from efforts by various levels of government to control and reduce costs and some services. Governments are again under pressure to reduce ballooning budget deficits. This chapter has several objectives. First, it reviews what is known about organisational restructuring and downsizing in general. Second, it presents findings from several analyses of the effects of health care restructuring and hospital downsizing on nursing staff in Ontario, Canada, and in other jurisdictions, undertaken in the late 1990s and early 2000s. Third, it considers current discussions targeted at reducing health care expenditures and presents results of recently collected 2009/2010 data. Fourth, it offers practical recommendations for managing hospital restructuring and downsizing efforts to minimise their adverse effects.

WHAT DO WE KNOW ABOUT ORGANISATIONAL RESTRUCTURINGS AND DOWNSIZINGS?

During the early 1990s, organisations engaged in widespread and dramatic restructuring. This resulted from the globalization of business, greater competition, the use of new technologies, and changes in the employer-employee relationship (Martin and Freeman, 1998). Restructurings, mergers and acquisitions, downsizings and plant closings were common (Gowing et al., 1998).

Studies of these processes have typically shown significant impacts on employees –those that survived and those that were terminated (Gowing et al., 1998; Noer, 1993; Marks, 1994). Common individual responses included anger, depression, low satisfaction, and heightened levels of both job insecurity and anxiety (Burke and Nelson, 1997, 1998; Burke and

Leiter, 2000; Spreitzer and Mishra, 2000). Downsized organisations lose the impetus for creativity and their ability to learn (Amabile and Conti, 1999; Fisher and White, 2000; Dougherty and Bowman, 1999).

These individual reactions were found to be associated with low levels of organisational performance as well (Cameron et al., 1987; Cascio, 1998, 1993). About half of the restructurings failed to achieve the benefits that were expected from them (Cascio, 1998; Marks, 1994).

McKinsey and Company (2010) concluded that corporate cost cutting programs quickly fade over time. Only 10 per cent of cost-reduction programs sustained their effects three years on according to their research of Standard and Poor 500 companies. Sales, general, and administrative costs seemed to be particularly difficult to cut. Thus organisations committed to reducing costs were generally unable to do so over only a three year time period. Organisational downsizings and restructurings have proven to be complex and difficult transitions. It is difficult for organisations to shrink their way to greater success!

Survivor Syndrome

Noer (1993) coined this term to refer to common responses of survivors of organisational restructuring and downsizing. The syndrome consists of high levels of anxiety, anger, depression, cynicism, and dissatisfaction. Others (e.g., Devine et al., 2003; O'Neill and Lenn, 1995; Wright and Barling, 1998) have identified similar survivor responses to organisational downsizing and restructuring.

Private Sector Restructuring and Downsizing: What Have We Learned?

Cascio (2002), based on an 18 year study of Standard and Poor 500 firms, concluded that firms that downsized were not more effective or profitable than firms that did not. Instead he advocates 'responsible restructuring'. Central to his thesis is changing the view that employees are costs to be cut, to viewing them as assets to be developed.

He examines 13 'myths' about downsizing, finding that research evidence provides no support for any of them. These myths include: downsizing employees boosts profits; downsizing employees has no effect on the quality of products or services, since companies are just 'cutting fat' by downsizing employees; and there are no adverse reactions to it.

Cascio (2002, p. 4) cites both direct and indirect costs of downsizing through layoffs.

Direct costs include: severance pay, outplacement services, administrative processing costs, and, in some cases, costs of rehiring former employees. Indirect costs include low morale, potential lawsuits from some employees, reduced productivity, and loss of trust and of organisational memory. Indirect costs may be larger than direct costs in many cases.

Cameron et al. (1991) observed 12 dysfunctional characteristics within organisations undergoing decline and downsizing which they termed 'the dirty dozen'. These were: centralisation of decision making, stopping of long-range planning, reductions in innovation, leadership scapegoating, employee resistance to change, higher levels of turnover, declining morale, loss of slack resources leading to organisational paralysis, the emergence of special interest groups, the loss of management credibility, increasing conflict among employees, and the use of across the board staffing cuts instead of more prioritised and focused reductions.

HEALTH CARE AND HOSPITAL RESTRUCTURING AND DOWNSIZING

During this same time period, various levels of government realised that growing budget deficits made it important to control and lessen their budget expenditures. Health care was then and continues to be the largest single budget allocation making it an attractive target for reduction in financial support.

Thus the Government of Ontario made a commitment to a balanced budget in the early 1990s, coupled with lower levels of financial support from the Federal government, resulting in lower levels of funding for health care. It created the Hospital Services Restructuring Commission (HSRC) which conducted a study indicating that the city of Toronto should reduce the number of hospitals from 45 to 32 through mergers and amalgamation of services, hospital closings and outsourcing and rationalisation of services. Health care restructuring in Canada took two forms: hospital closures and mergers, and bed reductions and downsizing through cuts in health human resources. By 1999, over 200 hospitals had morphed into 171, and merged hospitals had been reorganised to combine services and get rid of duplication. In the US, 828 hospitals closed between 1980 and 1992. Hospitals also made greater use of day surgery, decreased the average length of stay and shifted some of the burden of patient care to the community. Downsizing was common in almost every case, with nurses, being the largest employee group, most affected. Both nursing middle managers and front-line nursing service providers were targeted. Fewer nurse managers now had wider spans of control. Many full-time nursing positions were eliminated, creating a nursing workforce with more part time staff and casual nurses. Younger nurses were 'bumped' by longer tenured nurses. The number of registered nurses in Ontario fell by 8000 between 1995 and 1998. During this time period, thousands of nurses in Canada lost their jobs (Davidson, 1996). A 1996 survey of 20,000 nurses reported that 85 per cent believed that understaffing resulting from budget cuts and downsizings had created unsafe conditions for patients (Ontario Nurses' Association, 1996). With fewer staff, nurses' workload had increased. Nurses reported higher levels of stress and job insecurity, and lower levels of job satisfaction (Baumann et al., 1995; Richard Ivey School of Business, 1997).

Other initiatives included cost cuts for supplies and support services. Maintenance and replacement of equipment was delayed, increasing concern about occupational health and safety. Some services were outsourced, supplies were replaced by cheaper alternatives, cafeterias were closed, and counseling services and programs to protect nurses from abuse and violence were terminated.

A colleague, Esther Greenglass, and I, along with a few other researchers in Ontario. decided to examine the effects of these initiatives on nursing staff and their perceptions of the effects on aspects of hospital function. The Ontario Nurses' Association, one of two nurses unions in Ontario, cooperated in our work. We designed a longitudinal study with two waves of data collection from the same sample of nursing respondents with three years between data collections. All participants were employed in various hospitals in Ontario as nursing staff at T1, most were employed as nursing staff at T2, but some respondents had left the nursing profession (voluntarily or otherwise) and were now employed elsewhere.

Findings

Workload

Workload among the nursing samples was generally rated high. Workload was positively related to emotional exhaustion, with emotional exhaustion leading to both cynicism and psychosomatic symptoms, with cynicism also found to be negatively related to nurse ratings of their professional efficacy.

Changing units

We observed that 14 per cent of nursing staff had changed units in the preceding year, typically the result of hospital restructuring and downsizing. The effects on nurses of these changes were generally small; staff nurses changing units indicated higher levels of work stressors, lower levels of job satisfaction and lower levels of psychological well-being.

Number of downsizing and restructuring initiatives undertaken

A greater number of downsizing and restructuring initiatives was found to be significantly and positively correlated with a more negative impact on staff and quality of health care, lower levels of hospital facilities upkeep and a greater workload. In addition, impact on hospital facilities upkeep, impact on staff and quality of health care, and workload were themselves significantly and positively correlated.

Survivor responses

Mishra and Spreitzer (1998) identified four archetypal survivor responses to organisational restructuring and downsizing: Hopeful, Obliging, Cynical and Fearful.

Two dimensions underlay these types: an active/passive dimension based on the belief that individuals can/cannot cope with the restructuring/downsizing, and a constructive/destructive dimension based on perceptions of the presence/absence of threat or harm from the restructuring/downsizing.

- Fearful survivors – low ability to cope and high threat and harm – 'walking wounded'
- Obliging survivors –low ability to cope but low threat or harm –'faithful followers'
- Cynical survivors – high ability to cope and high harm or threat – 'carping critics'
- Hopeful survivors – high ability to cope and low threat or harm – 'active advocates'

Data were collected from long-term survivors (the T2 1999 sample) of Ontario hospital restructuring efforts. Nursing staff received scores indicating the extent to which each of the four survivor responses characterised them. Nurses indicating a higher number of restructuring initiatives were more cynical and more fearful. Nursing staff indicating higher levels of hospital support were more hopeful, more obliging, less cynical and less fearful.

Effects of hospital restructuring processes

Measures of the implementation of hospital restructuring were obtained in 1996 T1 and indications of hospital unit functioning were obtained in 1999 T2. Five restructuring processes were included: communication efforts, vision of the process, staff participation in the restructuring and downsizing process, revitalisation efforts during the restructuring and downsizing process, and levels of hospital support. Unit effectiveness consisted of four indicators: frequency of errors and injuries, coordination across nursing units, general assessment of patient care, and having adequate time for patients. The findings indicated moderate but positive relationships between more favorable perceptions of restructuring processes in 1996 and perceptions of hospital functioning in 1999.

Longitudinal effects

We found that measures of restructuring stressors (e.g., workload, use of staff bumping, and use of lower skilled generic workers), and of hospital support, obtained at T1 in 1996 were associated with nursing staff perceptions of their unit functioning (e.g., errors and injuries, patient care, coordination, time for patients, quality service culture, and overall unit functioning). Restructuring stressors had negative relationships with many of the outcomes, whereas level of hospital support had positive relationships with them.

We then computed difference scores between 1996 T1 and 1999 T2 measures of restructuring stressors, restructuring processes and nurse satisfaction and well-being. There were positive but moderate relationships between reductions in restructuring stressors over time and increased perception of use of more favorable restructuring processes over time, and increases in nursing staff satisfaction, level of psychological well-being and perceptions of hospital functioning.

Nurse coping resources

We also examined what role, if any, is played by individual nurse coping resources and found that nursing staff making greater use of control coping, less use of escape coping, and nurses indicating higher levels of self-efficacy, indicated lower levels of psychological distress during the hospital downsizing.

Nurses now working elsewhere

We compared work experiences and psychological well-being of hospital-based nursing staff who left their hospitals and moved to other jobs (n=36) using T1 and T2 data. Former hospital-based nurses now working elsewhere indicated higher levels of job satisfaction and psychological well-being (fewer psychosomatic symptoms), less job insecurity, lower levels of exhaustion and cynicism and higher levels of professional efficacy.

In other analyses, respondents described their new jobs as generally superior to their previous hospital-based nursing jobs. New jobs were judged better in terms of work hours, less stress, a lower workload and more satisfying job content, but were judged worse in terms of pay and union representation.

Other Research Findings on Health Care Restructuring

Baumann and Blythe (2003) offered an overview of health care restructuring in the 1990s. Workforce cuts and withdrawal of workplace supports without consideration of the human consequences resulted in a demoralised and short-staffed workforce with little or no cost containment benefits. They examine strategies used during this time and offer innovative approaches to change that make better use of nursing talents, capabilities and commitments.

Armstrong-Stassen and Cameron (2003) studied job satisfaction and turnover intentions among 111 nurses over a six-year period (1991–1997). Three hospital restructurings took place during this period in response to budget cutbacks (1992), hospital amalgamation (1995), and hospital downsizing (1997). Nursing staff indicated reduced satisfaction with their future career prospects, and reduced turnover intentions following the hospital restructuring. In 1997, nurses indicated lower job satisfaction and satisfaction with their workload, the type of work they were performing, their physical working conditions, their career futures, and their hospitals. They also indicated a significant increase in their turnover intentions.

Cummings and Estabrooks (2003) undertook a systematic literature review of the impact of hospital restructuring on survivors identifying 22 such studies. Consistent findings included decreases in job satisfaction, professional efficacy, ability to provide quality care, physical and emotional wellbeing, and increases in turnover and disruption in health care team relationships. Less experienced nurses, and nurses experiencing several rounds of restructuring, reported more negative reactions.

Rondeau and Wagar (2003) examined the effects of both hospital restructuring and hospital downsizing on hospital functioning in a sample of 285 Canadian acute care hospitals, collecting data from senior hospital executives. They reported that restructuring and downsizing had different effects on hospital performance. Hospitals embarking on restructuring without downsizing fared best, followed by hospitals undertaking both restructuring and downsizing, and those undertaking downsizing without restructuring.

Negative effects were significantly reduced when implementation processes were considered. That is, hospitals undertaking either restructuring or downsizing, or both, but implementing these more in keeping with suggested best practices (e.g., communication, fairness, staff participation) showed fewer negative performance effects of the transitions.

HOSPITAL RESTRUCTURING AND DOWNSIZING – 2010

A psychiatrist is reputed to have said 'Insanity is doing the same thing but expecting a different result.'

In 2009–2010, several countries, states and provinces, much like in the early 1990s, were facing budget deficits, partly due to the current world-wide economic crisis. These jurisdictions were again facing pressure to cut spending, and health care, the largest expenditure, was a prime target. The province of Ontario, in which I live, has reduced transfer payments to hospitals as a result. A few Ontario hospitals have recently reported being 'in the red'.

Perhaps the largest effort to balance budgets and related costs was the US state of California. California has been strongly affected by the current economic downturn. As a consequence, the state has terminated employees, required employees to take unpaid days off work, and cut support for both health care and education.

We had an opportunity (Burke et al., 2010) to partially replicate our 1996 Ontario health care restructuring study in California. We collected data from over 200 nursing staff in late 2009 and early 2010 as their restructuring efforts were being implemented using many of the same measures.

Results

Let us now consider some of the US results.

Respondents reported considerable hospital downsizing and restructuring initiatives

The most common restructuring initiatives were: budget cuts (82.6 per cent), a hiring freeze (76.9 per cent), overtime restrictions (73.6 per cent), not filling job vacancies (63.7 per cent), a wage freeze (44.9 per cent), beds closed (37.7 per cent), staff layoffs (33.2 per cent), and units closed (32.9 per cent).

Four predictor variables will be discussed here: number of restructuring initiatives undertaken in their hospitals, over the past year, increases in job insecurity, levels of hospital and union support, and activities undertaken by their hospitals to maintain or increase staff morale.

Restructuring initiatives

Nursing staff indicating a greater number of downsizing and restructuring initiatives also indicated lower levels of job satisfaction, greater intent to quit, more psychosomatic symptoms, lower levels of hospital maintenance and cleanliness, more negative impact on hospital functioning and effectiveness, and higher levels of job insecurity. Number of restructuring initiatives had no relationship however with levels of self-reported absenteeism and medication use.

Job insecurity

Including job insecurity as a predictor, after the number of restructuring initiatives undertaken in their hospitals was controlled, showed that nursing staff indicating higher levels of job insecurity as a result also indicated low levels of hospital maintenance and cleanliness and a more negative impact on hospital functioning and effectiveness.

Hospital and union support

Including levels of hospital support as a predictor, following a number of restructuring initiatives, showed that nursing staff reporting higher levels of hospital support also reported higher levels of hospital maintenance and cleanliness, a less negative impact of restructuring on hospital functioning and effectiveness, and fewer threats to their job security. Union support had almost no effect on any of the outcome measures, a finding similar to that obtained in our earlier Canadian study. The typical union-employer contract would not address increases in job demands, job strains and psychological distress resulting from downsizing and restructuring. Nursing unions do have a role in maintaining and improving the health and wellbeing of nursing staff and the quality of patient care however.

Initiatives to improve nursing staff morale

Including efforts by senior hospital administration to improve nursing staff morale, following a number of restructuring initiatives undertaken in their hospitals, showed that nursing staff indicating more efforts to improve morale reported a smaller deterioration in hospital maintenance and cleanliness.

Job insecurity

Job insecurity deserves a special mention. Job insecurity has been shown to increase during organisational restructurings and downsizings, in the general population at large during times of economic recession such as now. Research on job insecurity has increased in line with increasing research on organisational restructuring and downsizing.

Several reviews of the job insecurity literature have been undertaken (e.g., Cheng and Chan 2008; Sverke Hellgren and Naswall, 2002; Reisel and Probst, 2010). Job insecurity has been found to have similar relationships with a range of individual and organisational outcomes. It has been shown to have effects similar to those of actual unemployment, on individuals and their families. Job insecurity has been associated with diminished psychological well-being, physical health conditions, increased doctor visits, levels of anxiety, depression and overall distress. In addition individual job insecurity can increase feelings of insecurity in partners and children, and negatively affect children's school performance. Job insecurity can also impact organisations. It has been found to be associated with lower levels of job involvement, greater intent to quit, less trust of management, more job-related stress, more withdrawal behaviors such as absenteeism, tardiness and work task avoidance, lower levels of customer service, less employee flexibility, less creativity and innovation, lower levels of organisational citizenship behavior, reduced employee safety, and lower job and work unit performance. Job insecurity has important individual, family and organisational effects.

COSTS OF HEALTH CARE RESTRUCTURING AND DOWNSIZING, AND RECOMMENDATIONS

Let us now summarise the costs of restructuring and downsizing from studies undertaken in the health care sector. Evidence gathered in a number of countries showed that hospital restructuring and downsizing failed to reduce costs (see Baumann and Blythe, 2003, for a review of this literature). Instead most restructurings and downsizings had devastating effects on hospital staff. Hospitals also began experiencing nursing shortages which exist today. Nurses working in hospitals reported heavier workloads, dealing with sicker patients, working longer hours, more stress-related illness and workplace injuries, higher levels of absenteeism, and dissatisfaction (Aiken et al., 1994; Aiken et al., 2001).

Hospital executives, working with leaders of the nursing profession, must work together to address significant hospital organisation and management concerns. Hospital leadership must take proactive steps to maintain, and in some cases revitalise, a demoralised nursing staff (see Burke, 2003; Cameron 1994; Spreitzer and Mishsra, 2000; and Mishra et al., 1998, for suggestions on how best to proceed).

Implications for Practice

Cascio (2002, Chapter 5) offers considerable guidance to organisations considering restructuring involving downsizing. First he proposes several alternatives to downsizing, offering company examples of each. These include: using downsizing as a last resort, managing those that survive well, creating goodwill, even loyalty, among those laid off, providing other benefits (financial unemployment benefits) to employees whose hours are reduced, and getting employee input on how costs should be cut. Cascio believes that two concepts are central to restructuring and downsizing: justice and fairness, and communication. He again offers concrete suggestions on how organisations should best implement these transitions. The hospital CEO must develop a communications strategy that addresses the concerns of important stakeholders (employees, clients or customers, local community). Then the CEO must communicate with them using channels they can access and understand. CEOs must communicate a story that is honest, straightforward and consistent, and achievable. All managers must receive and understand where the organisation is heading, why, and how it is going to get there.

Cascio (2002, Chapter 7) lists 10 mistakes to avoid. These include: not being clear about short- and long-term goals; using downsizing as a first rather than last resort; using nonselective (e.g., across the board) downsizing; not involving employees in the restructuring process; not communicating honestly and openly; dealing poorly with those who will lose their jobs; not managing survivors effectively; not addressing needs of patients, customers or clients; and not evaluating progress, results and learning from mistakes.

Cascio (2002, Chapter 7) concludes with tips for 'restructuring responsibly'. These include:

- build the restructuring plan into the overall plan for the organisation;
- be clear on the reasons and rationale for restructuring;
- consider the benefits of a no layoff approach;
- before proceeding, make issues and potential need for restructuring clear for employees and get their input;
- make some financial cuts without 'nickel and dimeing' employees (e.g., cutting free coffee) and looking cheap and mean spirited;
- if employees will be laid off, do it in a way that is seen as fair, just and consistent; communicate often, using a variety of communication channels to keep all staff aware of what is going on;
- provide survivors with reasons for staying and contributing; and
- examine all human resource systems to make them supportive of the new vision and operation.

Hanes (2011) describes a work-sharing web-site started in Toronto by the entrepreneur Hannah McKinnon, that allows firms to share employees to avoid layoffs. It links firms with surplus staff with those needing employees. Thus hospitals can make staff available to nursing homes, for example, for a period of time until they have a need for them.

Probst (2009) suggests three levels of intervention to deal with feelings of job insecurity and threats to employment, common during restructuring and downsizings: primary – targeting organisational level sources of job insecurity (changing the organisation); secondary – increasing employee 'resilience' to feelings of job insecurity (changing individuals); and tertiary – reducing negative reactions of employees to their feelings of job insecurity (minimising negative effects). She offers the following practical organisational initiatives:

- inform employees about upcoming changes that could increase feelings of job insecurity;
- increase levels of organisational communication to employees;
- encourage greater employee participation and involvement in potential organisational changes;
- offer employees a 'realistic' preview of potential organisational changes;
- increase amounts of control employees have over their work; and
- help employees adapt to upcoming changes.

CONCLUSIONS

Private sector organisations embarked on widespread restructuring and downsizing efforts in the 1990s to become more competitive. Evaluations of these efforts indicate that most failed to achieve their business and financial objectives, while creating far-reaching dissatisfaction and anger among employees, both survivors and victims. Health care organisations, primarily hospitals, also undertook massive restructuring and downsizing efforts at the same time, following the approaches taken by the private sector, in response to government funding cutbacks. These efforts also were found not to reduce costs, but to create demoralisation in staff and place patient care at risk (Flint, 2003). Baumann and Blythe (2003) believe that the application of the business cost cutting model to health care settings was inappropriate since patient care relies on knowledge, skills and social relations.

But these efforts, though most failed, led to considerable learning on how to better go about organisational restructuring and downsizing (Cascio, 2002; Nelson and Burke, 1998). Organisations today faced with these difficult and complex transitions should be better prepared to undertake them.

Now, almost two decades later, the health care sectors in many provinces/ states and countries are contemplating restructuring and downsizing in response to another round of budget deficits – déjà vu all over again. In some cases (e.g., California), it seems as if they are going about it in the same way as the health care sector and hospitals in the 1990s that approached this crisis by using widespread layoffs. We know this will not work out well.

Hopefully some hospitals or health care regions will use research findings documenting the earlier failures and suggesting a 'better way forward' as they proceed.

NOTE

1. Preparation of this chapter was supported in part by York University. My colleagues Esther Greenglass, Lisa Fiksenbaum, Eddy Ng, Cobi Wolpin and Graeme MacDermid contributed to the research projects reported here. The Ontario Nurses' Association was of great help in data collection in some of these projects.

REFERENCES

Aiken, L.H., H.L. Smith and E.T. Lake (1994), 'Lower medicare mortality among a set of hospitals known for good nursing care', *Medical Care*, **32**, 771–787.

Aiken, L.H., S.P. Clarke, D.M. Sloane and J.A. Sochalski (2001), 'An international perspective on hospital nurses' work environments: the case for reform', *Policy, Politics and Nursing*, **2**, 255–263.

Amabile, T., and R. Conti (1999), 'Changes in the work environment for creativity during downsizing', *Academy of Management Journal*, **42**, 7630–640.

Armstrong-Stassen, M. and S.J. Cameron (2003), 'Dimensions of control and nurses' reactions to hospital amalgamation', *International Journal of Sociology and Social Policy*, **23**, 104–128.

Baumann, A., and J. Blythe (2003), 'Restructuring, reconsidering, reconstructing: implications for health human resources', *International Journal of Public Administration*, **26**, 1561–1580.

Baumann, A., L. O'Brien-Pallas, R. Deber, G. Donner, D. Semogas and B. Silverman (1995), 'The process of downsizing in selected Ontario acute care hospitals: budget reduction strategies and planning process', Toronto: Quality of Nursing Worklife Research Unit, University of Toronto.

Burke, R.J. (2003), 'Introduction. Health care restructuring in Canada', *International Journal of Sociology and Social Policy*, **23**, 1–7.

Burke, R.J., and M.P. Leiter (2000), 'Contemporary organizational realities and profession efficacy: downsizing, reorganization and transition', in P. Dewe, M.P. Leiter and T. Cox (eds), *Coping and Health in Organizations*, London: Taylor and Francis, pp. 237–258.

Burke, R.J., and D.L. Nelson (1997), 'Downsizing and restructuring: lessons from the firing line for revitalizing organizations', *Leadership and Organizational Development Journal*, **18**, 325–334.

Burke, R.J., and D.L. Nelson (1998), 'Downsizing, restructuring and privatization: a North American perspective', in M.K. Gowing, J.D. Kraft and J.C. Quick (eds) 'The new organizational reality: downsizing, restructuring and revitalization', Washington, D C: American Psychological Association, pp. 21–54.

Burke, R.J., E.W.S. Ng and J. Wolpin (2010), 'Effects of hospital downsizing and restructuring on nursing staff and hospital functioning: one more time', unpublished manuscript, Schulich School of Business, York University, Toronto.

Cameron, K. (1994), 'Strategies for successful organizational downsizing', *Human Resources Management*, **33**, 189–221.

Cameron, K.S., D. Whetten and M. Kim (1987), 'Organizational dysfunctions of decline', *Academy of Management Journal*, **30**, 126–137.

Cameron, K., S.J. Freeman and A.K. Mishra (1991), 'Best practices in white-collar downsizing: managing contradictions', *Academy of Management Executive*, **5**, 57–73.

Cascio, W.F. (1998), 'Learning from outcomes: financial experiences from 311 firms that have downsized', in M.K. Gowing, J.D. Kraft and J.C. Quick (eds), 'The new organizational reality: downsizing, restructuring and revitalization', Washington, DC: American Psychological Association, pp. 55–70.

Cascio, W.F. (1993), 'Downsizing: What do we know? What have we learned?', *Academy of Management Executive*, **7**, 95–104.

Cascio, W.F. (2002), *Responsible Restructuring: Creative and Profitable Alternatives to Layoffs*, San Francisco: Berrett-Koehler.

Cheng, G.H., and D.K. Chan (2008), 'Who suffers more from job insecurity? A meta-analytic review', *Applied Psychology: An International Review*, **57**, 272–303.

Cummings, G., and C.A. Estabrooks (2003), 'The effects of hospital restructuring that included layoffs on individual nurses who remained employed: a systematic review of impact', *International Journal of Sociology and Social Policy*, **23**, 8–53.

Davidson, J. (1996), Cited in D. Bell, 'Costing the cure', *CA Magazine*, 28 September.

Devine, K., T. Reay, L. Stainton and R. Collins-Nakai (2003), 'The stress of downsizing: comparing survivors and victims', *Human Resource Management*, **42**, 109–124.

Dougherty, D., and E. Bowman (1999), 'The effects of organizational downsizing on product innovation', *California Management Review*, **37**, 28–44.

Fisher, S.R., and M.A. White (2000), 'Downsizing in a learning organization: are there hidden costs?', *Academy of Management Review*, **25**, 244–251.

Flint, D.H. (2003), 'Downsizing in the public sector: Metro-Toronto's hospitals', *Journal of Health Organization and Management*, **17**, 438–46.

Gowing, M.K., J.D. Kraft and J.C. Quick (1998), *The New Organizational Reality: Downsizing, Restructuring and Revitalization*,Washington, DC: American Psychological Association.

Hanes, T. (2011), 'Sharing your employees to avoid layoffs', *Toronto Star*, 13 April, B8.

Marks, M.L. (1994), *From Turmoil To Triumph*, New York: Lexington Books.

Martin, R.E., and S.J. Freeman (1998), 'The economic contest of the new organizational reality', in M.K. Gowing, J.D. Kraft and J.C. Quick (eds), *The New Organizational Reality: Downsizing, Restructuring and Revitalization*, Washington, DC: American Psychological Association, pp. 5–20.

McKinsey and Company (2010), *Five Ways CFOs Can Make Cost Cuts Stick*, New York: McKinsey and Company.
Mishra, A.K., and G.M. Spreitzer (1998), 'Explaining how survivors respond to downsizing: the roles of trust, empowerment, justice and work redesign', *Academy of Management Review*, **23**, 567–588.
Mishra, K.E., G.M. Spreitzer and A.K. Mishra (1998), 'Preserving employee morale during the downsize', *Sloan Management Review*, **39**, 83–95.
Nelson, D.L., and R.J. Burke (1998), 'Lessons learned', *Canadian Journal of Administrative Sciences*, **5**, 372–381.
Noer, D. (1993), *Healing the Wounds: Overcoming the Trauma of Layoffs and Revitalizing Downsized Organizations*, San Francisco: Jossey-Bass.
O'Neill, H.M., and J. Lenn (1995), 'Voices of survivors: words that downsizing CEOs should hear', *Academy of Management Executive*, **9**, 23–34.
Ontario Nurses' Association (1996), *Dialogue on Health Reform*, May, Toronto: Ontario Nurses' Association.
Probst, T. (2009), 'Job insecurity, unemployment, and organizational well-being: oxymoron or possibility?', in S. Cartwright and C.L. Cooper (eds), *Oxford Handbook of Organizational Well-being*, Oxford: Oxford University Press, pp. 387–410.
Reisel, W.D., and T.M. Probst (2010), 'Twenty-five years of studies of job insecurity', *International Studies of Management and Organization*, **40**, 3–5.
Richard Ivey School of Business (1997), *Leading the Management of Change: A Study of 12 Ontario Hospitals*, London, ON: Richard Ivey School of Business.
Rondeau, K.V., and T. Wagar (2003), 'Downsizing and organizational restructuring: what is the impact on hospital performance?', *International Journal of Public Administration*, **26**, 1647–1667.
Spreitzer, G.M., and A.K. Mishra (2000), 'An empirical examination of a stress-based framework of survivor responses to downsizing', in R.J. Burke and C.L. Cooper (eds), *The Organization In Crisis*, London: Blackwell, pp. 77–118.
Sverke, M., J. Helgren and K. Naswall (2002), 'A meta-analysis and review of job insecurity and its consequences', *Journal of Occupational Health Psychology*, **7**, 242–264.
Wright, B., and J. Barling (1998), 'The executioner's song: listening to downsizers reflect on their experiences', *Canadian Journal of Administrative Sciences*, **15**, 339–355.

8. A better model of managing sickness absence

Hugh Flanagan, Fred Barwell, Patti Mazelan and Peter Spurgeon

INTRODUCTION

There is a very large literature on the problem created by absence at work, but, as Walker and Bamford (2011) note, the voluminous literature also contains many gaps. Most notably they identify a lack of attention to the wider organisational context (Dunn and Wilkinson 2002), to cultural aspects of absenteeism (Steel et al. 1995) and a relative weakness in assessing the effectiveness of proposed solutions (Spurgeon 2002). It is safe to conclude that sickness absence is a significant cost to the economy even if actual figures vary in accord with the method and approach to recording data. Willmott (2007) reports that less than half of the organisations (surveyed) actually cost absence, making any figure quoted subject to a fair degree of extrapolation. Perhaps the most important weakness to be found in the area is the fragmentation of approaches to managing absence, with organisations becoming very active when absenteeism is high but letting the topic drift when the actual rate drops (Carrington 2007). It is unlikely in such circumstances that a coherent evidence based approach will emerge.

The focus of this chapter is to consider, with respect to the health service in particular, how an improved model of sickness management can contribute to a reduction in costs from absenteeism and improved efficiency in the running of health organisations.

ABSENTEEISM IN THE HEALTH SECTOR

The wider financial pressures facing the UK health service are well documented, with efficiency savings of £20 billion required by 2014. Population projections only seem to intensify the magnitude of this challenge, with an increase of 17 per cent by 2033 giving a total population of 71.6 million, and of these 3.3 million being over 85 years old.

Better management of sickness absence could certainly contribute, with the Audit Commission report on absenteeism in the NHS suggesting that £290 million of the NHS's total sickness bill of £1.7 billion being an achievable target. However, a very significant managerial response is required if this is to happen, as the Commission also note that to reach the target, all Trusts would have to manage sickness absence as well as the top 25 per cent of Trusts currently do.

The Problem

NHS sickness absence is higher than in most other public and private sector organisations. There is real money to be saved by tackling the problem, though there are diverging views on how much. There is a strong view and some evidence that raw absence due to sickness should be seen in a wider context of the impact on clinical safety and quality and patient experience, and that it may indicate wider issues about staff engagement due to management practices.

Boorman

The Boorman interim report (2009a) describes NHS absence rates as high and not reducing.

> 10.3 million working days are lost in the NHS in England each year.
>
> - This is the equivalent of 45,000 wholetime equivalent (WTE) staff or some 4.5 per cent of the current workforce.
> - The annual direct cost of absence is some £1.7 billion a year.

Reducing absence by a third across the board would gain 3.4 million working days a year, equivalent to 14,900 extra WTEs and an estimated annual direct cost saving of £555 million.

There are indirect costs from sickness absence and poor staff health and wellbeing, resulting from the arrangements needed to cope with reduced availability of permanent staff, i.e.:

- Using agency and other temporary staff to cover staff absence (some £1.45 billion a year)
- Recruitment costs to replace staff who leave because of illness or stress. The Chartered Institute of Personnel and Development estimate £4,500 to fill a vacancy, higher for senior clinical and managerial staff.

- Ill-health retirement, which the NHS Employers Partnership Review estimated a cost to the NHS of £150 million a year.
- Cost of overtime and employing staff for additional discretionary hours, with the associated risks of stress due to long hours.

Additionally, Boorman (2009a) states there are 'significant benefits to the quality of service to patients, with better outcomes and improved patient experience. Our analysis showed a clear relationship between staff health and well-being and patient satisfaction'. Presenteeism, individuals attending work when unwell, which often reduces performance, is another issue, with many staff coming into work when they are sick enough to merit staying at home because they feel a sense of obligation to colleagues or managerial pressure. Staff also reported significant levels of stress and the belief that their employer did not take a positive interest in their health and wellbeing.

In summary, the Boorman report describes the key findings in relation to the state of the NHS in relation to health and wellbeing as:

- NHS staff have relatively high levels of sickness absence. On average, staff are absent for some 10.7 days a year, more than the public sector as a whole (9.7 days) and the private sector (6.4 days).
- These levels of sickness absence are reducing, but not as significantly as in other organisations. In the public sector as a whole, sickness absence fell from 9.8 to 9.7 days, while across the private sector it reduced from 7.2 to 6.4 days.
- Respondents report high levels of presenteeism, with many staff reporting that they come to work when they feel sufficiently unwell to justify staying at home.
- Many staff report significant levels of stress.
- Many staff do not believe that senior managers or their employer as an organisation take a positive interest in their health and well-being.
- Most staff believe that their state of health affects patient care.

Audit Commission

The Audit Commission (2011) found that the average NHS sickness rate is around 4.4 per cent, which equates to almost one day per month per staff member. Rates for individual organisations range from 1.6–6.8 per cent. Health care assistants are the staff group with the highest rate of 6.5 per cent (17 per cent in one organisation), ambulance workers 6.3 per cent, then nursing and midwifery staff at 5.2 per cent. Other frontline staff such as Trust doctors and dental staff have relatively low rates around 2.1 per cent.

Their analysis explored why there is such a large variation. They found that local economic deprivation together with staff grade mix explains 61 per cent of the local variation in sickness absence in trusts and 38 per cent in PCTs and that 'these are factors that management cannot control'. Deprivation and sickness absence are correlated, with deprivation explaining 17 per cent of the variation in trusts and 6 per cent in PCTs. Organisations with a higher proportion of staff at lower grades have higher sickness absence rates. Frontline staff generally have a higher rate. There is a general correlation in most organisations between pay grade and sickness absence. Staff on lower Agenda for Change grades have higher sickness rates and it is likely that this is affected by factors such as the ability to control one's work. Of course, some sickness absence is not due to genuine sickness but according to the Chartered Institute of Personnel and Development this is higher in the private sector. The Commission also identify indirect costs (temporary staff etc.) estimating them at nearly £740 million for NHS trusts and FTs and £180 million for PCTs. They also identify the cost of presenteeism, the loss in productivity due to employee ill-health at work, which could be as high as one and a half times that of actual sickness absence.

The direct cost estimated by the Audit Commission is similar to Boorman, £1.3 billion to NHS trusts and FTs and £0.33 billion to PCTs. The estimated cost to individual organisations varied between less than £900 and just over £2,700 per full-time equivalent member of staff. They also estimated indirect cost as nearly £740 million for NHS trusts and FTs and £180 million for PCTs.

In calculating savings the Commission state that:

> at least 61 per cent of the variation in NHS trusts and FTs and 38 per cent in PCTs is related to factors outside the control of management. This is important when estimating potential savings from improving sickness absence management. If all PCTs, NHS trusts and FTs were able to reduce the cost of absence to the lowest quartile of their group of nearest statistical neighbours, after allowing for deprivation and grade mix, the estimated potential savings would be £290 million. Reducing it to the median would produce estimated cost savings of £150 million. (Audit Commission 2011)

The Audit Commission estimated the median cost of sickness absence for NHS organisations is £3.2m a year with an additional cost of £1.9m a year for temporary staff cover.

The potential for savings is less optimistic than Boorman. Deprivation and staff mix were apparently not factored into the Boorman review's £555m target, even though they account for much of the variation between organisations' sickness rates, according to the commission.

The Audit Commission review also revealed that more than half of the days lost at a sample of trusts and PCTs were due to long term sickness lasting more than 20 working days, compared with just 5 per cent in the private sector and 8 per cent in the public sector overall.

A BETTER APPROACH?

Any approach to managing sickness absence and reducing some of the direct and indirect cost to the NHS, as well as the negative impact on safety, quality and the patient experience needs to be based on two factors:

1. Locating better management of sickness absence in a strategic context aimed at improving the health and well-being of staff, not only because it is the right thing to do but because it makes sound business sense, enabling the NHS to meet the quality and productivity challenge it faces through a focus on innovation and prevention. To achieve this on a sustainable basis requires engaging with staff to identify the problems, the underlying causes, the improvements that would address them, the ensuing impact on services and how changes would be implemented.
2. More effective and innovative data gathering to enable, at minimum, an understanding of the cost of sickness absence in each health organisation and at best, to provide some insight into the reasons for and patterns of sickness between staff groups/parts of the organisation and predict the likely problem areas/individuals based on the early pattern of absence.

Engagement

Research undertaken by the Institute of Employment Services on engagement in the public and private sector, shows clear links to employee attitudes towards other aspects of working life (Robinson et al. 2004), with the strongest driver being a sense of feeling valued and involved. The components of this are:

- involvement in decision-making
- the extent to which employees feel able to voice their ideas, and to which managers listen to these views, and value employees' contributions
- the opportunities employees have to develop their jobs
- the extent to which the organisation is concerned for employees' health and well-being.

These issues cover similar areas to those factors that build employee commitment, as can be found in the literature. But 'employee commitment' is seen as different and a lesser state to 'employee engagement'. Employee commitment may include those committed to the organisation for the 'wrong' reason. Structural commitment suggests that employees may stay with the organisation due more to a lack of alternatives than out of a positive affiliation – inertia re leaving a job they are dissatisfied with, or staying to get the pension (a form of long-term 'presenteeism'?). 'Employee engagement does not suffer from this problem as it involves working with staff to build alignment with the goals of the organisation and staff being prepared to 'go the extra mile' on behalf of the organisation' (NHS Institute for Innovation and Improvement 2007). Demonstrated concern and genuine co-action on employee health and wellbeing is fundamental to building an engaged workforce.

Boorman (2009b) and also the Audit Commission (2011) echo these ideas.

> While important steps have already been made in raising awareness of the importance of staff health and well-being to high-quality patient care, and areas of excellent practice already exist in the NHS, there remains much scope for improving staff health and welfare across the NHS as a whole. While the best NHS organisations already outperform private sector comparators, and we found clear examples of Trusts securing enhanced performance by targeting improved staff support, our research confirmed marked variations between NHS organisations and, worryingly, we received strong feedback that staff are not convinced that their health and well-being is seen as important to their employer.
>
> It is important to emphasise here that staff health and well-being is more than just the absence of disease. Rather, it puts an emphasis on achieving physical, mental and social contentment. There is a strong business case for investing in staff health and well-being. Organisations that prioritised staff health and well-being performed better, with improved patient satisfaction, stronger quality scores, better outcomes, higher levels of staff retention and lower rates of sickness absence.
>
> Making improvements in well-being services is not something that NHS leaders and managers can do alone. They need to work in close partnership with staff and staff representatives to design services that meet staff needs, and to reshape those services over time as needs change. (Boorman 2009b)

The Audit Commission state 'As well as making cost savings, there are many positive benefits from improving employee health and wellbeing. These include increased staff productivity, better morale and improved communication between teams. This in turn could lead to better quality services, improved patient satisfaction and a decrease in staff turnover.'

They emphasise the criticality of data collection and management in order to understand the sickness absence problem in a particular Trust. Understanding and diagnosing the problem effectively is a critical prerequisite to developing both strategic and tactical interventions.

- Review staff sickness absence rates in your organisation and check how you compare to similar organisations.
- Look in more detail at whether different staff groups or different parts of your organisation are well above or below the average. The NHS Information Centre's iView**ii** tool is available to do this.
- Calculate the cost of sickness absence to your organisation. If your organisation's cost improvement plan includes reducing sickness absence, then check whether the figures are reasonable.
- Consider whether your organisation could reduce its sickness absence rate and how that could produce savings – either cashable or through increased productivity. (Audit Commission 2011).

The Importance of Effective HRM

The largest employer in Europe, the NHS employs over 1.2 million people. There have been huge changes offering patients increasing choice over their health care through the continuing development of the market. Resource constraints and the continuing change make it necessary for increasing efficiency and improving patient outcomes through creative human resource management (HRM).

Over the years there have been a number of initiatives to take a more proactive approach to the health and wellbeing of staff, including Improving Working Lives. This approach and its 'principles of good HR practice underpins all of the current government initiatives and assists with the delivery of your organisation's objectives. For example, it will help organisations to meet their obligations under the NHS Constitution which embodies staff rights to representation, fair treatment, flexible working opportunities and a safe and healthy workplace' (NHS Employers 2009).

The Institute report discusses how HR practices affect the quality of services NHS patients receive. Progressive HR activity has been found to increase productivity in other organisations and sectors. Increasing the skills and knowledge of staff and enabling them to use those skills and knowledge, increases the likelihood of a positive attitude towards their work (Penna 2002, 2003; Watson Wyatt 2002). Similarly positive outcomes could be gained within the NHS when such HR practices are adopted (Hyde et al. 2006).

It is not unreasonable to assert that most NHS managers hold an instinctive belief that better employee engagement and wellness lead to better productivity, quality and safety. But they also know that this simple belief requires time, persistence and resilience to develop and implement what is likely to be a complex agenda. Faced with immediate resource reductions across the board and cut-backs in management costs, the reasonable response is to focus on the urgent and tactical, and to put off the strategic change that could provide the foundation for a more fundamental and sustained approach. However, there are good examples of organisations instigating initiatives and realising significant benefits:

> Capita launched a formal and accurate system to collect absence data to identify trends and absence patterns. As a trigger for reducing persistent short term absence we included the Bradford Factor and 'day one' referrals for all musculo-skeletal and stress-related absences. We also introduced a direct point of contact, with case management and treatment services for employees when triggers were met; it supports employees and managers. The system, together with absence management training for line managers, has reduced absence by 30 per cent over two years and saved £400 per employee. (Capita 2009)

> It's been reported that Portsmouth Hospitals trust has saved £9m from its overall pay bill for 2010–11, partly due to a 'renewed emphasis' being placed on the management of sickness absence and other employee relations activity. Over the last year it has formed a team within its existing workforce directorate with the objective of reducing sickness-related absence. Managers were trained by the team to manage sickness absence and to deliver informal sickness management meetings. (Portsmouth NHS Trust 2011)

The Portsmouth Trust dismissed 75 people through a 'formal management process'. It reveals that 56 of the dismissals related to sickness absence. However, the trust was able to help 85 members of staff back to work after long-term absence.

We propose that taking a strategic approach that builds in sustained improvement in:

- productivity through reducing direct and indirect cost of absence
- clinical quality through a balanced approach to the presence-absence of permanent staff e.g. through supporting staff who are unwell and whose presence at work would be detrimental (a shift in pressure to stay away when unwell rather than turn-up in spite of being unwell)
- safety through reducing risk of harm due to stress e.g. through poor team working or lack of time for training or handovers . . .

. . . is a sine qua non, in spite of any immediate sense of being overwhelmed. Some Trusts are already doing it and the NHS is going to be around in some form or other, still employing a million plus people, for a long time to come. Our proposed starting point is to implement a better system for measuring and monitoring sickness absence.

Measuring and Monitoring

Monitoring sickness absence always requires that attendance records are kept and maintained in a reliable and accurate way. At a bare minimum these records should be capable of capturing individual spells of absenteeism together with an indication of their duration and the reasons that led to non-attendance. At this minimal level HR absenteeism records should allow line managers to identify reasonable and unreasonable patterns of sickness absence. One of the main functions of such a database is to highlight those staff on whom managers may choose to focus their attention in an attempt to improve attendance through interventions which range from medical support for genuine reasons to disciplinary action for non-genuine reasons.

Few organisations make the best use of the sickness absence information that they have, which is unfortunate since improving monitoring and ensuring the availability of relevant statistics to line managers is one of the most practical and effective strategies to reduce sickness absence.

Even crude absence rates (usually simply calculated as percentage of contracted time lost within a defined period) can help identify problem areas, although comparison of these summary statistics may be misleading. Using these measures, absence rates may appear stable, but clearly similar amounts of lost time may result from either a few staff absent for long periods or many staff absent for short periods. For this reason, measures of absence frequency provide a better indicator of short-term absence than the crude absence rate and may be a more sensitive measure on which to design strategies to combat sickness absence. Of course, frequent short term absences may be more problematic than occasional long term absences, particularly in organisations where employees work shifts and rotas.

The Bradford system is a popular technique to characterise an employee's attendance, by combining measures of both absence frequency and absence duration. For an individual employee, the Bradford score is calculated as follows:

$$\text{Bradford Points Score} = (S)^2 \times D$$

where S is the number of spells of absence in a time frame (usually the last 52 weeks) and D is the number of days' absence within the same period. So for employees with 10 days' absence, for example, in one rolling 52 week period, distributed differently, the Bradford score can vary enormously:

- One absence of 10 days corresponds to 10 points (i.e. $1\times1\times10$)
- Five absences of two days each corresponds to 250 points (i.e. $5\times5\times10$)

- Ten absences of one day each corresponds to 1000 points (i.e. 10×10×10)

These scores are often used to identify 'trigger' points which are used to either signal the need for management to informally intervene or may be used more specifically to decide whether or not to introduce interventions such as a formal review, counselling, referral to occupational health, or taking disciplinary action.

The merit of the Bradford system is its simplicity but there are four underlying problems with this increasingly popular approach.

- The scores are weighted to give scores for disruptive impact of frequency rather than duration of spells of absence.
- The scores are based on a retrospective time period (therefore they are unable to incorporate absence spells as they occur).
- The formula for deriving scores takes no account of the reasons for absenteeism.
- The scores do not distinguish between employees who have more or less time off than would be expected and takes no account of patterns of absenteeism.

The attraction of the Bradford system is that it provides a simple and easy-to-understand method of linking sickness absence records and management interventions. However, this type of management trigger approach has a number of limitations that reduce its usefulness to line managers and human resource staff in tackling the problems of sickness absence at the organisational 'sharp end'.

An Integrated Perspective

As Lu et al. (2011) have recently observed, the sickness absence literature is dominated by cross-sectional studies and this is not always an appropriate design. Longitudinal studies are often a more appropriate way of considering sickness absence although in both cross-sectional and longitudinal studies, sickness absence data are often highly skewed and clustered at zero. This non-normal data is often inappropriately analysed using linear regression. In this section, some of the results previously reported in the jointly funded CIPD/AHP study of sickness absence (Spurgeon et al. 2007) are briefly presented to illustrate a visual model of sickness absence based on integrating cross-sectional and longitudinal data to highlight the 'sickness absence journeys' of employees. In this integrated model both cross-sectional and longitudinal data are seen as essential

Reasons for Absence

Gastrointestinal
Infection
Non Medical Reason
etc

Can be related to various categories

Gender	Men [n = 49770] Women [n = 32506]
Age groups	Up to 25 years [n = 15495] Between 25–35 years [n = 28340] Between 35–45 years [n = 20436] Between 45–55 years [n = 12025] Over 55 years [n = 5625]
Sector	Public Sector [n = 10290] Private Sector [n = 71987]
Accident	YES [n = 1270] NO [n = 81004]
OHI	YES [n = 5219] NO [n = 77055]
Industry	Education [n = 4085] Retail [n = 1309] Call centres [n = 1078] Financial services [n = 3875] Support services [n = 4937] NHS [n = 2808] Transport/Logistic [n = 26380] Telecom [n = 23973] Utility [n = 3095] Manufacturing [n = 598] Cent/Loc Gov [n = 6015] Housing assoc [n = 4124]

Figure 8.1 Key variables in AHP database

to understanding and effectively managing individual cases of sickness absence.

This study was based on privileged access to analyse a unique sickness absence database which had been collated and was being used by Allied Health Professionals (AHP), who offered absence management services to a wide range of organisations. The AHP database represented a large set of companies drawn from a wide range of industries and sectors (roughly one-third public sector and two-thirds private sector, including transport, finance, logistics, manufacturing, telecom, call centres, utilities, education and support services). In all, the sickness absence records had been collected from 40 different organisations and this comprised over 80,000 individual absence spells associated with approximately 30,000 individual employees. The key variables in the absence database are summarised in Figure 8.1.

This extensive database was designed to support AHP's business

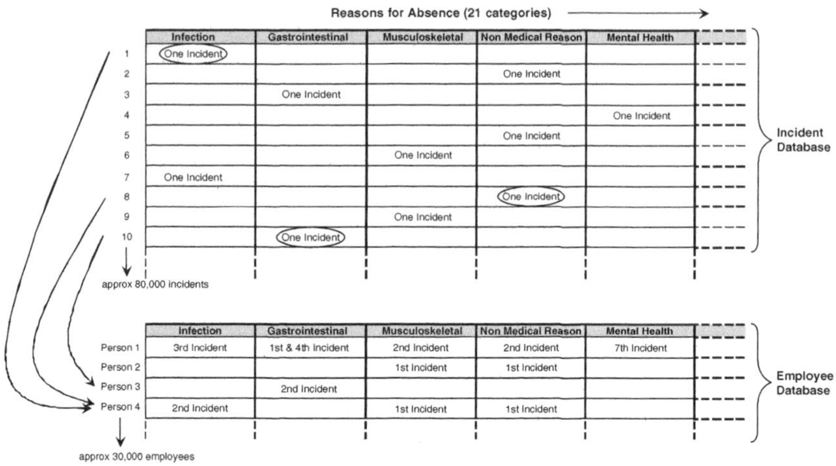

Figure 8.2 Two types of data base structure

activities of monitoring and managing sickness absence, whereby employees were required to report all unplanned absence to a contact centre on a 24-hour, seven-day a week basis. Qualified nurses, trained in occupational health, handled these sickness absence calls and used a standardised software package to code reasons for absence using a hierarchical coding framework based on the ICD10 system.

The structure of the working AHP database was suitable for aggregating the types and frequencies of sickness absence spells into various categories, but the database structure was not designed to allow easy identification of the absenteeism 'journey' of any particular employee. Since the ability to 'track' an individual's sequence and duration of sickness absence spells was essential to our approach, the original database was initially screened to check for outliers and identify missing data, and then restructured in order to provide a more flexible way of examining the sequence and progression of patterns of absenteeism for any individual employee. Figure 8.2 illustrates the two types of database structure:

The restructured database enabled an individual's absenteeism record to be accessible to statistical examination. The absenteeism database now existed in two forms – the original one based on absence spells and the rearranged one based on people. The first was labelled the 'incident' database and the second the 'employee' database.

Details of many thousands of absence spells were stored in the 'incident' database, categorised into 21 broad categories of reasons for absence (referred to as 'management reasons'). In the database, these higher-order

Table 8.1 Management reasons for sickness absence

Management reason	Frequency (per cent)	Mean days	SD days	Median days
Gastrointestinal	16811 (20.4)	2.70	6.85	1.5
Infection	13492 (16.4)	2.88	4.05	2
Non medical reason	11717 (14.2)	2.17	4.00	1
Musculoskeletal	8888 (10.8)	9.25	19.69	3
Neurological	5283 (6.4)	3.18	10.46	1
ENT and eyes	5281 (6.4)	3.97	8.90	2
Medical other	3550 (4.3)	6.47	21.90	2
Respiratory	3139 (3.8)	5.42	12.17	3
Mental health	2918 (3.5)	20.84	30.14	10
Injuries and poisoning	2243 (2.7)	10.47	21.36	3.75
Genito-urinary	2142 (2.6)	5.82	13.14	2
Complications of pregnancy and childbirth	1667 (2.0)	7.89	15.52	3
Dental	1575 (1.9)	2.49	4.99	2
Medical appointment	1241 (1.5)	2.12	7.26	1
Skin	863 (1.0)	5.70	10.55	3
Cardiovascular	660 (0.8)	16.76	35.67	4
Surgery	354 (0.4)	21.83	28.15	12.25
Endocrine	286 (0.3)	9.48	22.60	2
Tumours	102 (0.1)	38.21	59.96	10
Blood	61 (0.1)	12.01	21.43	5
Exposure	*3 (0)*	*7.67*	*5.86*	*10*

reasons were split into approximately 400 or so specific reasons for absence. Table 8.1 summarises these 'higher-order' reasons for sickness absence in the database, in descending order of frequency for all 21 management reasons.

The table shows that more than 60 per cent of all spells of absenteeism are accounted for by four reasons:

- Gastrointestinal problem (20.4 per cent)
- Infection (16.4 per cent)
- Non-medical factors (14.2 per cent)
- Musculoskeletal problem (10.8 per cent)

Furthermore, the table reveals that over 90 per cent of all spells of absenteeism are accounted for by the top 12 management reasons. Further analysis revealed that these patterns are related to age, gender and nature of the industry. For example, absence due to a musculoskeletal problem rises from an average of 5.89 days for the under-25s to 22.06 days for those aged 65 and over. In terms of total time lost due to absence, the top two causes are first, musculoskeletal problems and second, mental health problems. In the area of mental health the most prevalent reasons are stress and depression, and together, these accounted for some 50 per cent of the sickness absence spells. The spells too can be lengthy, suggesting relatively high impact upon the organisation.

- The average spell of absence for a mental health problem is 20.84 days
- The average spell of absence for stress is 21.48 days
- The average spell of absence for depression is 29.83 days

After minor illnesses (colds, flu, stomach upsets and headaches), stress and mental health, musculo-skeletal injuries and back pain are the major *medical* reasons for absence from work. There are however, many *non-medical* reasons for absence from work including:

- Personal/family crises/ childcare responsibilities
- Feeling bored and too unmotivated to attend
- Feeling undervalued
- Being intimidated/bullied/harassed
- Not able to cope with workplace pressures
- Hangover/overslept

A major message from the detailed analysis of the incident data is that a range of important variables simultaneously influences the pattern of individual sickness absence. This suggests that stereotypes or generalisations sometimes made in relation to sickness absence should be viewed with caution. For example, the aggregated results indicate that the average number of working days lost per absence spell is 6.35 days for the public sector, compared to 4.89 days for the private sector. Although this confirms the expected pattern overall, disaggregating by gender, age and job type, reveals that the magnitude and direction of these differences vary depending on which sub-groups are compared. Furthermore, there are very clear differences in average working days lost per absence spell between the industries in the database, ranging from 3.28 days to 7.31 days. It is clear that the frequency of absence spells as well as the working days lost per absence spell must be considered along with the particular job demands and the management intervention policy, because they can all combine to influence the pattern observed.

Designing the sickness absence database is fundamental not only in influencing data-capture strategies but also in how it may be used by HR professionals to understand the causes, consequences, potential implications and identification of absenteeism appropriateness. 'Incident' databases are particularly suitable for cross-sectional comparisons and this type of information is important in providing the 'big picture' of sickness absence. Aggregated cross-sectional sickness absence information is essential for the development of statistical reference groups based on age, gender, and occupation.

From Data to Management Action

It is clear that aggregated data on its own is only half of the sickness absence story and is not capable of guiding line managers to make the most effective interventions about individual cases of sickness absence. We suggest that a better strategy might be to use the available evidence (derived from both the incident and employee perspectives) to target case based decision making for individual employees and to intervene at an organisational level on underlying causes which impact on groups of employees. The components of this integrated strategy would include the following:

- Establish normative reference groups
- Identify overall patterns of absenteeism in database and investigate causes
- Identify individual patterns of evolving sickness absence 'symptomatology'
- Use management triggers based on normative reference data appropriate to individual
- Determine if individual absenteeism 'journey' is within acceptable boundaries
- Act on overall patterns to manage underlying causes.

Construction of the 'employee' database enabled the sequence and progression of the absence record for individual employees to be examined so that the patterns of duration and episodes of lost working days could be analysed in a more flexible way. Although inevitably skewed, Figure 8.3 illustrates that different reasons for sickness absence have different shapes of distribution.

On the face of it these distributional variations would seem to make comparisons practically impossible. However, all distributions can be made comparable by splitting the area under the curve (whatever shape the curve is) into equivalent areas based on equal percentages of employees

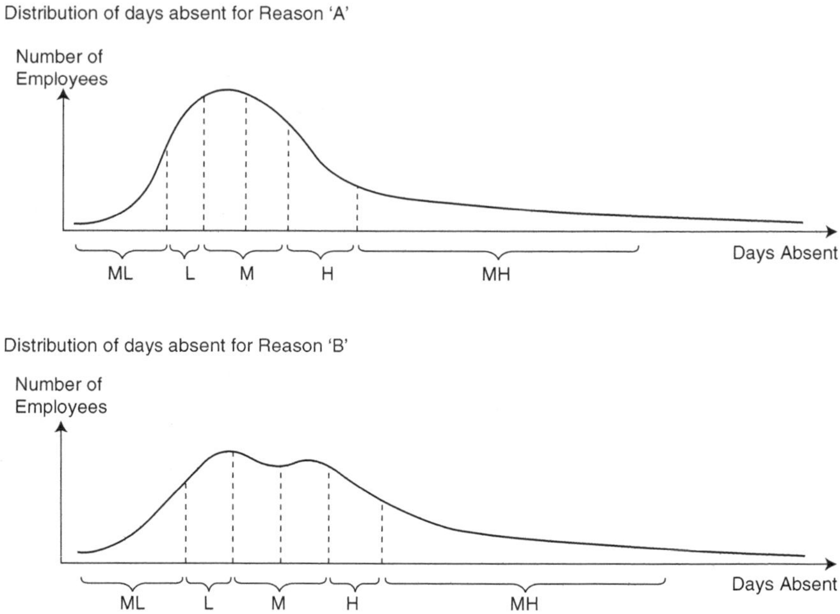

Note: ML=Much Lower= $^1/_6$ (weighted score -2); L =Lower= $^1/_6$ (weighted score -1); M=Mid-Range = $^1/_3$ (weighted score 0); H=Higher= $^1/_6$ (weighted score +2); MH =Much Higher=$^1/_6$ (weighted score +2).

Figure 8.3 Different shapes of absence distributions

in each section. In this way the area under any distribution could be split into bands as shown in Figure 8.3 (we have selected five bands for ease of explanation).

These bands provide a useful means of understanding how absenteeism records may be more flexibly interpreted than is generally undertaken at present. Two contrasting examples of how this may be achieved are shown in Figure 8.4.

An examination of the scenarios above shows how these may be used as a means of understanding the absenteeism 'journeys' of particular employees. Specifically, this type of visual aid is based upon benchmarking an individual's record of absence spells against reference data, enabling line managers to ask more targeted questions, such as:

- Is the individual absent for more or less time than expected?
- Does the individual have stress or bullying problems at work?
- Is this an example of habitual absenteeism?

(i) Two contrasting examples of individual employees' absence records

RECORD 1) Male, Aged 45–55 years

Possible Scenario:

Following two absence spells with relatively long durations of absence, the individual's reasons for this are explored in a management interview. The situation improves for the next two spells of sickness/absence. At the fifth spell, there now may be a slight issue of returning too quickly - the situation will need to be monitored closely for the next few sickness/absence spells.

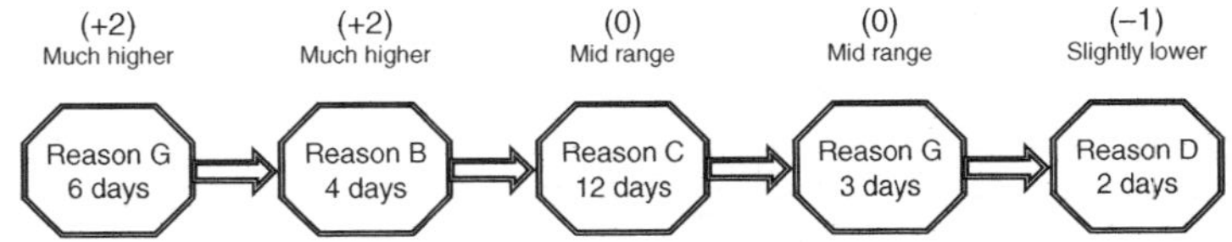

Total number of working days lost = 27 days
Relative weighting of absence record = Σ (+2, +2, 0, 0, −1)
= +3 more than expected

RECORD 2) Female, Aged 25–35 years

Possible Scenario:

Although the sickness/absence record shows that the amount of days lost per sickness/absence spell is neither more or less than expected, the repetition of the reason might imply that this is chronic or perhaps untreatable. Management action is needed to explore the root cause of this sickness/absence record.

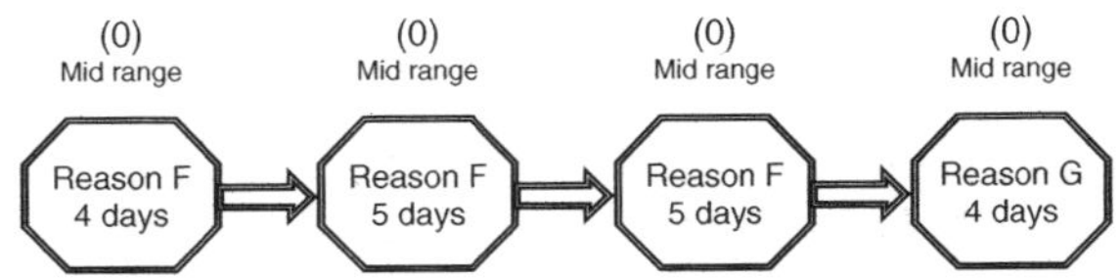

Total number of working days lost = 18 days
Relative weighting of absence record = Σ (0, 0, 0, 0)
= 0 more than expected

Figure 8.4 Two contrasting examples of individual absence records

- Is the individual highly motivated or not sufficiently resilient for their work duties?

The ability to obtain answers to important questions such as these exemplifies the potential benefits of building the sickness absence database with reference group data. Clearly, early intervention is essential to tightly controlling absenteeism in organisations. In other words, not only are absenteeism levels lowest where line managers are able to adopt an early and active responsibility for management, but future and repetitive spells of absenteeism can be moderated through the early application of appropriate HR strategies. One of the important outcomes of this research is the suggestion that intervention can occur at a much earlier time when it relies on a scenario based understanding of the patterns of individual absenteeism.

STAFF DECISIONS AND PRODUCTIVITY IN THE NHS

The longstanding research into sickness absence and the more recent interest in presenteeism has been driven by the high organisational costs of both to effective performance at work. Within the NHS, the Boorman report has highlighted that productivity is significantly constrained because of high levels of both sickness absence and presenteeism. Many NHS staff have reported spending several days at work when they were not well and this has prompted a demand for better management of health-at-work issues.

The decision to attend work or be absent (for both good and bad reasons) is often portrayed as a rational choice that a member of staff makes between competing alternatives. This individual model of sickness absence is rooted in work by Rhodes and Steers (1990; Steers and Rhodes 1978), who suggested that the decision to go to work not only depends upon the ability to attend but is also influenced by the motivation to do so. From this angle, employee attendance or absence depends upon the joint influence of job satisfaction and pressures to attend and consequently the determinants of attendance or absence are such factors as job monotony, stress, satisfaction, work involvement, leadership and co-worker support.

Others have argued that the individual decision to attend work is also moderated by both economic considerations and the ‘absence culture’ of an organisation. Time away from work has a positive value and if the personal utility of leisure exceeds the rewards of work then individuals may be more likely to make the rational choice to absent themselves (Kaiser,

1998). Furthermore, lost pay and training, reduced chances of promotion, and greater risks of being sacked may all be taken into account when the attendance decision is made (Broström et al., 2002). The prevailing 'absence culture' is also influential in the individual's decision to attend or not and this refers to what a member of staff has learnt to be acceptable (Rentsch and Steel, 2003) through taking on board the shared perception about absence legitimacy and the prevailing 'custom and practice' surrounding absence behaviours (Nicholson and Johns 1985).

Understanding the individual decision that individuals make with respect to attending or being absent from work has the potential to shed light on the wide continuum between absenteeism (i.e. no productivity) and active engagement (i.e. full productivity). Johns (2010) has pointed out that we know little about how absence episodes start and how they evolve over time. Adopting a longitudinal perspective about how individual members of staff make a sequence of decisions to remain absent or return to work is the approach recommended in this chapter and this is critical in designing management interventions which strike the appropriate balance in discouraging inappropriate absence or attendance. Clearly, the attendance decision is influenced by an interaction between the person's perception of their illness and their occupation. For example, Nicholson (1977) has pointed out that a sore throat will probably lead to absenteeism for a singer and presenteeism for a pianist – similarly a heart attack is very likely to result in absence whilst a diagnosis of hypertension is likely to result in attendance at work.

Clearly there are many reasons for both absenteeism and presenteeism, and the context of the working environment is crucial to understanding these. For example, in the NHS presenteeism is often fuelled by feelings of moral obligation, typically in the form of reluctance to let colleagues or patients down, and this feeling is often heightened by difficulties in arranging cover because of inadequate back-up arrangements. Increasing productivity in the NHS rests on designing management practices that are informed by an understanding of why particular staff choose to attend or to absent themselves from work.

IN SUMMARY

There is little doubt that absence from work is a significant and costly problem. The increasing recognition by HR departments that absence should be tackled as a strategic priority linked to broad concepts such as wellbeing at work is to be welcomed. However the persistence of the level of the problem, albeit with several local successes, suggests that generalised approaches, well intentioned as they are, do not seem to be achieving sustainable reductions.

HR managers face a difficult balance as an overly aggressive bearing down on staff may well have a range of negative consequences in the wider context of employee relationships. Equally repetition of policy guidelines tends to lose impact. It is our contention that HR managers are generally not given the proper tools, particularly in terms of the data collected. Working from averages or frequency of an employees' absence provides little real insight and places considerable weight on the absenteeism interview, with both parties seeing it essentially as a warning but with little real change in the situation.

The nature of the data discussed here is different in type and allows the absence pattern of an individual to be placed within a normative database for similar groups of staff and by sector, or indeed a range of variables. There is a vital phase of data collection and creation of the appropriate comparative material, but once this is achieved the individual case based approach enabled by such data has significant advantages for both employee and employer. Because patterns of absence can be seen and predicted, any significant discrepancy from the norm for that individual facilitates informed and targeted interventions benefiting the longer term health condition of the individual as well as allowing the employer to proactively prepare for a future (and largely predictable) issue.

The decision to attend work or to be absent, beyond an obvious and uncontestable illness, is a very individual and personal one. Many factors and different circumstances are involved. This 'motivational fulcrum' or tipping point is identifiable in the case based approach and as a consequence tailored and relevant initiatives can be used rather than the more hopeful universal approach based on averaged data which may well miss the point for any particular individual. Until there is investment in the appropriate data and analysis tools, it seems that absence from work will continue to be a problem, with initiatives of varying types having marginal impact.

REFERENCES

Audit Commission (2011), 'Managing sickness absence in the NHS: health briefing', London.

Broström, G., P. Johansson and M. Palme (2002), 'Economic incentives and gender differences in work absence behavior', *Swedish Economic Policy Review*, **11** (1), 33–63.

Boorman, S. (2009a), 'NHS health and wellbeing review: interim report', August, Leeds: Department of Health.

Boorman, S. (2009b), 'NHS health and wellbeing: final report', November, Leeds: Department of Health.
Capita (2009), http://www.capitahealthandwellbeing.co.uk/news/articles/nhs-in-a-competitive-health-care-market.aspx.
Carrington, L.A. (2007), 'A suitable case for treatment', in S. Harrington (ed.), *Human Resources*, London: Haymarket Publishing.
Chartered Institute of Personnel and Development (2010), *Absence Management Annual Survey Report 2010*, London: Chartered Institute of Personnel and Development.
Dunn, C., and A. Wilkinson (2002), 'Wish you were here: managing absence', *Personnel Review*, **31**, 228–246.
Hyde, P., et al. (2006), *Improving Health through Human Resource Management: Mapping the Territory*, London: Chartered Institute of Personnel and Development/Department of Health.
Johns, G. (2010), 'Presenteeism in the workplace: a review and research agenda', *Journal of Organizational Behavior*, **31**, 519–542.
Kaiser, C.P. (1998), 'What do we know about employee absence behavior? An interdisciplinary interpretation', *Journal of Socio-Economics*, **27** (1), 79–96.
Lu, X., P. Leino-Arjas, K. Piha, A. Aittomäki, P. Saastamoinen, O. Rahkonen and E. Lahelma (2011), 'On methodologies for analysing sickness absence data: an insight into a new method', *International Journal of Biological and Life Sciences*, **7**, 2.
Nicholson, N. (1977), 'Absence behavior and attendance motivation. A conceptual synthesis', *Journal of Management Studies*, 14, 231–252.
Nicholson, N., and G. Johns (1985), 'The absence culture and the psychological contract: who's in control of absence', *Academy of Management Review*, **10**, 397–407.
NHS Institute for Innovation and Improvement (2007), 'Human resource management, organisational and workforce development in the NHS: from current thinking to future models: an interim report', Report researched by Institute for Employment Studies (IES), Coventry.
NHS Employers (2009), 'Improving working lives in the NHS – a framework developed by the NHS Staff Council'. Available at: www.nhsemployers.org.
Penna (2002), 'Unleashing the chain reaction: using human capital management to tap the power in your people', criticaleye.net.
Penna (2003), 'Taking measures: harnessing people measures to drive business performance', criticaleye.net.
Portsmouth NHS Trust (2011), http://www.health4work.nhs.uk/blog/2011/06/rein-costs-managing-sickness-absence/.
Rentsch, J.R., and R.P. Steel (2003), 'What does unit-level absence mean? Issues for future unit-level absence research', *Human Resource Management Review*, **13**, 185–202.
Robinson, D., S. Perryman and S. Hayday (2004), 'The drivers of employee engagement', IES Report 408, Brighton: Institute for Employment Studies.
Rhodes, S., and R.M. Steers (1990), *Managing Employee Absenteeism*, Reading, MA: Addison-Wesley.
Spurgeon, A. (2002), 'Managing attendance at work: an evidence based review', British Occupational Health Research Foundation. bohrf.org.uk.
Spurgeon, P., P. Mazelan, F. Barwell and H. Flanagan (2007), 'New directions in

managing employee absence: an evidence-based approach', Chartered Institute of Personnel and Development.
Steel, R.P., J.R. Rentsch and W.H. Hendrix (1995), 'Cross-level replication and extension of Steel and Rentsch's (1995) longitudinal observe findings', *Journal of Business Psychology*, **16**, 447–456.
Steers, R.M., and S.R. Rhodes (1978), 'Major influences on employee attendance: a process model', *Journal of Applied Psychology*, **63**, 391–407.
Walker, V., and D. Bamford (2011), 'An empirical investigation into health sector absenteeism', *Health Services Management Research*, **21**, 142–150.
Watson-Wyatt (2002), 'Human Capital Index'. www.watsonwyatt.com.
Willmott, B. (2007), 'Absence management: annual survey report 2007', London: Chartered Institute of Personnel and Development. www.cipd.co.uk.

PART III

Better leadership, better organisational performance

9. Nurse leaders: partners in health care leadership

Margaret M. Hopkins and Deborah A. O'Neil

OVERVIEW

In this chapter we open with a brief description of the history and current context of the field of nursing. Second, we review the role of nurse leaders and the extant literature on their effective characteristics and required competencies. Third, we report our findings from two surveys of nurses at various institutions and levels. Finally, we draw several conclusions about effective nurse leadership and provide summary recommendations.

HISTORY OF NURSING

Florence Nightingale is widely credited with establishing the foundation for nursing as a profession (AAHN, 2011; Judd et al., 2010). She served as the head of a hospital that tended to sick and elderly women in England and established a school of nursing for the professional education of nurses at a London hospital.

Nightingale received permission to travel with a group of other women to the Crimean War front to tend to the sick and wounded, seeing a need since the British Army did not have any kind of nurses. Within months, the death rate in the British Army decreased substantially.

During the United States Civil War there were no provisions for military nurses, yet it was estimated that 3000 women served in a voluntary capacity as nurses (AAHN, 2011; Judd et al., 2010). In the Second World War, over 77,000 nurses served officially in the US armed forces.

The first permanent US schools of nursing were established in 1872 in the Women's Hospital of Philadelphia followed by one at the New England Hospital for Women and Children. By the end of the 19th century, only one-tenth of practicing nurses were graduates of hospital nurse training schools. The mid to late 20th century saw increased formal consideration of nursing education and requirements for the nursing profession. The number of graduate programs grew during this time as well as new advanced practice roles for nurses such as clinical nurse specialist, nurse practitioner and nurse administrator.

Today there are more than 3 million members of the nursing profession in the United States, which represents the largest segment of the health care workforce (Institute of Medicine, 2010). Nurses practice in a variety of settings such as hospitals, clinics, schools, community centers, homes, and war zones. Most nurses are registered nurses (RNs), while more than a quarter million are advanced practice nurses (APRNs) holding advanced degrees and national certifications. Nursing administration is recognised as a leadership role that requires graduate education to prepare for complex health care settings.

Current Context for Nursing

Numerous challenges face health care leaders today including increasing consumer demands, changing priorities and incentives, and insufficient resources. There is escalating pressure to do more with less. The quality of health care delivery and access to affordable, cost-effective health care are the fundamental drivers of change in the industry (Vlasses and Smeltzer, 2007). Shifting demographics (e.g., increasingly aging and diverse populations) and societal norms, innovations in technology, scientific advances, financial reforms, patient expectations, new models of patient care and personalised medicine are specific illustrations of these primary forces for change (O'Neil and Morjikian, 2003). One particularly troublesome factor in the field of nursing which affects the entire health care industry is the persistent shortage of nurses (Judd et al., 2010).

Given this evolving and challenging environment, leaders in health care must have the ability to lead change effectively. In addition, with increased emphasis on an integrated approach to patient care, teamwork and collaboration become critical skills for health care leadership (Vlasses and Smeltzer, 2007). A report concluded that academic institutions must begin educating health professionals to work collaboratively (IPEC, 2011). While leading change and leading teams are two focal areas for leadership, the preparatory education and the professional development of health care professionals including nurses remain largely focused on clinical competence and not on the development of these two domains of leadership (Weston et al., 2008).

THE ROLE OF THE NURSE LEADER

In response to these enumerated changes in the health care field, the role of the nurse leader has evolved considerably over the past decade, and the requisite skills to meet the evolving role have also changed. Increased responsibilities for budgeting, staffing and regulatory compliance as well as multiple unit management are primary examples of the shifts in nursing responsibilities (Sherman and Pross, 2010). Learning new technologies is another ongoing requirement for nurse leaders (Kowalski, 2004). In addition, as mentioned above, leading change and leading teams have become two critical skills for the optimal performance of nurse leaders.

The nurse leaders' role is moving toward requiring a transformational style of leadership (Sherman and Pross, 2010; Thyer, 2003). Transformational leaders challenge the status quo, encourage followers to be creative, foster supportive relationships, have a clear vision and motivate their followers toward achieving that vision, and serve as a role model for others (Bass, 1985). Thus, nurse leaders who are transformational develop shared values, a common vision, and cultures of engagement (Sherman and Pross, 2010). Their leadership contributes to staff commitment and retention (Acree, 2006; McGuire and Kennerly, 2006). Their staffs are involved in decision-making which contributes to building stronger teams (Thyer, 2003). The contemporary role of the nurse leader requires a collaborative approach to leadership which in turn maximises and strengthens team effectiveness (Akerjordet and Severinsson, 2008).

Interviews conducted with nurse leaders identified two areas of concern for nursing leadership (Sieg, 2009). First, there is a need for stronger models of developing nurse leaders including better educational programs, mentoring programs and ongoing training and professional development. The education and professional development programs for nurses remain primarily centered on the clinical aspects of the role and not on the requisite leadership qualities. Second, due to an overall nursing shortage there are serious difficulties with present and future staffing needs. Considering the critical nature of this shortage, nurse leadership becomes even more imperative since the quality of leadership exhibited directly impacts staff nurse retention (Kowalski, 2004).

Characteristics of Effective Nurse Leaders

Due to the changing nature of nurse leadership in response to the evolution in the field of health care, it is important to identify the qualities, behaviors and characteristics that successful nurse leaders exemplify. The literature reports a wide array of essential qualities for outstanding nurse leaders. However, we can identify some common themes among the predominant characteristics.

First, the ability to lead teams is paramount to effective nurse leadership. In one study of women in the health care professions, nurses identified team leadership as one of the top three attributes of effective leadership in their organisations (Hopkins et al., 2006). Another study examined missed nursing care, which is defined as ‘any aspect of required patient care that is omitted or significantly delayed’ (Kalisch, 2009, p. 485). The results demonstrated that a lack of resources and a lack of teamwork were the two most-often cited causes of these errors. Issues such as closed loop communication, lack of trust and of shared models of patient care contributed to the lack of teamwork. Nursing leadership in high performing teams was found to foster cohesive, goal-directed teamwork through open communication which ultimately resulted in effective problem solving and better patient care (Vogelsmeier, 2008).

Building effective relationships is another essential characteristic for nurse leaders (Anthony et al., 2005; Laschinger et al., 2009; Manion, 2004). The quality of unit level leader-member exchange had a direct and an indirect effect on nurses’ psychological empowerment and job commitment (Laschinger et al., 2009). Two of the five themes of excellent nurse leadership identified by Manion (2004) were those of forging authentic connections and partnering with staff. Developing collaborative relationships, which also relates to effective teamwork, contributes to demonstrating effective nurse leadership (Anthony et al., 2005). One critical set of relationships for nurse leaders are those with physicians (Balke, 2006).

Communication is a third factor contributing to outstanding nurse leadership (Anthony et al., 2005). Studies illustrating the importance of communication reported that giving and seeking information (Hemman, 1998), listening to staff and providing positive feedback (Duffield et al., 2011) were important aspects of communication resulting in effective nurse leadership. The work of Kalisch (2009) also underscored how communication is vital to effective teamwork and quality patient care.

Decision making is a fourth theme from the extant literature illustrating the abilities of nurse leaders. Nurse executives receiving the highest scores from their staff demonstrated a willingness to make decisions (Dunham-Taylor, 1995). A study to determine the leadership behavior profile of senior nurse leaders found that decision making was the first of four primary behaviors, followed by building relationships, giving and seeking information, and influencing people (Hemman, 1998).

A fifth area of importance for nurse leaders is emotional intelligence. Emotional intelligence is the ability to be aware of one’s own and others’ emotions and to effectively manage those emotions (Goleman et al., 2002).

A high degree of emotional intelligence would enable nurse leaders to cope with their demanding and stressful roles in a knowledgeable and supportive manner (Akerjordet and Severinsson, 2008; Landa and Lopez-Zafra, 2010).

Visibility is another element of effective nurse leadership. Indicators of quality nurse leaders identified visibility as a predominant characteristic (Anderson et al., 2010; Duffield et al., 2011). Nurse leaders who were visible, accessible, and regularly consulted and recognised their staff contributed to an overall positive work environment with staff satisfaction and increased staff retention (Duffield et al., 2011; Manion, 2004). Exceptional nurse leaders, defined as those who scored above the mean in the National Database of Nursing Quality Indicators RN survey, reported visibility as the first of two key components of their leadership, with communication a close second (Anderson et al., 2010).

Each of these six thematic areas associated with outstanding nurse leadership relates to the 'soft skills' of leadership and not the technical or knowledge-based aspects of leadership. O'Neil and Morjikian (2003) highlighted the need to reintegrate the psycho-social behaviors of care with the traditional bio-medical aspects of care, which these six primary characteristics of effective nurse leadership illustrate.

Competency Models for Nurse Leadership

Several competency models exist for the spectrum of health care professions. For example, the Interprofessional Education Collaborative (IPEC) consists of six US associations of health profession schools: nursing, medicine, pharmacy, dental, public health, and osteopathic medicine (IPEC, 2011). IPEC formed an interprofessional panel to create a list of core competencies with the purpose of advancing interprofessional learning and team-based care. They identified four competency domain areas – values and ethics; roles and responsibilities for collaborative practice; interprofessional communication; and teamwork and team-based care – and specific competencies within each of the four domains.

There are also a number of competency models that have been developed by professional nursing associations for the purpose of identifying the core competencies for nurse leaders. The American Association of Critical Care Nurses (AACN) Synergy Model contains eight focal areas: clinical judgment; caring practices; facilitation of learning; advocacy or moral agency; response to diversity; collaboration; clinical inquiry; and systems thinking (AACN, 2011; Hardin and Kaplow, 2005).

Another competency model used for nursing leadership development at the unit level is the Nurse Manager Leadership Collaborative (NMLC)

Learning Domain Framework (NMLC, 2006). To address the need for leadership development in the nursing field, the American Organization of Nurse Executives and the American Association of Critical Care Nurses worked together to create a model that identifies competency domains needed by current and future nurse leaders. There are three domains and numerous competencies within each domain. The first domain is the *Leader Within* and includes areas such as personal and professional accountability, career planning, and reflective practice. The second domain, the *Art of Leadership*, encompasses such areas as human resource skills, relationship management and influence skills, diversity management, and shared decision making. The *Science of Leadership* is the third domain, which contains financial management, performance improvement, strategic management and clinical practice knowledge among others.

The National Clinical Nurse Specialist (CNS) Competency Task Force identified and validated core CNS competencies and behaviors (2010). The core CNS competencies are competencies and behaviors expected of graduates of master's and post-master's programs that prepare clinical nurse specialists. The core CNS competencies and behaviors were validated through a national web-based survey to the members of participating organisations (e.g., American Organization of Nurse Executives, National Association of Clinical Nurse Specialists, American Association of Colleges of Nursing, and Board of Certification for Emergency Nursing). The CNS competency model consists of the following: direct care; consultation; systems leadership; collaboration; coaching; research; and ethical decision making, moral agency and advocacy.

Finally, a study of 120 nurse managers concluded that six competency areas were essential for nurse leaders: personal mastery; financial management; human resource management; interpersonal effectiveness; caring; and systems thinking (Sherman et al., 2007).

Although there are various competencies and a wide range of behaviors listed in each competency model for nurse leaders, we can identify some commonalities across these models. The three primary areas contained in each of the models are collaboration, systems thinking, and clinical judgment and knowledge. Additional universal themes which appear across the nurse leadership competency models are the following: advocacy/moral agency; caring; diversity; financial management; human resource management; and interpersonal skills or relationship management.

Several of the common themes from the nurse leadership competency models align with the previously reported results from literature studies which identified the characteristics of effective nurse leaders. Teamwork and collaboration as well as relationship management or interpersonal skills are paramount for nurse leaders. All aspects of human resource management appear to be critical as well, which encompass staffing, employee relations and employee development. Thus, attending to the people aspect of the nurse leader role through leading people effectively is recognised as a core role and responsibility for nurse leaders.

FINDINGS FROM NURSE LEADERSHIP SURVEYS

Two surveys of nurses revealed findings relevant to our discussion of nurse leadership in health care organisations. We collected data from two groups of nurses engaged in different health care leadership seminars at two universities in the Midwestern region of the United States (Sample 1 and Sample 2). We used thematic analysis (Boyatzis, 1998) to ascertain prevalent themes in the respondents' answers to sets of questions (described below), and themes and frequency counts are presented in the tables that follow.

The first sample of 37 nurses from a variety of health care institutions comprised the participants shown in Table 9.1.

The majority of participants in Sample 1 were employed in academic medical centers (80 per cent), and the remaining were employed in a variety of segments of the health care sector, including private practice nursing, urban hospital nursing, and schools of nursing.

Participants in Sample 1 were asked three questions related to their leadership:

1. How would you define your opportunities to play a leadership role in your organisation?
2. What do you need to do to develop your leadership skills?
3. What does your organisation need to do to develop your leadership skills?

Table 9.1 Sample 1 Demographics

Position	%/# of sample (N = 37)
Nurse Manager	41% (15)
Registered Nurse	16% (6)
Nursing Student	14% (5)
Nursing Director	11% (4)
Clinical Nurse Specialist	11% (4)
Nurse Practitioner	8% (3)

Table 9.2 Opportunities to play a leadership role in your organisation

Descriptor	%/# of sample (N = 37)
Excellent	32% (12)
Good	51% (19)
Fair	14% (5)
Poor	3% (1)

Responses to these questions are reported in Tables 9.2–9.4. Note that multiple themes could be identified in an individual's response to questions 2 and 3.

Responses to the first question (see Table 9.2) suggest that an overwhelming percentage of the nurses in our sample (83 per cent) describe their opportunities to play a leadership role in their organisations as being either 'Excellent' (12 respondents or 32 per cent) or 'Good' (19 respondents or 51 per cent).

Representative comments describing opportunities for leadership are listed below:

1. 'I am currently working in a new developing program. This is allowing me to develop my role as the program is evolving' (Nurse Practitioner who describes her opportunities as 'Excellent').
2. 'We have many opportunities to participate in leadership until you get to the highest levels then communication is less' (Nurse Manager who describes her opportunities as 'Good').
3. 'Within nursing my contributions and talents have been recognised; however, I have been ignored as have other nurses in important decisions and processes as well' (Clinical Nurse Specialist who describes her opportunities as 'Excellent' within nursing and 'Poor' in the larger hospital system).
4. 'Small practice, roles very well defined, and physicians limit [nurse's opportunities to demonstrate leadership] (Private Practice Nurse Practitioner who describes her opportunities as 'Fair').

Responses to the second question regarding what individuals needed to do to develop their leadership skills and abilities (see Table 9.3) focused on such themes as 'access to coaching and mentoring' from senior leaders, 'additional education and training', and becoming 'more confident and assertive' in their roles in the health care system. Also mentioned were 'gaining more experience through practice', 'effectively managing staff', and working more as members of 'teams' in their organisations.

Table 9.3 What do you need to do to develop your leadership skills and abilities?

Themes	%/# of respondents
Access to coaching, mentoring, role models and networks	24% (9)
Additional education, training, learn new skills	22% (8)
Be more confident, assertive, take ownership	22% (8)
Gain more experience, practice my craft	16% (6)
Delegation and effective management of employees	14% (5)
Teamwork	5% (2)

Table 9.4 What does your organisation need to do to develop your leadership skills and abilities?

Themes	%/# of respondents
Promote education, training and development	35% (13)
Support (e.g., resources, time, etc.)	32% (12)
Recognition, respect, responsibility	22% (8)
Coach, mentor, be patient	11% (4)

Responses to the third question, about what the nurses believed their organisations needed to do to help them develop as leaders (see Table 9.4) revealed themes of promoting 'educational opportunities' including on the job training and seminars as well as advanced degrees; providing 'support' in terms of time and resources; 'recognising and respecting' nurses' contributions as well as affording them responsibility; and finally, 'coaching, mentoring' and demonstrating patience as they developed their skills and abilities.

The second sample of 15 nurses from one US Midwestern university medical center comprised the participants shown in Table 9.5.

Participants in Sample 2 were asked four questions related to their leadership:

1. What inhibits your ability to play a leadership role?
2. What are the major challenges you face in your role?
3. What current strengths do you bring to your role as a nurse?
4. What skills, abilities, etc. do you need to further develop?

Major themes reflected in the responses to the four questions are reported in Tables 9.6–9.9. Note that multiple themes could be identified in an individual's response.

Table 9.5 Sample 2 Demographics

Position	%/# of sample (N = 15)
Nurse Manager	67% (10)
Nursing Director	13% (2)
Registered Nurse	13% (2)
Clinical Nurse Specialist	7% (1)

Table 9.6 Factors that inhibit your ability to play a leadership role

Themes	%/# of respondents
Lack of management direction and support, lack of decision-making authority	47% (7)
Lack of time	27% (4)
Individuals who are not team oriented	27% (4)
Entitlement issues from staff, staff that challenge authority to lead	20% (3)

Table 9.7 Major challenges faced in your role

Themes	%/# of respondents
Staff morale and attitude, lack of accountability, resistance to change	93% (14)
Needing to do more with fewer resources	53% (8)
Individuals who are not team oriented, a 'Dr. vs. Nurse mentality'	47% (7)
Lack of management support	40% (6)

One theme was a clear front-runner in responses to the first question (see Table 9.6) about the inhibitors to nurse leadership – 'lack of upper management direction and support'. Nurses reported ambiguity about decision-making authority and confusion about the types of conditions under which they were allowed to make decisions. Being left out of upper management decisions was also related to this theme. Additional factors were 'time considerations', a 'lack of team orientation' among colleagues, and challenges in 'exercising authority with staff members'.

In response to the second question, regarding major challenges to nurses, four themes were identified (see Table 9.7). The most prevalent theme was 'dealing with challenging staff members', i.e., poor morale

Table 9.8 Current strengths you bring to your role

Themes	%/# of respondents
People person, fair in dealing with others	60% (9)
Team orientation	47% (7)
Listening, open-mindedness	33% (5)
Knowledgeable	33% (5)
Organised, see big picture, change agent	33% (5)
Hard working	27% (4)
Communication	13% (2)

Table 9.9 Skills and abilities needing further development

Themes	%/# of respondents
Team building	40% (6)
Group dynamics, handling difficult employees, handling conflict	33% (5)
Listening, empathy, patience	33% (5)
Confidence	27% (4)
Organisation skills, time management, delegation	13% (2)
Business thinking	13% (2)

and negative attitudes, lack of accountability and responsibility, and those who resisted change. In addition, the theme of 'lack of management support' was identified here as a challenge as well as in the prior question about inhibitors. It seems that lack of management direction and support is a major barrier to nurse leaders' effectiveness. Another theme that was mentioned as an inhibitor also showed up here as a challenge – the 'lack of team orientation'. In particular comments about doctors and nurses not being on the same team were common. The final theme was that of 'doing more with less': less staff, less resources, less time, etc.

In question 3, participants were asked to identify the current strengths they bring to their role as nurses. Responses to this question reflected a focus on relationship management and interpersonal skills as well as nursing knowledge and organisation skills (see Table 9.8). For example, being a 'people person,' a 'fair person,' a 'team builder and a team player' as well as 'being open to listen and to learn from others' were the major themes to summarise the responses.

The developmental needs of the nurses listed in participants' answers to question 4 revealed many of the same themes mentioned in their list of strengths (see Table 9.9). The respondents stated that 'team building' and 'group dynamics,' including 'handling difficult people' and 'conflict management' as well as 'listening skills' were several important areas for their continued leadership development.

CONCLUSIONS AND RECOMMENDATIONS

Based on the results of our two surveys and the extant literature, we have identified four meta-themes relative to nurse leadership: Management Direction and Support; Staffing and Resources; Teamwork; and Education, Training and Development. As discussed earlier in the chapter, the existing literature has noted the latter three meta-themes present in our data. However, the issue of management direction and support is distinctive, and our results provide further insight into its impact on effective nurse leadership.

'Management Direction and Support' presents significant organisational challenges for nurses and their ability to lead. A widespread comment throughout the surveys was the lack of manager support, illustrated predominantly in terms of recognition, respect and clarifying decision-making authority for the nurses. In addition, the nurses in our two samples were seeking support in terms of opportunities, resources and time to develop their leadership skills and continue their professional development. The respondents were also asking for mentoring, coaching and role modeling from their upper-level managers and access to these senior-level networks.

The nurses believed that they had very good opportunities to demonstrate leadership in their organisations. However, examining these survey results further revealed that the nurses were distinguishing those occasions for leading within their defined roles and strict organisational boundaries. Their ability to exhibit leadership was primarily shown laterally with their peers and downward with their staff. They thought that their leadership capabilities were largely ignored or marginalised by those above them in the hierarchy. Obstacles presented by upper management and other professionals (i.e., physicians) were a constant source of tension and concern for the nurses. Not only does this issue prevent nurses from realising their full leadership potential, it also inhibits the teamwork and collaboration needed for optimal health care delivery.

The second meta-theme is 'Staffing and Resources.' A persistent problem in the health care field is inadequate resources to meet the demand for quality and efficient health care. The shortage in the nursing profession has been acute for the past decade. In addition to a nurse staffing shortage, there are pressures throughout the health care environment to do more with less. Squeezing efficiencies in all aspects of health care delivery has become the norm. Thus, nurses and other professionals in this field feel the impact of operating with limited means.

The 'Staffing' component of the second meta-theme encompasses several concerns about effectively leading and managing staff. Examples of this issue included problems with staff morale and attitude (perhaps due in part to environmental constraints), accountability, and resistance to change. Effective delegation as well as how to manage employees in a changing and challenging environment were two additional factors mentioned in our survey results. For the most part the focus on 'Staffing' came from concerns and issues with staff and how to deal with these problems effectively.

'Teamwork' is the third meta-theme from our survey data. The ability to build and develop teams was identified as a challenge as well as an opportunity. Difficulties presented in leading individuals who were not team-oriented, and a doctor versus nurse mentality, were presented as two challenging issues. In addition, both of our sample groups named teamwork as an opportunity area for their own leadership development. An interesting finding is that teamwork was also a predominant strength area mentioned by the nurses in our study. While nurses believe that teamwork is a strength area for them, it is such a crucial factor in health care that it is likely recognised as a work-in-progress requiring ongoing attention and not a static end state.

Finally, 'Education, Training and Development' is the fourth meta-theme. To gain more experience through education, training and development in order to improve their craft was an area consistently mentioned in the survey data. This was discussed as an area of responsibility for both the nursing staff and their organisational leadership. The nurses were eager to learn additional knowledge, skills and abilities; and they felt that the leadership in their organisations needed to more strongly promote and support these types of opportunities.

Based on our research, we propose three fundamental recommendations to enhance nurse leadership. First, the ability to lead change is a crucial requirement for health care leadership and must be highlighted in professional development efforts. This topic was named by only one-third of the respondents to our survey as an area of strength for them. In addition, staff resistance to change was a major concern of a majority of both sample groups. Numerous models already exist (e.g., in the business literature) that could inform health care organisational change efforts as well as individual development activities for leading change effectively. Placing a high priority in this area will assist nurse leaders in strengthening their ability to lead change and to lead others through the change.

Second, nurses and nurse leaders must be considered by physicians and senior management as true partners in health care. Nurse leaders should be invited and encouraged to share their knowledge and be 'at the table' to contribute their skills and abilities. Especially with the increased emphasis on teamwork, health care leadership must foster the development of team-building skills and must model these skills themselves in order to create and sustain high-performing teams at all levels of the industry.

Finally, we echo the call made by others (e.g., O'Neil and Morjikian, 2003) to shift the balance in nurse training and development by more fully integrating the psycho-social behaviors of care with the traditional clinical aspects of care. An increased emphasis on these behaviors should cover the entire spectrum from nursing schools to ongoing professional development. In this way, nurse leaders will become stronger at all levels in health care organisations and no longer play a supporting role but a leading role in health care delivery.

REFERENCES

Acree, C.M. (2006), 'The relationship between nursing leadership practices and hospital nursing retention', *Newborn and Infant Nursing Reviews*, **6** (1), 34–40.

Akerjordet, K., and E. Severinsson (2008), 'Emotionally intelligent nurse leadership: a literature review study', *Journal of Nursing Management*, **16**, 565–577.

American Association for the History of Nursing, Inc. (AAHN), *Nursing history calendar*. Retrieved 15 May 2011 from http://www.aahn.org/nursinghistory calendar.html.

American Association of Clinical Care Nurses (AACN) (2011), *The American Association of Critical-Care Nurses (AACN) Synergy Model for Patient Care*. Retrieved 1 May 2011 from http://www.aacn.org:88/wd/certifications/content/synmodel.pcms?pid=1&&menu=#Nurse.

Anderson, B.J., M. Manno, P. O'Connor and E. Gallagher (2010), 'Listening to nursing leaders: using national database of nursing quality indicators data to study excellence in nursing leadership', *Journal of Nursing Administration*, **40** (4), 182–187.

Anthony, M.K., T.S. Standing, J. Glick, M. Duffy, F. Paschall, M.R. Sauer, D.K. Sweeney, M.B. Modic and M.L. Dumpe (2005), 'Leadership and nurse retention: the pivotal role of nurse managers', *Journal of Nursing Administration*, **35** (3), 146–154.

Balke, J.M. (2006), 'Nurse executives: a grounded theory study of dynamic competencies', Unpublished doctoral dissertation, Capella University.

Bass, B.M. (1985), *Leadership and Performance*, NY: Free Press.

Boyatzis, R.E. (1998), *Thematic Analysis*, Thousand Oaks, CA: Sage Publications.

Duffield, C.M., M.A. Roche, N. Blay and H. Stasa (2011), 'Nursing unit managers, staff retention and the work environment', *Journal of Clinical Nursing*, **20** (1/2), 23–33.

Dunham-Taylor, J. (1995), 'Identifying the best in nurse executive leadership, part II: interview results', *Journal of Nursing Administration*, **25** (7/8), 24–31.

Goleman, D., R. Boyatzis and A. McKee (2002), *Primal Leadership: Realizing the Power of Emotional Intelligence*, Boston: Harvard Business Press.
Hardin, S. and R. Kaplow (2005), *Synergy for Clinical Excellence: The AACN Synergy Model for Patient Care*, Sudbury, MA: Jones and Bartlett Publishers.
Hemman, E.A. (1998), 'Leadership profiles of senior nurse executives', Unpublished doctoral dissertation, Seattle University.
Hopkins, M.M., D.A. O'Neil and D. Bilimoria (2006), 'Effective leadership and successful career advancement: perspectives from women in health care', *Equal Opportunities International*, **25** (4), 251–271.
Institute of Medicine (2010), 'The future of nursing: leading change, advancing health', Report Brief, October, 1–4. Retrieved 15 May 2011 from http://www.iom.edu/~/media/Files/Report%20Files/2010/The-Future-of-Nursing/Future of Nursing 2010 Report Brief.pdf.
Interprofessional Education Collaborative Expert Panel (IPEC) (2011), 'Core competencies for interprofessional collaborative practice: report of an expert panel', Washington, D.C.: Interprofessional Education Collaborative. Retrieved 1 May 2011 from http://www.aacn.nche.edu/Education/pdf/IPECProceedings.pdf.
Judd, D., K. Sitzman and G.M. Davis (2010), *A History of American Nursing: Trends and Eras*, Sudbury, MA: Jones and Bartlett Publishers.
Kalisch, B.J. (2009), 'Nurse and nurse assistant perceptions of missed nursing care: what does it tell us about teamwork?', *Journal of Nursing Administration*, **39** (11), 485–493.
Kowalski, K. (2004), 'Growing future leaders: developing perinatal managers from within', *Journal of Obstetric, Gynecologic and Neonatal Nursing*, **33** (3), 362–370.
Landa, J.M.A., and E. Lopez-Zafra (2010), 'The impact of emotional intelligence on nursing: an overview', *Psychology*, **1**, 50–58.
Laschinger, H.K., J. Finegan and P. Wilk (2009), 'Context matters: the impact of unit leadership and empowerment on nurses' organizational commitment', *Journal of Nursing Administration*, **39** (5), 228–235.
Manion, J. (2004), 'Nurture a culture of retention', *Nursing Management*, **35** (4), 28–39.
McGuire, E., and S.M. Kennerly (2006), 'Nurse managers as transformational and transactional leaders', *Nursing Economics*, **24** (4), 179–186.
National Clinical Nurse Specialist Competency Task Force (2010), 'Clinical nurse specialist core competencies', Retrieved 1 May 2011 from http://www.nursingcertification.org/pdf/Exec Summary – Core CNS Competencies.pdf.
Nurse Manager Leadership Collaborative (NMLC) (2006), 'Nurse manager leadership partnership learning domain framework', Retrieved 1 May 2011 from http://www.aone.org/aone/resource/NMLC/nmlcLEARNING.html.
O'Neil, E., and R. Morjikian (2003), 'Nursing leadership: challenges and opportunities', *Policy, Politics and Nursing Practice*, **4** (3), 173–179.
Sherman, R., and E. Pross (2010), 'Growing future nurse leaders to build and sustain healthy work environments at the unit level', *Online Journal of Issues in Nursing*, **15**, 1.
Sherman, R.O., M. Bishop, T. Eggenberger and R. Karden (2007), 'Development of a leadership competency model', *Journal of Nursing Administration*, **37** (2), 85–94.
Sieg, D. (2009), 'Reflections on nursing leadership', Retrieved 15 May 2011 from

http://www.reflectionsonnursingleadership.org/pages/vol35_3_sieg_nursingleaders.aspx.

Thyer, G.L. (2003), 'Dare to be different: transformational leadership may hold the key to reducing the nursing shortage', *Journal of Nursing Management*, **11**, 73–79.

Vlasses, F.R., and C.H. Smeltzer (2007), 'Toward a new future for healthcare and nursing practice', *Journal of Nursing Administration*, **37** (9), 375–380.

Vogelsmeier, A.A. (2008), 'Leadership, communication and teamwork: differences between high and low performing nursing homes', Unpublished doctoral dissertation, University of Missouri, Columbia.

Weston, M.J., B. Falter, G.S. Lamb, G. Mahon, K. Malloch, K.G. Provan, S. Roe and L. Werbylo (2008), 'Health care leadership academy: a statewide collaboration to enhance nursing leadership competencies', *Journal of Continuing Education in Nursing*, **39** (10), 468–472.

10. Enhancing medical leadership and engagement: impact upon organisational performance

Peter Spurgeon

INTRODUCTION

The term 'engagement' has emerged within the literature on work psychology as a development from job satisfaction and staff commitment. It has become popular and is used in many contexts, usually without definition and seemingly on the basis that all involved in the discussion have a shared understanding. Once a term reaches such a level of popular usage – for example leadership – then the lack of precision can also be a source of confusion.

Politicians, when being interviewed and in a situation where opposition clearly exists to their viewpoint, will frequently retreat to phrases such as 'we must engage the public in a debate about this'. In this sense engagement is a rather unspecified dialogue and part of a general process of communication. Also reference is sometimes made to engaging with a source of opposition or conflict, and again engagement is part of a communication process with a focus on influencing the other party. We can find strands of these rather lay concepts of engagement when we consider a more academic application to the notion of engagement in a work setting.

Towers Perrin (2009) describe three aspects of employee engagement as the basis of a survey tool they use to help businesses enhance their performance. The three key components are:

1. A rational, cognitive understanding of the organisation's strategic goals, values and how they 'fit' within it
2. An emotional or affective attachment to these goals
3. A motivation or willingness to do more than the minimum effort in their role.

In a study of 50 multinational companies they report the impact employee engagement has on financial performance. Over 12 months companies with high levels of engagement outperformed those with less engaged employees in three key financial measures, operating income, net income growth and earnings per share.

Earlier notions of engagement suggested that it might be seen as a dimension with disengagement at one end. Although this was subsequently regarded as over simplistic it does resonate here in the context of organisational performance. It is at a common-sense level difficult to argue how a disengaged, disaffected and alienated workforce is likely to be able to sustain high levels of performance.

Schaufel and Bakker (2003) describe engagement as 'a persistent, positive affective motivational state of fulfilment in employees that is characterised by vigour, dedication and absorption'. In the context of health care, Paller (2005) reported that the degree of engagement of the physicians had a direct impact on the financial bottom-line of the hospital. More recently in the UK, West (2011) reports work using the NHS Annual Survey that higher levels of staff engagement are associated with higher quality services, better financial performance, higher patient satisfaction and lower staff absenteeism.

One of the more significant documents in the area of engagement is the report commissioned by the Cabinet Office in the UK (MacLeod and Clarke 2009). Looking across a range of sectors they confirm that there is no universal agreed meaning to the term and moreover approaches to measuring engagement are themselves variable, with many internal company specific tools and little externally accessible psychometric data on the robustness of the measure. Even allowing for this they conclude that (a) engagement correlates with performance and with innovation and (b) engagement levels in the UK are relatively low. There is in their words 'a compelling case' to link engagement with performance and in the context of this text and its concern to promote innovation, a requirement to understand how we might work towards enhancing levels of engagement in health services.

MEASURING ENGAGEMENT

Ham and Dickinson (2008) comment in their review of medical leadership, engagement and organisational performance that very few robust measures of engagement are to be found. Reinertsen et al. (2007), with colleagues from the Institute for Health Improvement (IHI), have been active in encouraging organisations to focus on engagement. They express surprise at how few hospitals in the USA have made improving engagement a significant component of their strategic plan. IHI have devised a checklist of issues to consider when contemplating how to go about improving levels of engagement. However there is a distinction between a measure and a checklist. The latter relies on self-report and what a particular set (usually selective) of individuals feel about the issues highlighted.

A recent national project in the UK, 'Enhancing Engagement in Medical Leadership', conducted jointly by the NHS Institute for Innovation and Improvement and the Academy of Medical Royal Colleges and led by the author, set out to address both the training requirement in medical leadership and the issue of engagement. With respect to the second methodological aspect the project objectives were to:

1. Develop a reliable and valid measure of medical engagement which will be quick and relatively unobtrusive to complete
2. To differentiate within the scale a measure of personal engagement at an individual level (the motivation of the individual to perform in relevant managerial and leadership roles) from the organisational context (which may foster or constrain engagement)
3. To develop a framework for recommending organisational strategies to enhance medical engagement and performance within the organisation.

It should be noted that the work reported here from this project was directed to the medical workforce as particular challenges were perceived around the crucial role of the profession in taking forward radical change and indeed their capacity to resist if they were not motivated to do so, i.e. were disengaged. However, the concept of engagement can certainly be applied more widely and aspects of the project have subsequently been broadened out to include other clinical staff.

The Enhancing Engagement in Medical Leadership project is reported more fully in Spurgeon et al. (2011) but in developing the Medical Engagement Scale it employed three key conceptual premises:

1. Medical engagement is critical to achieving the service improvements sought in the NHS.
2. That both the individual employee and the employer are involved and this is reflected in the definition of engagement used in the process of developing the scale: 'The active and positive contribution of doctors within their normal working roles to maintaining and enhancing the performance of the organisation which itself recognises this commitment in supporting and encouraging high quality care' (Spurgeon et al. 2008).

3. That a distinction is made between competence (what people have been trained to do and can do and performance which is the result of choosing to do (motivation) and therefore the issue specifically addressed in the Medical Engagement Scale (MES).

The full development process is described in Spurgeon et al. (2008). The resulting measurement tool (MES) consists of an overall Index of Medical Engagement for the entire organisation and then three sub-scales (Working in an Open Culture; Having Purpose and Direction and Feeling Valued and Empowered). Both the individual perspective and the organisational response are built into the measure. The overall measure and subscales were also found to be reliable with Cronbach alpha coefficients from .70 to .93.

MEDICAL ENGAGEMENT AND ORGANISATIONAL PERFORMANCE

The MES has now been used with approximately 50 secondary care Trusts in the UK NHS, involving nearly 5000 doctors from all specialties and grades. This set of UK based norms has recently been supplemented by data from other countries (Australia, Malta, Denmark and Italy). Each organisation using MES is therefore now able to benchmark its level of medical engagement against a large total database as well as against organisations of a similar type to themselves e.g. Mental Health.

Within the Enhancing Engagement in Medical Leadership project a specific sub-set of 30 secondary care Trusts were used to consider the issue of how far engagement levels related to a range of independently collected performance data. The Care Quality Commission has annually rated UK Trusts in terms of performance (Finance, Achieving Targets, User Experience, and Quality and Safety).

Table 10.1 shows how the Top 10/ Bottom 10 Trusts in the sample fared against these ratings.

With the odd exception it is clear that the more engaged organisations performed better than Trusts with low levels of engagement.

Table 10.2 illustrates this numerically in terms of correlations with a whole range of performance measures (NPSA Safety Data, Standardised Mortality Rates, Patient Experience).

Virtually all the correlations are positive and whilst they do not prove that engagement causes differential level of performance, the number, size and consistency of the data make (as MacLeod and Clarke said earlier) a compelling case.

Table 10.1 Comparison of MES Index (30 secondary care Trusts) to overall Care Quality Commission ratings

	Trust ID (Trust names withheld for confidentiality	Overall Medical Engagement Scale Index (in descending order)	CQC - NHS performance ratings 2008/09				
			Overall quality score	Financial management score	Core standards score (as a provider of services)	Existing commitment score (as a provider of services)	National priorities score (as a provider of services)
Top 10 Trusts	21	65.8	Good	Excellent	Fully Met	Fully Met	Good
	12	65.2	Good	Good	Fully Met	–	Good
	15	63.4	Excellent	Good	Fully Met	Fully Met	Excellent
	5	62.0	Excellent	Excellent	Fully Met	Fully Met	Excellent
	24	60.8	Good	Excellent	Fully Met	–	Good
	1	60.4	Excellent	Excellent	Fully Met	Fully Met	Excellent
	10	59.9	Good	Excellent	Almost Met	Fully Met	Good
	16	59.8	Good	Fair	Fully Met	Almost Met	Excellent
	14	59.7	Excellent	Excellent	Fully Met	Fully Met	Excellent
	11	58.8	Excellent	Excellent	Fully Met	Fully Met	Excellent
Bottom 10 Trusts	25	56.8	Fair	Fair	Almost Met	Fully Met	Poor
	4	56.7	Fair	Fair	Almost Met	Fully Met	Fair
	22	55.7	Fair	Fair	Partly Met	Almost Met	Good
	23	55.3	Fair	Good	Almost Met	Partly Met	Excellent
	29	54.4	Good	Excellent	Fully Met	Fully Met	Good
	3	54.3	Fair	Excellent	Fully Met	Fully Met	Poor
	26	53.1	Fair	Fair	Almost Met	Almost Met	Fair
	8	52.7	Good	Good	Fully Met	Almost Met	Good
	18	52.1	Fair	Fair	Fully Met	Partly Met	Good
	20	47.0	Poor	Poor	Almost Met	Not Met	Fair

Table 10.2 Care Quality Commission NHS performance ratings correlated with levels of engagement

The Care Quality Commission - NHS performance ratings 2008/09	Medical Engagement Index	Meta 1: Working in a Collaborative Culture	Meta 2: Having Purpose & Direction	Meta 3: Being Valued and Empowered	Sub 1: Climate for Positive Learning	Sub 2: Good Interpersonal Relationships	Sub 3: Appraisal & Rewards Effectively Aligned	Sub 4: Participation in Decision Making & Change	Sub 5: Development Orientation	Sub 6: Work Satisfaction	n Trusts
Overall quality score	0.68 ***	0.63 ***	0.70 ***	0.65 ***	0.68 ***	0.46 **	0.73 ***	0.49 **	0.62 ***	0.62 ***	30
08/09 financial management score	0.47 **	0.48 **	0.44 **	0.46 **	0.50 **	0.37 *	0.52 **	0.24	0.47 **	0.41 **	30
08/09 core standards score (as a provider of services)	0.34 *	0.37 *	0.25	0.36 *	0.37 *	0.31 *	0.31 *	0.12	0.41 *	0.28	30
08/09 existing commitments score (as a provider of services)	0.64 ***	0.59 ***	0.67 ***	0.60 ***	0.64 ***	0.45 *	0.69 ***	0.53 **	0.61 ***	0.55 **	25

2008/09 NHS performance ratings existing commitments and national priorities indicator scores (frequency of 'achieved')	0.69	0.54	0.75	0.70	0.56	0.44	0.76	0.62	0.66	0.68	
	***	**	***	***	**	*	***	***	***	***	25
Total time in A&E: four hours or less (% level 'achievement')	0.55	0.55	0.47	0.59	0.52	0.53	0.52	0.33	0.70	0.46	
	**	**	*	***	**	**	**		***	*	24
Inpatients waiting longer than the 26 week standard (% level 'underachievement')	−0.57	−0.59	−0.41	−0.64	−0.52	−0.62	−0.44	−0.30	−0.72	−0.52	
	***	***	*	***	**	***	*		***	*	25
All cancers: two month urgent referral to treatment (% level 'achievement')	0.54	0.52	0.42	0.61	0.49	0.50	0.35	0.46	0.60	0.57	
	**	**	*	***	**	**	*	*	***	**	24

Note:
[1] Attenuated range of performance ratings
Levels of significance; * = $p < 0.05$, ** = $p < 0.01$, *** = $p < 0.001$.

BOX 10.1 COMMON STRATEGIES FOUND IN TRUSTS WITH HIGH LEVELS OF ENGAGEMENT

- Stable leadership within the Executive team.
- Selecting and appointing the most suitable doctors through an open meritocratic system, e.g. using 1-2 day assessment processes to evaluate competencies beyond medical skills.
- Developing mutual trust and respect between managers and doctors, e.g. by promoting open and honest bi-directional communication, allowing for challenge to existing systems and accepting the need for change.
- Providing clear role responsibilities, accountability and empowerment structures for doctors and managers, e.g. by encouraging doctors to accept responsibility and accountability, while ensuring that the organisation allows doctors to take decisions, rather than requiring them to refer these for management approval.
- Clarifying expectations, firm decision-making and enforcing professional behaviour, e.g. by reminding staff that behaviour which is disruptive and unreasonable will not be accepted.
- Offering support, professional development and leadership opportunities to doctors, e.g. by offering development opportunities for medical staff which encourage the awareness of their wider role and the behaviours that are required.

(After Atkinson et al. 2011)

Current work is attempting to establish whether the highly engaged Trusts have utilised common strategies or approaches that could be useful for others. Box 10.1 summarises some of the key features found in these highly engaged Trusts.

Two messages emerge from this – continuity of leadership allows relationships to be established between management and doctors, and secondly, engagement doesn't just happen. Those organisations that develop it, work at it.

Figure 10.1 Medical Leadership Competency Framework (MLCF)

ENGAGEMENT AND LEADERSHIP

The Enhancing Engagement in Medical Leadership project had at least two aims, one of which was to develop and apply the Medical Engagement Scale as described above. The second aim is nicely captured by Armit and Roberts (2010) who suggest that the medical engagement sought is more likely to be achieved by equipping doctors themselves with the medical leadership skills to promote this engagement.

The project responded to this requirement by developing the Medical Leadership Competency Framework (MLCF). The basic components of this are shown in Figure 10.1.

Each of the domains contains four further elements and these are elaborated further in terms of learning contexts and examples. The MLCF has been endorsed by the General Medical Council (GMC) through its incorporation into *Tomorrow's Doctors*, the document that describes the required content of undergraduate medical education. Subsequently the MLCF has been integrated into the curriculum of all the Royal Medical Colleges representing each of the medical specialties at post-graduate level. Thus the key skills of leadership are becoming a required part of training for all doctors at undergraduate and post-graduate level. This should therefore make participation in wider leadership roles of health organisations a natural and normal part of the medical role. In itself this would be a very significant culture change and hopefully go some way to seeing levels of engagement rise as a natural consequence of greater involvement in the organisations' overall goals.

CONCLUSION

Health organisations are going to need to promote innovation and encompass radical change to meet the challenges described in the Introduction to this chapter. Other chapters have made clear the importance of leadership to this challenge. Here it is suggested that leadership and medical leadership in particular will need to promote medical engagement to ensure that the changes happen. Both leadership and engagement have been shown to be part of sustaining high levels of performance and together form a powerful component of more effective management of organisations and the staff that work in them.

REFERENCES

Armit, K., and H. Roberts (2010), 'Engaging doctors: the NHS needs the very best leaders', *Asia Pacific Journal of Health Management*, **4** (2), 47–52.

Atkinson, S., P. Spurgeon, J. Clark and K. Armit (2011), *Engaging Doctors: What Can We Learn from Trusts with High Levels of Medical Engagement?*, University of Warwick, Coventry: NHS Institute for Innovation and Improvement and Academy of Medical Royal Colleges. Available at: www.institute.nhs.uk/ building_capability/building_leadership_capability/project_documents.html.

Ham, C., and H. Dickinson (2008), 'Engaging doctors in leadership: review of the literature', HSMC, University of Birmingham.

MacLeod, D., and N. Clarke (2009), 'Engaging for success: enhancing performance through employee engagement. A report to Government'. http://www.bis.gov.uk/files/file52215.pdf.

Paller, D.A. (2005), 'What the doctor ordered: the best hospitals create emotional bonds with their physicians', The Gallup Organisation. http://gmj.gallup.com/content/18361/what-the-doctor-ordered.aspx.

Reinertsen, J.L., A.G. Gosfield, W. Rupp and J.U. Whittington (2007), 'Engaging physicians in a shared quality agenda', Innovation Series, IHI, Boston, USA.

Schaufel, W.B., and A.B. Bakker (2003), *Utrecht Work Engagement Scale: Preliminary Manual* (version1), Occupational Health Psychology Unit, Utrecht University, Netherlands.

Spurgeon, P., P. Mazelan and F. Barwell (2008), 'Developing a measure of medical engagement', *International Journal of Clinical Leadership*, **17**, 213–223.

Spurgeon, P., J. Clark and C. Ham (2011), *Medical Leadership: From the Dark Side to Centre Stage*, Oxford: Radcliffe.

Towers Perrin (2009), *Employee Engagement Underpins Business Transformation*, New York, NY: Towers Perrin HR Services. Available at. http://www.towersperrin.com/tp/getwebcachedoc?country=gbr&webc=GBR/2008/200807/TP_ISR_July08.pdf. Accessed March 2012.

West, P. (2011), 'Developing staff engagement to improve health service quality: presenting the evidence'. www.dh.gov.uk/eu/publicationsandstatistics/publicationspolicyandguidance/DH129643.

11. A review of quality improvement in health care and recommendations for the future

Amy L. Grove and James O. Meredith

INTRODUCTION

In recent years public spending on health care has increased by approximately £8 billion per year to £118 billion in 2011(HM Treasury 2011). Between 1997 and 2005 this funded an increase in management staff of 77.7 per cent compared with only 26.8 per cent for qualified nurses (Mintel 2009). The extent to which this increase in expenditure has resulted in concomitant quality improvements within the NHS is under question (Klein 2007). Worldwide there is an ever increasing demand for health services, brought about by an ageing population and greater social, cultural, racial and geographical diversity, which needs to be delivered with reducing budgets (Department of Health 2010). Efficiency gains and bureaucracy reduction are anticipated to deliver the required savings within the UK NHS (Department of Health 2011). Recognition of actual and potential deficits in services over the past two decades has prompted many health care organisations to introduce a wide range of initiatives and programmes to improve efficiency (Schouten et al. 2008). However these are often branded as Quality Improvement (QI) programmes although their focus is often on cost saving and efficiency rather than quality. The existing literature on these is wide and expanding but quality and generalisability are lacking.

QUALITY IMPROVEMENT

Quality improvement methods date back to the late 19th century and machine based manufacturing, when it became necessary to understand quality and productivity. Frederick Taylor introduced his theory of 'scientific management' in 1890, which aimed to increase productivity through detailed time studies. At the same time Frank and Lilian Gilbreth used motion studies to improve efficiency combined with psychology to understand how to improve worker morale. Arguably the first report of QI in health care was in 1910 when Frank Gilbreth observed that surgeons spent more time searching for instruments than performing the operation. This led to the American Medical Association recommending a scrubbed nurse to assist the surgeon by passing instruments (NHS 2002).

In the post war period a decimated Japan listened carefully to the Western quality gurus such as Taylor, Deming and Juran and rebuilt their industry using their philosophies. Taichii Ohno began the Toyota Production System (TPS) with a desire to create the perfect factory (Esain et al. 2008). He started by understanding the critical role of inventory and waste, and introduced principles such as 'just in time' and 'quality circles', both of which are the foundation of Toyota's ability to produce high quality cars at low cost (Weinstock 2008). The use of QI methods in UK health care began in the 1990s with Business Process Re-engineering (BPR). Since this time there have been numerous attempts to improve health care by transferring the philosophies, tools and methods from other industry sectors. These include Total Quality Management (TQM) (Locock 2003), the Toyota Production System (TPS) (Thompson et al. 2003), lean six sigma (Schroeder et al. 2008; Ben-Tovim et al. 2008), six sigma (Fillingham 2007) and lean (de Koning et al. 2006; NHS 2004). A quality improvement timeline since 1900 is included in Figure 11.1 *The quality improvement timeline*, which depicts some of the key events in QI history. A brief summary and history of each follows below.

Total Quality Management (TQM)

Total Quality Management is an integrative philosophy of management for continuously improving the quality of processes and products. It was developed by Deming, a US statistician but evolved in Japan from the 1950s. It emphasises that the quality of a process is the responsibility of everyone who is involved in its creation. Continuous improvements are an ongoing activity focused on the needs of internal and external customers. TQM has nine common practices as cross-functional design, process management, supplier quality management, customer involvement, information and feedback, committed leadership, strategic planning, cross-functional training, and employee involvement (Cua et al. 2001).

Business Process Re-engineering (BPR)

Business process re-engineering developed from work by Michael Hammer in 1990 (Hammer and Champy 1993). It is the analysis and design of

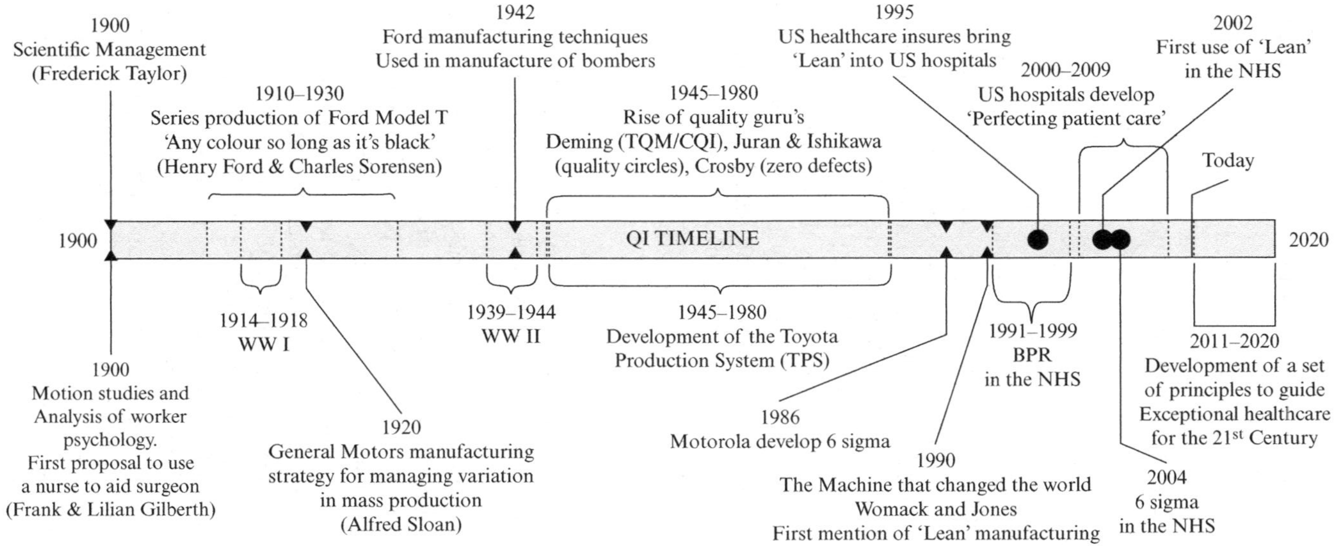

Figure 11.1 The quality improvement timeline

workflows and processes within an organisation. A business process is a set of logically related tasks performed to achieve a defined business outcome. It emphasised a radical 'clean break' approach to organisational change, but has rarely been implemented to its full extent, whether in health care or in other settings. It is frequently associated with large workforce reductions although its main champions, Hammer and Champy, stated that it was for quality improvement not cost reduction.

Rapid Cycle Change (PDSA)

Rapid cycle change is based on Langley's Model for Improvement (Langley et al. 2009), which is a simple tool for accelerating improvement. The model is meant to add to the QI methods that organisations may already be using rather than replacing them. The model is based on the Plan-Do-Study-Act cycle (PDSAs), first developed by Deming and also known as a Shewhart cycle (Deming 1986). PDSA cycles have been widely used in the initiatives promoted by the US Institute for Healthcare Improvement, and particularly in quality improvement collaboratives in the NHS. Rapid cycle changes allow front line staff to implement low-risk tests of change based on the improvement ideas and therefore encourage staff engagement in QI.

Lean

'Lean thinking' was introduced in 1996 by Womack and Jones (Womack et al. 1990). It developed from the Toyota Production System (TPS) and has been applied in many competitive sectors (Westwood et al. 2006; Ben-Tovim et al. 2008). Lean contains a series of tools focused on reducing waste, synchronising waste flows and managing variability (Ben-Tovim et al. 2008). Lean organisations strive for perfection, which comes from a continuous stream of small improvements. The principles of lean aid in the formation of a more controlled environment from which to improve by standardising processes and introducing methods of work to reduce peaks and troughs in work flow (Westwood et al. 2006).

The NHS began its own lean initiative in the early 2000s, which has resulted in a number of reported successes in hospital Trusts (Fillingham 2007; Wilson 2009). These initiatives used techniques introduced by the NHS Modernisation Agency (Brown and Duthe 2009; Proudlove et al. 2008) and later developed into The Productive Ward series by the NHSIII (NHSI 2008). It is most suited to organisations with high volume repeated tasks where staff are empowered to make changes (Radnor et al. 2006).

Six Sigma (6σ)

Six sigma was developed by Motorola in the 1980s and is grounded in the rules of normal distribution, in that everything produced should be within six standard deviations of the mean or have only 3.4 defects per million. Six sigma uses a structured approach known as the Define Measure Analyse Improve Control (DMAIC) methodology. It makes extensive use of statistical tools such as statistical process control (SPC) to identify variations in a process and to distinguish between chance (or common cause) variation and assignable (or special cause) variation (Schroeder et al. 2008). Six sigma has had limited application in health care, most likely because its rigorous methodology does not suit busy health care professionals. Six sigma requires statistical expertise alongside reliable local data collection in order to produce worthwhile improvements (Powell et al. 2008).

Quality Improvement in Health Care

QI methods have been applied in various clinical areas and organisational contexts in the UK and elsewhere since the early 1990s (Grove et al. 2010b). The models vary in their emphasis and underlying principles but they have considerable similarities in implementation. Despite this there has been little consistency in their application. There is now a body of evidence to suggest that quality improvement methods such as lean are beneficial in the UK health care service, although there is no consensus on which is the ideal method (Locock 2003; Thompson et al. 2003; Schroeder et al. 2008; Ben-Tovim et al. 2008; Fillingham 2007; de Koning et al. 2006; Proudlove et al. 2008). There are currently few published studies which demonstrate measurable and sustained improvements. Equally, data on the cost-effectiveness of QI approaches are largely unavailable (Powell et al. 2008; Ayers et al. 2005; Øvretveit et al. 2002). A systematic review by Schouten and colleges (Schouten et al. 2008) identified only seven studies (from 1104 reviewed) which reported improved outcomes from QI implementations in health care.

The link between QI and profitability is not always clear. A QI method such as six sigma will deliver profitability by improving efficiency and so reducing cost. Hence, effectiveness can be easily assessed. QI methods reduce the input of resources, e.g. labour and materials required for a particular output, thereby reducing costs. They may also increase customer satisfaction by producing a more reliable output at a lower cost. For example, a patient presenting with a common complaint may experience treatment that varies from below to above expectation. If it is below expectation it is likely that the patient will present a second time leading to additional cost, if above expectation then the treatment will have cost more than it needed to. The ideal solution is to give the right treatment at the right time leading to minimal waste and satisfied customers (Rust et al. 1995, 2002; Payson 1998).

Improvements to customer satisfaction and service will lead to greater profitability, although the pathway from customer satisfaction to revenue is indirect and hard to measure. A customer focus will enhance customer attraction, customer retention and word of mouth, all of which lead to revenue expansion. Programmes to improve quality are more likely to increase costs although there is extensive research linking customer satisfaction with positive business outcomes and revenue generating ability. A focus on customer satisfaction and retention has been shown to be more effective at generating revenue than focusing purely on cost or indeed both of these together (Rust et al. 1995, 2002; Payson 1998).

It cannot be said that QI methods in health care are not effective. The evidence gap is indicative of the lack of systematic implementation and evaluation that is employed, coupled with an under reporting of positive improvements. The nature of QI programmes means they are often complex interventions that need to be understood and examined in the context within which they occur. The research methodology used to study QI must take a more holistic approach, incorporating observation, case study and mixed method action research alongside the traditional controlled experimental design. The following section reviews a case study implementation of one of the most common QI approaches, Lean Thinking in the NHS, and explores the lessons that have been learned about effective implementation and recommendations for the future.

CASE STUDY

This case study examines the use of lean in a UK health care setting, which has proved successful in manufacturing and service sectors. The majority of research to date has been in hospitals, which raises questions regarding the extent to which lean is, or can be, applied within the community setting. The aim of the lean transformation was to achieve an improved service with the same or less resource across a health visiting service. Health visiting forms an integral part of child and family services in the NHS (Department of Health 2007). Like other organisations, they are now required to improve services and reduce cost whilst providing safe, quality care for patients.

Business consultants were commissioned by NHS management to deliver the implementation and a ‘Lean Thinking’ collaborative team was established. Staff were selected from a range of roles across the service, including clinical, managerial and administrative staff. They met at regular intervals throughout the project and were supported by the consultants who specialised in lean. There were no formalised roles or allocated project champions. During the research both qualitative and quantitative data detailing the outcome and process of the lean implementation were collected via semi-structured interviews and focus groups, time and motion studies, document analysis and value stream mapping. The detailed research designs are published elsewhere (Grove et al. 2010a, 2010b).

The results can be segmented into two streams, those which impact the service and those which contribute to the body of knowledge regarding QI in health care. In terms of impact on the service, value stream mapping (VSM) of the patient pathways was the method of most interest for the project team. 'Value added', 'Non value-added but business essential' and 'Waste' tasks for staff were defined by the project team and are presented in Figure 11.2. Results from analysing 10 days of activity across 12 staff with time-and-motion studies demonstrated that administrative support staff spent 0 per cent of their time on value added work and 53 per cent was spent on non value-added but business essential tasks. The remaining 47 per cent was categorised as wasted time. Clinical staff spent 56 per cent of their time on value added activity, 29 per cent on non value-added activities and 15 per cent on wasteful activities. Value stream mapping of the birth notification pathway identified 29 process steps of which 25 were defined as waste. To arrange a first home visit required 38 process steps of which 33 were waste. In each case, 86 per cent of the processes were categorised as waste.

The main focus for the lean thinking team was to redesign selected patient pathways to eliminate the waste process steps. The decisions on which steps and activities to remove were made through workshop discussions between staff. Figure 11.3 shows the current state map for the service, the redesigned process map is presented in Figure 11.4. The revised map contains 23 steps versus the original 67. This represents a 65 per cent decrease in the number of processes required to carry out the birth notification and arrange first visit tasks.

The qualitative results proved more fruitful to the study of QI in health care. The semi-structured interviews, focus groups, document analysis and direct observation gave rich data regarding the process of QI. The data was categorised into themes or *challenges* that the service faced during the early stages of the lean implementation. The six challenges that acted as barriers preventing the lean implementation from being completely successful are detailed below.

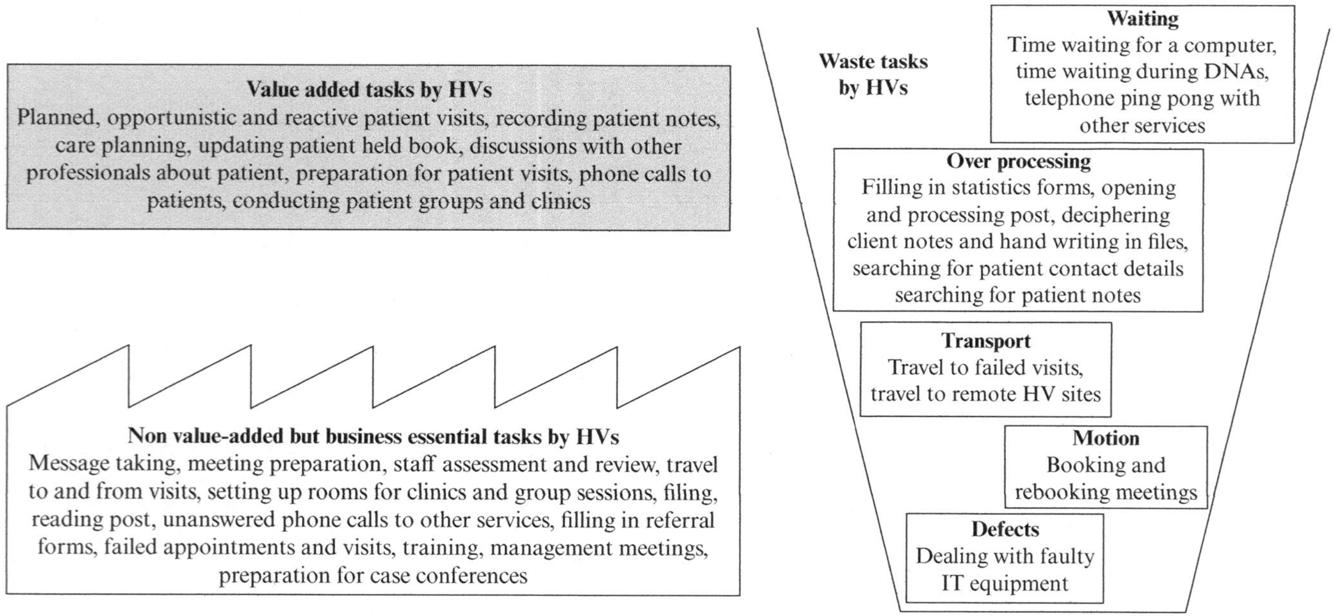

Figure 11.2 Categorisation of activities into waste and value added

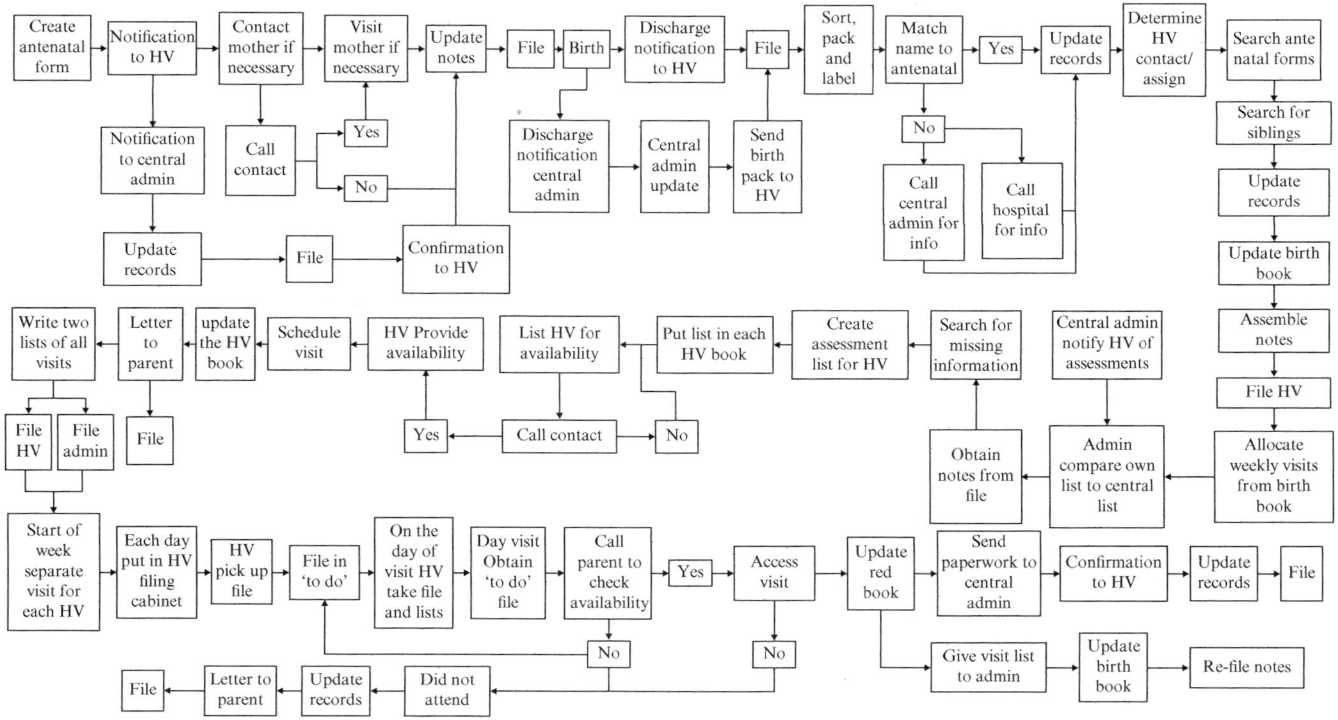

Figure 11.3 Current state map of a process in the Health Visiting service

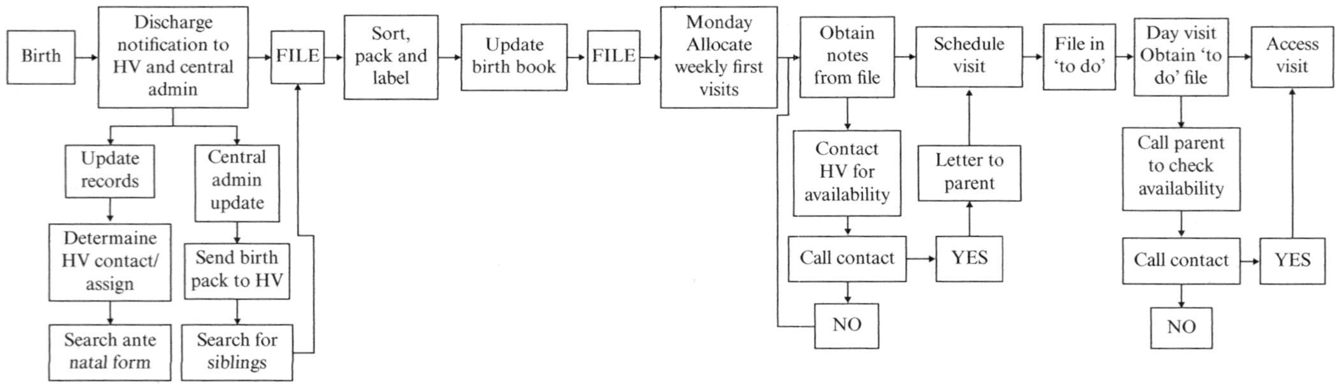

Figure 11.4 Future state map of a process in the Health Visiting service

Process Variability

A high degree of process variability existed throughout the service between members of staff who worked in both the same and different locations. This lack of standardisation made applying lean tools such as value stream mapping extremely difficult. For example, a regularly occurring event such as a new birth triggers a number of processes to occur. It would be expected that these would be the same across all sites but in fact they were significantly different. This lack of standardisation made it extremely challenging to map out processes and agree on which tasks needed to be done by who and when. Staff were unable to converge on a common approach for specific tasks, thereby making it difficult to identify which processes added value and which were waste.

Understanding of Lean

The focus for this case study was on lean tools and techniques rather than on the overall philosophy. Thus there was a poor understanding of the lean philosophy and in many cases it was seen as another passing quality fad. This, combined with the fact that key stakeholders had not been informed of the exercise taking place, meant that meaningful changes were difficult to implement and limited the transformation's acceptability and sustainability. Lean implementation requires a thorough understanding of the underlying principles rather than simply selecting lean tools developed elsewhere and applying them.

Communication and Leadership

There was an overall lack of communication and leadership. Silo working combined with flexible part-time staff and middle management control of the project led to poor communication and leadership. This was a significant limiting factor in the start up and success of the project. One of the key requirements for a lean implementation is management buy-in at all levels of the organisation, which was not evident in this case study.

Target Focused

Centrally defined targets shifted emphasis from local delivery of care to achieving national standards. These were rarely in line with what members of staff considered important for the service. There was little joint understanding of what a quality service was or what they should be working towards. NHS organisations strive to achieve numerous inappropriate targets, which drive perverse behaviour, particularly when they push the organisation to focus on achieving specific numbers rather than customer value or satisfaction. The project team realised that delivering quality care is about improving patient experience not improvement to the bottom line.

Defining Waste

Waste is so ingrained into the service that identifying it proved difficult, and removing it – unobtainable. Defining waste is challenging in this environment as each individual had a different way of undertaking a particular task. Therefore what constitutes waste depends on the individual involved. There was no central knowledge and understanding of what is and is not needed when you focus on what is 'value' to the patient as the customer.

Who is the Customer and What Do They Value?

Finally, there was considerable confusion about who is the customer of the service. Multiple customers such as patients, government agencies and families meant that the focus was rarely on achieving patient satisfaction. Various levels of the organisation were attempting to fulfil differing 'customer' requirements. A clear understanding of who the customer is will aid the service deliver quality care.

RECOMMENDATIONS: A MODEL FOR QI IMPLEMENTATION IN HEALTH CARE

Based on previous literature and our experience, a QI iceberg model was developed, displayed in Figure 11.5. The premise of the model is to demonstrate the relationship between QI 'tools and techniques' and the various organisational conditions that must be fulfilled prior to QI implementation to ensure success. The recent focus on efficiency gains and cost reduction, rather than delivering quality, has led to a number of partial implementations of QI programmes as health care managers have attempted to replicate the success of others without understanding the underlying principles and philosophy of improvement. There are critical core determinants that need to be put in place before organisations can embark on any QI programme (Dunn 2009). Experience tells us that many health care organisations start at the top of the iceberg, implementing new methods, buying work packages and employing consultants, while little thought is given to the necessary core determinants of QI 'below the water line'.

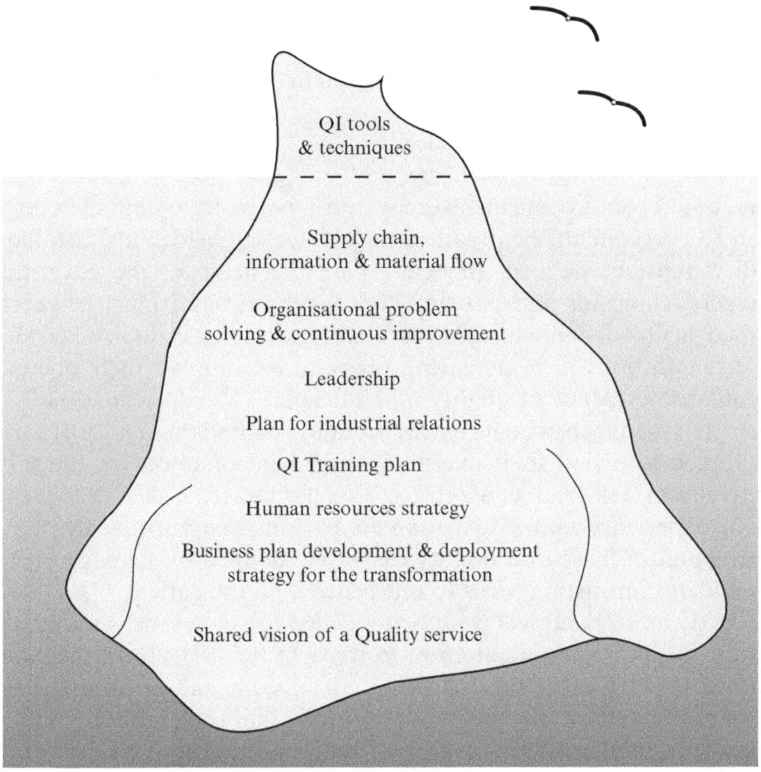

Figure 11.5 Quality improvement iceberg

There is no quick and easy way to become a quality organisation. Toyota has taken 50 years to get where it is, using a structured approach with continuous improvement ingrained throughout the entire organisation. If UK health care services wish to deliver world-class health care in the face of constrained resources and greater demand they need to adopt a long term vision for success. This will involve developing their own QI philosophy based on patient value and satisfaction, not simply applying tools and techniques developed by other industries.

A More Systematic Approach to QI in Health Care

The introduction of QI developed in industry is not a new phenomenon in the field of health care. Transformational efforts such as TQM, six sigma and BPR have been implemented, but often fail to translate into sustainable results in both the UK and the US (Bigelow and Arndt 2000;

Bahensky et al. 2005). This more often than not is due to the absence of the key factors which sustain improvements, such as leadership, communication, engagement and empowerment (Bateman and David 2002).

Shared Vision of a 'Quality Service'

Every quality improvement exercise must begin by communicating the vision to everyone in the organisation. However, before this can happen 'quality' must be defined. In health care the needs of the government, managers, clinicians and patients are all relevant and must be carefully weighed up to define what a high quality service will look like. Health care organisations face increasing pressure to improve their operations and provide evidence of quality and efficiency (Kujala et al. 2006). This means that managers who have traditionally focused on quality of care are now forced to review their overall management practices for the sake of effectiveness (Hellstrom et al. 2009). This has caused a shift in focus from patient experience and satisfaction to bottom line improvement. A QI implementation based on quality or 'value' defined by management will have widely contrasting focus to one centred on the patient.

As early as 1991 targets were being called for to set measurable objectives for health gain in an attempt to reorient the NHS towards outcome (Catford 1991). Central targets can be effective in concentrating the attention of NHS staff on specific issues provided that the incentives and punishments are sufficient. However, poorly thought out targets deliver weak or perverse outcomes (Bevan and Hood 2006; Appleby et al. 2005).

Often targets are counterintuitive and result in gaming – the manipulation of data to report good outcomes while hiding real performance. Indeed, performance monitoring that is done badly can be harmful and even destructive to the organisation (Barker et al. 2004; Young and MacLean 2008, 2009) as well as detrimental to patient health (Lewis and Appleby 2006). At the height of the UK Labour government it is estimated that there were 300 targets to be met by NHS managers (Klein 2007). This dependence on wasteful performance checking goes against the quality teachings of Deming who advises that focusing on customer satisfaction is more likely to lead to performance improvement (Deming 1986).

Strategy for the Transformation and Business Plan Development

A strong strategy, plan and vision developed right from the start of a QI implementation is crucial. Without it disagreement will arise as to what constitutes improvement due to the variations in working practices. Health care staff have become so used to issues and problems in everyday processes that they learn how to work around them. As a result problems are ignored or absorbed into the service and are not immediately obvious to staff. A typical view from staff is that 'this is the way that we have always done it', which is not acceptable. It requires a change of mindset and operating framework that cannot be achieved by teaching staff, often too simplistically, how to implement SPC charts and PDSA cycles. Ideally, the NHS requires a culture where looking for waste and solving problems is the norm, not a novelty as in the case study above. World class organisations understand that removing waste can deliver efficient and quality care. Identifying and focusing on waste removal will reduce cost and improve flow (Westwood et al. 2006). However, maximising value to patients, not cost reduction, must be at the heart of any improvement strategy.

The QI approach chosen by an organisation is less important than how and by whom it is used. Long term commitment is vital to finding worthwhile improvements. In fact it may actually be better to cherry pick the relevant parts from all QI methods in order to generate a health care specific system. Once the route is chosen a plan of how to achieve it is required. This simple stage is often ignored. The business plan will inform those involved how the organisation will transition from where they are to their quality service vision.

Human Resource Strategy

It is important to recognise the generic characteristics of all health care organisations that make QI particularly challenging. One of these is the ongoing relationship between efficiency programmes and job reduction. QI must not be used as a short term crisis measure to balance the books. Experience suggests that improvement initiatives rarely succeed unless staff employment is guaranteed in advance (Jones and Mitchell 2006). Improvement philosophies and quality gurus never advocate implementing improvement programmes as a means to enable reductions in the workforce. Capacity gained as a result of improved operations should be reallocated to other sections of the organisation which require extra support. Despite this, previous NHS initiatives branded as improvement programmes have resulted in job cuts, particularly from front line staff. This has produced a culture where efficiency is interpreted by the workforce as redundancy, leading to poorly motivated staff and failure of the initiative.

Job security must be guaranteed from the outset by senior management. People are key to any QI transformation. There is a multitude of literature on organisational change that should be consulted prior to initiation of a QI programme. Alterations to one part of the service have a ripple effect thoughout the organisation. Unless everyone involved understands the changes or the validated reasoning behind them, 'blocks' will be put in place. Each organisation and individual linked to the transformation needs to be informed about the process and its aims. Agents of change should be recruited to communicate with other members of staff and get them onside. The key is to reinforce the message that QI cannot be a mask for job reduction. This can be supported by consulting with unions and medical governing bodies from the outset.

Validated Quality Improvement Training Plan

Improvement programmes are not simple and quick routes to success, although they can deliver rapid small gains. They are not easy: regardless of the method selected, an understanding of the various theories, tools and language is always required. Staff working in health care may find this difficult or inappropriate to accept. A full lean transformation requires a minimum of seven years to implement, which is a significant investment of time (Womack et al. 1990). The current Toyota Production System has been in existence since 1945; it has had many years of development to arrive at where it is now. In terms of efficiency and processes, the NHS is 30 years behind world class manufacturing organisations whose staff understood the need for change and adapted in order to remain competitive. To date this sense of urgency has not existed in health care (Young and McClean 2009).

Generally only small scale training is provided to staff in the form of workshops or tool box packages. These approaches typically only review the various QI tools and techniques, as they are easily available and thus are used as a quick fix solution. Unfortunately there is very little 'low hanging fruit' in health care: problems are systemic and need sustained action to produce change towards quality. Poor training using a 'toolkit' approach leads to poor results, as people are unaware of the reasons for their actions and have no understanding of how to overcome problems. A back to basics training plan is essential.

Leadership for Improvement

Management support and commitment to provide necessary resource and training is critical for successful QI transformation. Managers need to be actively involved with QI for both symbolic and practical purposes, to ensure that QI activities are aligned with strategic objectives of the organisation and are resourced effectively to address systems barriers to changes.

Leadership support is key to enable staff to make improvements by giving them time and space to contribute towards change (Westwood et al. 2006). In order for the improvements to be sustainable staff must also be responsible for implementing solutions, with the full support of managers. Service changes which affect organisational operations need to be coordinated centrally and led from the top with a clear strategic framework to ensure they occur systematically throughout the organisation (Proudlove et al. 2008).

A major challenge for QI implementation in the NHS is a lack of communication and leadership within the services. In the case study, lean was applied within a small segment of the organisation using a middle down approach. The decisions and requests for improvement came from middle level managers but without a shared vision, a supporting strategic framework, or a plan as to how the aims would be achieved. Ideally the vision is set by the leaders and informs all operational plans, with stakeholders involved in the process. The complexity of the organisation means that a large number of stakeholders needed to be involved to implement even the simplest change. It is clear that to make any meaningful changes requires input from management across all departments.

Organisational Problem Solving and Continuous Improvement

Health care is complex and demand is variable and unpredictable (Shah et al. 2008). It provides a classic example of the challenges faced by many services in that it contains quasi-manufacturing processes combined with high input variability due to the individual differences between patients' needs. Nevertheless, NHS services are not necessarily more complex than the manufacturing industry where QI methods originated. The law of variability states that greater random variability will lead to a less productive process (Schmenner 1998). Whilst each patient is unquestionably different, as a population or group they will be normally distributed, and as such can be planned for. Car manufacturers have gone beyond mass production of vehicles and now build them 'made to order' to achieve high customer satisfaction. This is analogous with the potential to provide bespoke services to individual patients. It is not plausible to expect every patient's journey and treatment to be standardised, but much can be done to improve the efficiency and flow of processes between the various fractions.

The limiting factor which prevents patient treatment being 'made to order' is the current high level of variability in work processes. This variability in services is exaggerated as work is often performed by many independent staff and stakeholder organisations. It is difficult to establish any fixed processes as people and their actions cannot be easily segmented.

There is a tendency for health care workers to 'do things their own way', often based on popular belief rather than established evidence. The supply and demand relationships between the individuals and organisations are also overly complex. This restricts the ability to plan and predict which processes should and would be required for a redesigned quality service.

The inherent complexity makes implementing QI difficult as there is no consensus on what is 'good' or 'bad'. Without an overarching understanding by everyone regarding what is correct – or what is a quality service – then only limited improvement will be possible. This should be outlined from the outset. A true QI transformation requires that all stakeholders are supportive of the move towards a joint understanding of quality.

Understand the Supply Chain, Information and Material Flow

People working in health care can find it difficult to separate the 'process' steps required to achieve an outcome from the actual delivery of care that is given to a patient. Processes are often seen as secondary to the overall outcome. It is not important how a patient moves along a referral pathway, the main concern is only that the outcome, either clinical or target focused, is achieved.

Health visitors in the case study above stated that they had no time for planning and administration because patient care always comes first. This is counterproductive and resulted in variable operations to achieve the same goal, some using significantly more resource than others. The link between improved operations leading to patient benefit is not always obvious to staff undertaking QI. The focus of this improvement exercise was cost reduction; improvements must be focused on how they can improve value to the patient.

Varying degrees of poor communication and process definition led to high levels of staff stress and an inability to deliver care to all patients equally as would be expected. Services found it increasingly difficult to coordinate as levels of communication decreased. The case study consisted of groups of clinicians, managers and administrative staff who were responsible for managing the service and their daily activities. This works when teams are composed of self disciplined people who define rules that encourage self-organisation (Highsmith 2004). However, it requires intense collaboration and communication.

This was highlighted by flexible and part time working which reduces the ability to contact and engage with other members of staff, especially when attempting to motivate them towards change. The need to work closely and share information goes against the norm in segmented health care, particularly where autonomous silo working is expected and accepted, such as across shifts, wards and specialties. To sustain improvements made in both practice and culture, health care Trusts must plan transformational change across their whole organisations, not just selected parts (King 1997), otherwise only small incremental adjustments can be achieved.

Quality Improvement Tools and Techniques

Poor understanding of QI principles by staff are a barrier to success. QI tools and techniques are promoted as the wonder solution to many problems. It is questionable whether what is hailed as QI in health care is actually QI in practice. Many health care processes are unstable and require a radical redesign rather than minor adjustments. Staff being asked to produce improvements are introduced to only the top 10 per cent of the QI iceberg (MQIII) but are asked to perform complex tasks such as value stream mapping and the DMAIC method without any preparatory training or organisational development. Observations from our research demonstrated that NHS staff struggle to identify key steps that deliver value to patients. Staff believed that it was impossible to map processes as each individual patient pathway and its processes are different and their needs are varied.

There is an underlying belief that this type of simplicity does not exist in health care. This is symptomatic of the lack of understanding related to QI methods generally. NHS staff dislike lean and six sigma jargon, because it ignores cultural and interpersonal factors that are important in this environment. Simple 'exploratory data analysis' rather than in depth statistics are likely to deliver a great deal of knowledge related to a particular process or service. For example, in a study examining the efficiency of orthopaedic theatres (Meredith et al. 2011), high level timing data was used to generate Figure 11.6. This demonstrates theatre usage across multiple centres and theatre teams and enables greater understanding of what is occurring.

In Figure 11.6, each bar represents a day of surgery. The grey sections are surgery and white are gaps or waste. Some days, such as C3, were very efficient: five procedures were carried out with an early start, short surgeries and short waits. Others such as E6 are longer days overall and contain only two procedures. This simple data analysis helps guide which areas should be targeted for further analysis and improvement. A significant quantity of the data required for QI is already available within the NHS. As in this example the basic data was available from the theatre information system which most hospitals now own. Data should be utilised more effectively to help highlight problem areas and form a baseline against which to measure improvements.

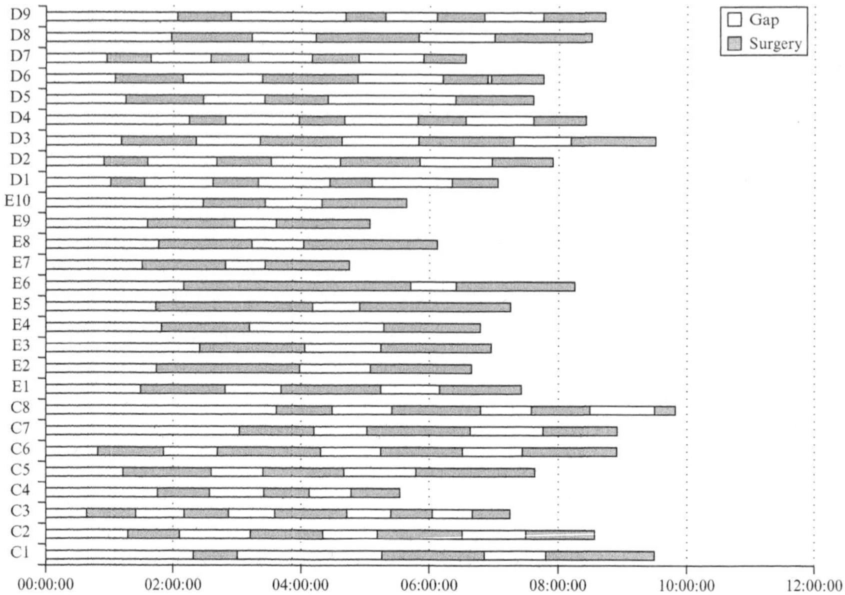

Figure 11.6 Gaps and surgery within orthopaedic theatres

Ever since Levitt's seminal work in 1972 and 1976, which took a production line approach to service processes, conventional operations management methods have increasingly been applied to service industries including health care. Health care organisations share a range of contextual characteristics that make it particularly challenging for QI programmes to succeed. These include:

- High degrees of variability and a lack of standardisation
- A need for process flexibility
- Multiple stakeholders with longstanding organisational divisions
- Challenging relationships between managers and health professionals
- A track record of top down reorganisation and change programmes

CONCLUSIONS

The recommendation to the NHS is to consider the contextual characteristics and challenges highlighted by our research experience for future QI implementations. These barriers to successful QI implementation can be overcome with the core determinants of QI which sit 'below the water line'. These include: upfront planning, transformational leadership, excellent communication, identification and sharing of best practice and above all a shared vision of the aims of the exercise so that all members of staff are highly motivated to improve the service. This may require significant alteration or selection of a 'best fit' approach from all improvement methodologies. There is no one 'right' QI method, instead the NHS should move towards a tailored approach that is suited to local needs and towards a shared vision, which may be improved patient satisfaction, reduced readmissions or reduced infection rates, but NOT efficiency improvements (or job reductions).

Health care is no more complex than any other industry where QI has been successful. If the NHS wish to deliver world class health care with constrained resources and greater demand they need to adopt a long term vision and develop their own QI philosophy based on quality to the customer (patient). The NHS is guilty of jumping on the bandwagon of one quality fad after another without having understood them and expecting fast results. Perhaps big promises by well paid consultants are to blame but the primary goal for the future should be to train their own staff in basic quality principles so they can decide how best to apply the various tools at their disposal towards achieving the shared vision. In so doing they will have already commenced their journey towards a bespoke QI method for health care which can be developed, tested and continually improved.

REFERENCES

Appleby, J., S. Boyle, N. Devlin, M. Harley, A. Harrison and R. Thorlby (2005), 'Do English NHS waiting time targets distort treatment priorities in orthopaedic surgery?', *Journal of Health Service Res. Policy*, **103** (2), 67–72.

Ayers, L.R., S.C. Beyea, M.M. Godfrey, D.C. Harper, E.C. Nelson and P.B. Batalden (2005), 'Quality improvement learning collaboratives', *Qual Manag Health Care*,**14**, 234–47.

Bahensky, J., J. Rose and R. Bolton (2005), 'Lean sigma – will it work for healthcare?', *Journal of Healthcare Information Management*, **191** (1), pp. 39–44.

Barker, R., M. Pearce and M. Irving (2004), 'Star wars, NHS style', *BMJ*, **329** (7457), pp. 107–9.

Bateman, N. and A. David (2002), 'Process improvement programmes: a model for assessing sustainability', *International Journal of Operations & Production Management*, **22** (5), 515–26.

Ben-Tovim, D., J. Bassham, D. Bennett, M. Dougherty, M. Martin, S. O'Neill, J. Sincock and M. Szwarcbord (2008), 'Redesigning care at the Flinders Medical Centre: clinical process redesign using "lean thinking"', *Medical Journal of Australia*, **188** (6), 27–31.

Bevan, G. and C. Hood (2006), 'Have targets improved performance in the English NHS?', *BMJ*, **332** (7538), 419–22.

Bigelow, B., and M. Arndt (2000), 'The more things change, the more they stay the same', *Health Care Management Review*, **25**, 65–72.

Brown T., and R. Duthe (2009), 'Getting "lean": hardwiring process excellence into Northeast Health', *J Healthc Inf Manag*, **23**, 34–8.

Catford, J. (1991), 'Health targets', *BMJ*, **302** (6783), 980–1.

Cua, K.O., K.E. McKone and R.G. Schroeder (2001), 'Relationships between implementation of TQM, JIT, and TPM and manufacturing performance', *Journal of Operations Management*, **19** (6), 675–694.

de Koning H., J.P. Verver, J. van den Heuvel et al. (2006), 'Lean six sigma in healthcare', *Journal for Healthcare Quality*, **28** (2), 4–11.

Deming, W. Edwards (1986), *Out of the Crisis*, MIT Press.

Department of Health (2007), 'Facing the future: a review of the role of Health Visitors', White paper, Department of Health, London.

Department of Health (2010), 'Equity and excellence: liberating the NHS', White Paper, Department of Health, London.

Department of Health (2011), 'The Health and Social Care Bill', Department of Health, London.

Dunn, A. (2009), 'Implementation of lean manufacturing in General Motors Manufacturing Luton (GMML)', unpublished EngD thesis, 19 January, University of Warwick, Coventry.

Esain, A., S. Williams and L. Massey (2008), 'Combining planned and emergent change in a healthcare lean transformation', *Public Money & Management*, **28**, 21–6.

Fillingham, D. (2007), 'Can lean save lives?', *Leadersh Health Serv*, **20**, 231–41.

Grove, A., J. Meredith, M. MacIntyre, J. Angelis and K. Neailey (2010a), 'Lean implementation in primary care health visiting services in NHS UK', *Quality and Safety in Health* Care, **19**, 1–5. doi:10.1136/qshc.2009.039719.

Grove, A., J. Meredith, M. MacIntyre, J. Angelis and K. Neailey (2010b), 'UK health visiting: challenges faced during lean implementation', *Leadership in Health Services*, **23** (3), 204–218. DOI 10.1108/17511871011061037.

Hammer, M., and J.A. Champy (1993), *Reengineering the Corporation: A Manifesto for Business Revolution*, New York: Harper Business Books.

Hellstrom, A., S. Lifvergren and J. Quist (2009), 'Applying process management in healthcare – investigating implementation difficulties', International Annual EurOMA 2009 Conference Proceedings of the 16th Annual International EurOMA Conference, Göteborg. Available at: www.euroma2009.org/Proceedings/Papers/FCXST-09068951-1564076-1.pdf (accessed 23 September 2009).

Highsmith, J. (2004), *Agile Project Management. Creating Innovative Products*, Boston, MA: Pearson Education.

HM Treasury (2011), *Public Expenditure Statistical Analyses*, HM Treasury, London.

Jones, D., and A. Mitchell (2006), *Lean Thinking for the NHS*, London: NHS Confederation.

King, W. (1997), 'Organizational transformation', *Information Systems Management*, **14**, 63–5.

Klein, R. (2007), 'The new model NHS: performance, perceptions and expectations', *British Medical Bulletin*, **81** (82), 1–12.

Kujala, P., P. Lillrank, V. Kronstrom and A. Peltokorpi (2006), 'Time-based management of patient processes', *Journal of Health Organisational and Management*, **20** (6), 512–24.

Langley, G.L., K.M. Nolan, T.W. Nolan, C.L. Norman and L.P. Provost (2009), *The Improvement Guide: A Practical Approach to Enhancing Organizational Performance (2nd edition)*, San Francisco: Jossey-Bass.

Lewis, R., and J. Appleby (2006), 'Can the English NHS meet the 18-week waiting list target?', *Journal of R. Soc. Med.*, **99** (1), 10–13.

Locock, L. (2003), 'Healthcare redesign: meaning, origins and application', *Qual Saf Health Care*, **12**, 53–7.

Meredith, J.O., A.G. Grove, P. Walley, F. Young and M. Macintyre (2011), 'Are we operating effectively? A lean analysis of operating theatre changeovers', *Operations Management* Research. DOI: 10.1007/s12063-011-0054-6.

Mintel (2009), *Medical equipment (industrial report)*. Available at: http://academic.mintel.com/ sinatra/oxygen/display/id¼439732 (accessed 10 September 2009).

NHS (2002), *NHS Improvement Leaders Guide to Process Mapping, Analysis and Redesign*, London: NHS Modernisation Agency.

NHS (2004), '10 High Impact Changes for service improvement delivery (Best Practice Guidelines)', NHS Modernisation Agency.

NHSI (2008), 'The Productive Ward. Releasing time to care', The Productive Ward project leaders' guide, London: NHSI.

Øvretveit J., P. Bate, P. Cleary, S. Cretin, D. Gustafson, K. McInnes et al. (2002), 'Quality collaboratives: lessons from research', *Qual Saf Health Care*, **11**, 345–51.

Payson, S. (1998), 'Quality improvement versus cost reduction: a broader perspective on evolutionary economic change', *Technology Analysis & Strategic Management*, **10**, 69–88.

Powell, A.E., R.K. Rushmer and H.T.O. Davies (2008), 'A systematic narrative review of quality improvement models in health care', NHS Quality Improvement Scotland (NHS QIS).

Proudlove, N., C. Moxham and R. Boaden (2008), 'Lessons for lean in healthcare from using six sigma in the NHS', *Public Money Manag*, **28**, 27–34.

Radnor, R., P. Walley, A. Stephens and G. Bucci (2006), 'Evaluation of the lean approach to business management and its use in the public sector', Social Research Scottish Executive Social Research.

Rust, R.T., A.J. Zahorik and T.I. Keiningham (1995), 'Return on quality (ROQ): making service quality financially accountable', *Journal of Marketing*, **59**, 58–70.

Rust, R.T., C. Moorman and P.R. Dickson (2002), 'Getting return on quality: revenue, expansion, cost reduction, or both?', *Journal of Marketing*, **66**, 7–24.

Schmenner, R.W. (1998), 'On theory in operations management', *Journal of Operations Management*, **17** (1), 97–113.

Schouten, L.M.T., M.E.J. Hulscher, J.J.E. Van Everdingen, R. Huisman and R.P.T.M. Grol (2008), 'Evidence for the impact of quality improvement collaborative: systematic review', *BMJ*, **336**, 1491–94.

Schroeder, R.G., K. Linderman, C. Liedtke et al. (2008), 'Six sigma: definition and underlying theory', *J Operat Manag*, **26**, 536–54.

Shah, R., S. Goldstein, B. Unger and T. Henry (2008), 'Explaining anomalous high performance in health care supply chain', *Decision Sciences*, **39** (4), 759–87.

Thompson, D.N., G.A. Wolf and S.J. Spear (2003), 'Driving improvement in patient care: lessons from Toyota', *J Nurs Adm*, **33**, 585–95.

Weinstock, D. (2008), 'Lean healthcare', *J Med Pract Manage*, **23** (6), 339–41.

Westwood, N., M. James-Moore and M. Cook (2006), *Going lean in the NHS*, London: NHSI.

Wilson, G. (2009), 'Implementation of releasing time to care: the productive ward', *J Nurs Manag*, **17**, 64–54.

Womack, James P., Daniel T. Jones and Daniel Roos (1990), *The Machine That Changed the World*, London: Simon & Schuster UK.

Young, T.P., and S.I. McClean (2008), 'A critical look at lean thinking in healthcare', *Quality and Safety in Health Care*, **17** (5), 382–6.

Young, T., and S. McClean (2009), 'Some challenges facing lean thinking in healthcare', *International Journal of Quality in Health Care*, **21** (5), 309–10.

12. Leadership across complex systems and boundaries

Jean Hartley

INTRODUCTION

Leadership research has traditionally focused on social influence within specified organisational boundaries, for example, by a leader over a defined group such as a team or an organisation and has also tended to focus on conventional, hierarchical organisations.This chapter examines leadership from a perspective which is gaining greater scholarly and practitioner interest: leadership across complex systems (e.g. Avolio et al., 2009; Gardner et al., 2010; Marion and Uhl-Bien, 2001; Uhl-Bien and Marion, 2009; Benington and Hartley, 2009; Schneider and Somers, 2006).This involves examining leadership where it is exercised across institutional boundaries (for example, across professional, organisational, sectoral, and governmental boundaries) and considering the implications of those contexts for the purposes, or challenges, of effective leadership in such contexts, and the capabilities which indicate effective leadership in such situations. Thus, the three concepts of context, challenge and capability in leadership arenas form the weft of the cloth about leadership across complex systems and boundaries in this chapter.

THE CONTEXTS IN WHICH LEADERSHIP IS EXERCISED

'One cannot separate the leader(s) from the context any more than one can separate a flavor from a food' (Osborn et al., 2002, p. 799). There is a growing interest in how the context both constrains leadership and also creates opportunities for leaders to shape or 'constitute' the context (e.g. Gardner et al., 2010; Leach et al., 2005; Grint, 2005). How leaders make sense of the context and explain their sense-making to others is a crucial part of the challenge of leadership (Hartley and Benington, 2010; Storey, 2004). But it has been argued that the context of leadership is like the weather, sometimes noticed but often only superficially commented on (Porter and McLaughlin, 2006). Osborn et al. (2002) argue that the effectiveness of leadership depends on the appropriateness of leadership actions in relation to the degree to which the environment is munificent, volatile and/or interdependent.

Health care organisations, it can be argued, currently operate in an environment which is far from munificent and which is also highly volatile and interdependent. First, there are new problems to be addressed in health care, including the changes in the nature of complex and long-term illnesses, the need to address not just illness but health and life-style choices, an ageing population, changing health goals with more 'predict and prevent' as well as treatment, higher expectations from patients and users about health care, and greater pressures on funding with the consequent need to consider step-change innovation, not just continuous improvement. These issues all call for a different approach to leadership, which recognises the complexity of the context and the interlocking nature of problems. Second, the wider national and global context also involves dynamism and uncertainty (Hartley and Benington, 2011a) – the collapse of confidence in global financial markets (and in economics as the dominant discipline for government discourse and decision-making); shifts in geo-political and economic power away from the USA and the UK towards India and China; the escalating revolution in information technologies, networked communications and social media; a growing loss of respect for politicians and representative democracy; ageing of the population, with a crisis in pensions and in care for elderly people; growing inequalities between rich and poor, both within and between countries; and volatile ecological and climate changes – each of these has implications for health care and how health care is organised. Third, in many countries and notably in the UK over the past couple of decades, leadership in the health service has taken place in a context of continuous change, upheaval and 'churn' in organisational structures, cultures and practices – which has both shaped and constrained the possibilities for leadership thinking and action. Recent legislation in the UK to abolish some of the current NHS structures and governance arrangements (e.g. to phase out strategic health authorities and primary care trusts, to hand over commissioning of services to groups of GPs, and to open up the NHS further to patient choice and private competition) will unleash a further period of large-scale organisational and cultural change, and fundamentally change the context for health leadership.

These complex cross-cutting problems do not fall neatly within the responsibilities of any single level of government or any single public service or a single organisation. They require a fundamentally different approach to leadership.

The dominant metaphors for organisation in the post-Second World War period have been mechanical – the machinery of government, levers of power, chain of command, and cogs in the machine, for example. This worked fairly well as a model for an industrial age, based upon mass production of standardised products and services, along linear assembly lines with a Taylorist division of labour between separate processes, taking place in a fairly stable political, economic, technological and social context. There are many aspects of organisations, including in health care, which still require the routines and reliability of these standardised forms of production. A well-ordered hierarchy and a clear command and control structure, together with a good bureaucracy, is an essential backbone for good governance and public leadership in many situations. However the pyramid-like structures of Weberian bureaucracy are often too rigid, inflexible and top heavy to be able to adapt to the deep and rapid changes in the external context.

So it is becoming increasingly clear that organisations in the public, private and voluntary sectors need to picture themselves not only in terms of machines and pyramids, but also in terms of organic living systems, continuously evolving and adapting as they interact with a changing external environment. This requires a new paradigm of government and public service leadership as part of a complex adaptive system, in which each part is closely interacting with other parts, as in the ecosphere (Uhl-Bien and Marion, 2009; Uhl-Bien, 2001). There is a growing recognition that the problems and leadership challenges outlined here need to be seen as part of a complex interactive and adaptive system, rather than as a simple, mechanical chain of cause and effect (Benington and Hartley, 2009; Benington and Moore, 2011; Stacey, 1995; Waldrop, 1992). The whole systems challenge is not just to achieve greater coordination or closer partnership between separate bodies, but to explore a collaborative sharing of ideas, budgets, and staff across the traditional boundaries between different sectors, services, and levels of government – and (most challenging of all) between the state and the citizen. The leadership challenges are huge – not only to learn to lead services across organisational and sectoral boundaries, but also to lead networks and movements within civil society. It also involves negotiating different pressures from different sources, for example, health care organisations which need to collaborate with public, private and voluntary organisations horizontally, but also manage vertical accountabilities to central government and to national policy priorities like QIPP (Quality, Innovation, Productivity and Prevention).

In addition, public leaders are increasingly recognising that citizens and communities are part of the whole complex adaptive system – within, not outside the system (Hartley and Benington, 2011a; Alford, 2009).

Traditionally the private and public sectors have made a clear distinction between producers and consumers. Public services have been 'delivered' (like post, or pizzas) to users, who are seen as waiting outside the boundary of the organisation. However, the boundaries between the traditional 'producers' of services and those of 'consumers' and users are increasingly blurred and bridged as there is increasing recognition that many services are co-produced. In the private sector this phenomenon of the co-creation of goods and services is creating a new breed of 'pro-sumers', who are both producers and consumers. Similar innovative approaches to co-creation with users and stakeholders are being explored and tested in many areas of public service (for example in school classrooms, hospital wards and neighbourhood communities). We can expect to see the development and testing of many innovative patterns of 'co-creation' of public services and of public value jointly between users, citizens and communities (Alford, 2009).

THE CHALLENGES OF LEADING ACROSS BOUNDARIES

The dynamic and complex context means that public policymakers, managers and professionals must learn how to lead processes of change beyond their sphere of formal control. In traditional models of governance the state retains control – over budgets, services and decision-making. Under the emerging model of networked governance, control has to be shared between many different organisations and actors – in the private, public, voluntary and informal community sectors. Developing and mobilising dialogue with other stakeholders about the goals and public purposes to be pursued, and the outcomes to be achieved, are now seen to be a critical part of the job of leadership (Osborn et al. 2002; Hartley and Benington, 2010; Grint, 2005).

The role of leadership in tackling and framing complex problems, and in sense-making and sense-breaking, has always lain at the heart of leadership studies though it is not always articulated as such. For example, Stogdill's (1950) seminal definition of leadership is about goal setting and goal achievement, and many other definitions are based on purpose or task.

A number of writers have distinguished different types of problem or challenge, arguing that they call for different types of leadership. The work of Heifetz (1994, 2011) has, over the last decade, been influential in drawing the distinction between technical and adaptive problems. 'Technical' problems include those that have been encountered before, where the causes are fairly well understood and/or agreed, for which known solutions already exist, and which can be addressed by a particular organisation, profession or service. Technical problems may be complicated but they are potentially resolvable through existing practices. The leadership challenge is to make it happen. One example of a technical problem in the health service is the need to wash hands to prevent the spread of infection within hospitals. Staff in hospitals know the evidence and they agree about what needs to be done (at least formally) – the challenge is to make it happen in practice.

By contrast, 'adaptive' problems are characterised by a lack of knowledge or agreement about either what causes the problem or what might solve it (or ameliorate it). Furthermore, adaptive problems often require changes in values, attitudes and/or behaviours, including among those who are involved in the problem field – they may be unwittingly or wittingly contributing to the problem along with other people. This may require a painful recognition by leaders and stakeholders that they are part of the problem as well as part of the solution. Part of the leadership purpose is to constructively challenge and to encourage the relinquishing of dearly held beliefs and attitudes where these constrain change to achieve public purposes.

Attempting to resolve an adaptive problem may throw up other challenges because the problems are cross-cutting and interrelated. Often, many different groups of people may have to join together to contribute to solving the problem, through changing their mind-sets and behaviours. An example of an adaptive problem is childhood obesity.

Clarifying the purpose of leadership is so close to the heart of the question for Heifetz that he defines adaptive leadership as 'mobilising people to tackle tough problems.' (1994, p. 15). Adaptive problems require a different kind of leadership in which the leader must refuse to collude with the fantasy that he or she has magic solutions to the problem and instead must persuade 'followers' and others that they may need to be involved in addressing the problem and may indeed be part of the problem as well as part of the solution. The leadership challenge in these circumstances is to confront the complexity of the problem and seek to orchestrate the work of a range of people to address it.

The work of Heifetz (1994) is particularly relevant for thinking about the leadership of complex and cross-cutting problems, where neither the means nor the outcomes are clear or agreed upon. His work is valuable not only in terms of framing and addressing the challenge, but also in terms of leadership as questioning the ways of working with various stakeholders involved in the problem – identifying the adaptive challenge; creating a safe but challenging holding environment; regulating the distress;

maintaining disciplined attention; protecting the voices of leadership from below; moving continuously between the balcony and the battlefield. Benington and Turbitt (2007) have tested ways (over a three-year period) in which leaders can address complex or uncertain challenges using the adaptive leadership framework in a very complex societal and policing situation in Northern Ireland.

Grint (2005), drawing on the work of Rittell and Webber (1973) and echoing the earlier work of John Stewart (2001), has drawn a similar distinction, in that he discusses 'tame' and 'wicked' problems. Certainly, the idea of 'wicked' problems has gained currency in public service organisations over the last few years. Tame problems are broadly equivalent to Heifetz's technical problems – we have the know-how to address and deal with the matter. Wicked problems are complex and often interrelated with a number of issues. These two approaches to challenges have major implications for leadership strategies, styles, processes and behaviours.

However, problems or challenges are not entirely objective. There is a constitutive aspect as well in that a problem may be seen and framed differently by different stakeholders. What is a crisis to a patient arriving at Accident and Emergency at a hospital may be a technical problem to the emergency team who have dealt with this kind of situation many times before. Part of the skill of leadership is in understanding how others frame the situation and then taking into account that framing and influencing it (Yukl, 2006; Storey, 2004).

In the past, perhaps, there was a tendency to assume that the qualities of the leader would define what was important and how leadership should be exercised. In contemporary thought on leadership, there is now the view that leadership starts with purpose or, in the terms used here, the challenges of leadership. So considering the question 'What is leadership for?' is the foundational question. Whether leadership is for organisational improvement or turnaround, whether it is concerned with societal change or team change, whether the problems to be addressed are tame or wicked – all of these are now increasingly being seen as central to understanding leadership, but the approach will be different for these different problems (Hartley and Benington, 2010; Dickinson et al., 2011; Grint, 2005). This is an argument that leaders need to adapt their strategy and their style according to the problems being encountered.

Adaptive leadership is increasingly recognised as a strategy for wicked, or 'adaptive' problems. It is intimately linked to the type of problem encountered; it should not become the latest leadership fad. It emphasises the value of asking questions, not just providing solutions.

WHO LEADS ACROSS SYSTEMS AND BOUNDARIES?

There is a range of definitions of leadership in the field, often reflecting differences in emphasis between competing concepts of leadership (Hartley and Benington, 2010). There is a need to conceptualise leadership beyond the boundaries of specific organisations (where the majority of leadership studies have been focused until recently) and also to consider a wider network of internal and external stakeholders over whom leaders now have to try to exercise influence.

Hartley and Allison (2000) consider three perspectives on leadership – the person, the position and the process. All three approaches may overlap, though different writers may emphasise one perspective more than another. Some writers, while recognising the value of an analysis of the person and/or the position, have theorised and researched the 'processes' or activities of leadership. For example, Heifetz (1994) writes: 'To capture these uses of the term [leadership] in a definition, we can use the word "mobilize", which connotes motivating, organizing, orienting and focusing attention' (p. 20).

Interest in not only formal leadership but also leadership beyond boundaries, and indeed, beyond authority, has been increasing among UK public policymakers and managers as they face raised expectations by citizens that governments and public services will respond to the complex cross-cutting problems in society.

There is an increasing research focus not on the individual or on a single leadership position, but on 'distributed leadership' across an organisation or network (Spillane, 2005; Gronn, 2002). This seems increasingly important in the context of partnership working, inter-organisational activity, and whole systems working, where leadership is often dispersed (Hartley and Allison, 2000), collaborative (Huxham and Vangen, 2000), collective (Denis et al., 2001), or contested (Currie and Lockett, 2007; Hartley and Benington, 2011b). Denis et al. (2001) go further and argue for the need to consider 'leadership constellations', by which they mean that the task of leadership may, formally or in practice, pass between different leaders with different skills and characteristics at different phases of a project or where different challenges have to be faced. Osborn et al. (2002) argue that in organisations experiencing considerable environmental dynamism the leadership role has to mobilise or draw on a wide range of stakeholders to shape outcomes.

Hartley and Benington (2010) set out the case for considering different types of leadership based on different roles and resources (including personal and positional power). The characteristics of leadership are likely to vary in differing situations – between formal and informal leadership; between direct (near, face to face leadership) and indirect (distant, aiming to influence others without direct contact) leadership; professional (e.g. clinical) and managerial leadership; and political and managerial leadership. There is also community leadership to consider.

Heifetz (1994) draws a distinction between leadership with authority and leadership without (or, Hartley and Benington argue, beyond) authority. By authority, he means power conferred through a formal source of legitimacy, e.g. appointment to an organisational position, such as chief executive, or election to a role such as MP. Leadership beyond authority has different sources of legitimation, often from below (e.g. from clients, citizens and/or communities) or horizontally (e.g. from peers, partners and other stakeholders), rather than only from above (e.g. by formal mandate).

The sources of legitimation for leadership beyond authority can include recognition by peers and the public (for example an opinion leader amongst doctors, or a health campaigner in the voluntary sector); and/or the authorisation that can come from creating a coalition between different organisations and interests to achieve a common goal (Benington and Moore, 2011).

Those leading with formal compared with informal authority have different sources of legitimacy, and access to different political, social and organisational resources to achieve their goals – including the use of hierarchy, command and control, and instruction as well as informal influence (Hartley and Benington, 2011a; Heifetz, 1994, 2011).

There is also growing recognition that the sources of organisational and individual leadership power may vary within public services. There has been a growth of interest in the roles and the resources of clinical leaders compared with managerial leaders in health (e.g. Edmonstone, 2009; Spurgeon et al., 2011; Baker and Denis, 2011). Edmonstone catalogues the differences between the sources of expertise for a health service manager compared with a clinical leader, and while this is not empirically derived it does point to important differences in the ways in which clinical leaders compared with managerial leaders are likely to address problems, take up the leadership of change, weigh up evidence, convince colleagues and so on.

The sources of authority, legitimacy and organisational and individual power for leadership are shaped by the wider policy and organisational context. The growing recognition of a more differentiated approach to leadership, which includes the roles and resources of leadership, means that there is now more space in the academic literature, and in policy and practice, to accept the varied contributions of different types of leadership.

Yukl (2011) argues for a more situation-based concept of leadership due to differences in sources of power and legitimacy in different organisational situations. This also takes us, again, into the wider recognition of distributed leadership (Spillane, 2005; Gronn, 2002; Hartley and Allison, 2000).

The idea of a 'great leader' was popular for a time in the policy literature (e.g. super-heads, directly elected mayors etc.) but the research evidence is not supportive (Currie et al., 2005). In fact, the research evidence is pointing in a different direction – that the model of an individual 'great leader' is not likely to work effectively in tackling the complex cross-cutting problems now facing citizens, communities, public services and governments. There is a stronger interest in the particular roles and resources of leadership 'constellations' and processes, in particular contexts, at particular times.

POLITICAL ASTUTENESS CAPABILITIES TO LEAD ACROSS BOUNDARIES

Selznick (1957) has argued that 'the theory of leadership is dependent on the theory of organization' (p. 23, quoted in Storey, 2004), so that as organisations change, theories of leadership need to change as well. There is growing evidence from this chapter and elsewhere that there is a need for leadership theory which takes account of pluralistic interests in and around organisations and which locates leadership processes in a network of influence across internal organisational boundaries and across organisations and groups in society. This section outlines the capabilities, sometimes called skills, which, it has been found from empirical research, leaders exhibit when they operate effectively in these conditions. The language of skill is used as a shorthand for a wide set of abilities that enable the non-specific, non-routine, discretionary and unstructured parts of the job or role to be achieved, including mind-sets, judgements, expertise, behaviours and other practices (Boyatzis, 2006; Fletcher, 2008).

Leadership across boundaries requires the effective use of political skills. This is because a leader needs to be able to understand and work with a range of stakeholders, who may have diverse interests, values and goals and who may sometimes collaborate but at other times compete. This is likely to happen inside the organisation as well as outside its formal boundaries, given the cliques and factions and the variety of professional, managerial and staff interests which exist within organisations. Externally, working across different organisational structures, cultures and subcultures, power dynamics and organisational processes of decision-making also requires political 'nous'. There is a need to anticipate and shape challenges arising from diverse interests, not just respond to them. The impact of politics (both formal and informal) may vary according to the sector the organisation is in, the degree to which it has a high and visible public profile, the sensitivity of some of its activities and its accountability and governance structures. However, all organisations must take account of politics – in the sense of diverse and sometimes competing interests – and senior and strategic managers and professionals in particular must be sensitive to the interplay of politics with organisational purpose. A range of skills for leading in these environments is as important for private sector managers as it is for public or voluntary sector managers, given the complex and increasingly media-visible world in which they are located and the amount of business that they undertake through commissioned or contracted work for public services.

Political astuteness skills are starting to be recognised in the management academic literature as elements of effective management (Baddeley and James, 1987; Buchanan and Badham, 2008; Buchanan, 2008; Hartley and Fletcher, 2008; Hartley et al., 2011; Gallop, 2011). These capabilities or skills have been recognised as particularly significant for health care professionals and managers in the context of resource scarcity and rationing (Dickinson et al., 2011). Some academics conceptualise politics as solely about self-interest (as noted by Vigoda-Gadot and Drory, 2006), but increasingly researchers are commenting that this is an unnecessarily limited view of politics, given that organisations operate in a pluralistic society, with a wide range of stakeholders and interest groups (Butcher and Clarke, 2008; Hartley and Fletcher, 2008; Baddeley and James, 1987). Leading with political awareness is about leadership skills for working with stakeholders and this inevitably means across boundaries, and often taking the whole system into account. Crick's (2004) view of politics as a means to achieve outcomes in situations where there are differences is critical to this view of politics. It means that effective leadership needs to be able to identify, reflect on and address differences in viewpoints and interests. Yet, this view of leadership as being concerned with variety and difference is not well articulated in current leadership frameworks.

Research by Hartley et al. (2007) in the UK in focus groups and interviews and particularly in a national survey of 1,495 middle and senior managers across all sectors (including health managers) developed, tested and confirmed a conceptual framework of political astuteness skills. The skills framework has been replicated in cross national comparison with over 1,000 senior public managers in Australia and New Zealand (Hartley et al., 2011). The framework has five dimensions:

Personal skills An essential foundation is to have self-awareness of one's own motives and behaviours, and the ability to exercise self-control. It is also essential to be open to and curious about the views of others; and to have a proactive disposition, initiating rather than waiting for things to happen.

Interpersonal skills These concern having the inter-personal capacity to influence the thinking and behaviour of others, getting buy-in from people over whom the person has no direct authority, and making people feel valued. These are 'tough' as well as 'soft' skills because the ability to negotiate, to stand up to pressures from other people, and to handle conflict in ways to achieve constructive outcomes is important. There are some elements which go beyond traditional leadership skills; for example, they include cultivating relationships which have potential rather than immediate value, and knowing when to rely on position and authority and when to rely on less direct methods of exerting influence.

Reading people and situations This dimension is based on thinking and intuition about the dynamics which can or might occur when stakeholders and agendas come together. There is a recognition of different interests and agendas of a variety of people and their organisations, and an interest in discerning what may be the underlying as opposed to the espoused agendas which people bring to situations. It includes thinking through the likely standpoints of varying interest groups in advance of dealing with them, and using a wider knowledge of institutions, political processes and social systems to understand what is or what might happen. It also includes recognising where you may be seen as a threat to others and their interests (rightly or wrongly, because this is about the ability to view situations from other people's perspectives).

Building alignment and alliances Building alignment and alliances is about recognising difference and plurality of interest but being able to forge these into collaborative actions even where there are substantial differences in outlook or emphasis. This dimension goes beyond much of the literature on partnerships where finding consensus and commonality is the key skill. This dimension recognises but works with difference and with conflicts of interest in order to forge new opportunities. It builds on the proactivity of the first dimension (personal skill) in actively seeking out alliances and partnerships rather than relying on those which are already in existence or which are expected to contribute. It includes being able to bring out into the open and deal with differences between stakeholders, rather than concealing them or hoping that if they are ignored they will somehow go away. It includes the capacity to craft a realistic and useful consensus without ending up with the lowest common denominator.

Strategic direction and scanning This dimension has two major elements. First is a sense of strategic thinking and action in relation to organisational purpose. This includes thinking long term and having a road map of where the manager wants to go so that he or she is not diverted by short-term pressures. Second is the skill of strategic scanning, which means noticing and thinking about longer-term issues thath may have the potential to have an impact. This is about not just looking at what is on the horizon, but considering what may be over the horizon. It requires analytical capacity to think through scenarios of possible futures, to think about small changes which may herald bigger shifts in society and the economy, and being able to find ways to analyse and manage (as far as possible) the uncertainty which lies outside the organisation.

This research indicates that effective leaders in a complex set of interrelationships across organisations deploy skills in each of these dimensions to achieve outcomes in complex and dynamic settings inside and outside the organisation where diverse interests are in play. Furthermore, from an HR perspective, the research indicates that such skills can be acquired and enhanced, particularly through experiences both inside and outside the workplace (Hartley et al., 2007, 2011). This means that there is scope for learning and development of these skills through the efforts of individual managers, through organisations and education and training establishments, and in professions.

There is a stronger emphasis currently about the range of social and emotional competencies to exercise leadership and this interest at least in part derives from the greater complexity of leading and managing across boundaries and complex systems, reflecting Selznick's (1957) comment. For example, the interest in emotional intelligence and leadership (e.g. Goleman et al., 2002) has emphasised skills of engaging with others, with authenticity, credibility and genuineness, but with relatively little said about some harder skills of managing conflict, dealing with pressure and on occasions the need to bang heads together. Huxham and Vangen (2005) have noted that working across boundaries is not about simple consensus-building but can sometimes include the need for 'collaborative thuggery'. For this reason, leadership theory which takes account of difference, not just collaborative efforts based on consensus, needs to be central to both theory-building and to policy and practice.

Leadership which is able to influence not only colleagues and subordinates, but stakeholders in the private, public and voluntary sectors is becoming increasingly important. This requires leadership across boundaries and across complex systems. An understanding of the contexts, challenges and capabilities (skills) of leadership outside as well as inside the organisation is, we have argued, critical to effectiveness in a dynamic changing world. Whether the boundaries are professional, organisational, sectoral, governmental or international, a conceptual understanding of leadership in complex systems is critical, along with practical skills to influence those systems and stakeholders.

REFERENCES

Alford, J. (2009), *Engaging Public Sector Clients: From Service Delivery to Co-production*, Basingstoke: Palgrave Macmillan.

Avolio, B., F. Walumbwa and T. Weber (2009), 'Leadership: current theories, research and future directions', *Annual Review of Psychology*, **60**, 421–449.

Baddeley, S., and K. James (1987), 'Owl, fox, donkey or sheep: political skills for managers', *Management Education and Development*, **18** (1), 3–19.

Baker, G.R., and J.-L. Denis (2011), 'Medical leadership in health care systems: from professional authority to organizational leadership', *Public Money and Management*, **31** (5), 355–362.

Benington, J., and J. Hartley (2009), 'Whole systems go! Leadership across the whole public service system', London: National School of Government.

Benington, J., and J. Moore (2011), *Public Value: Theory and Practice*, Basingstoke: Palgrave Macmillan.

Benington, J., and I. Turbitt (2007), 'Policing the Drumcree demonstrations in Northern Ireland: testing leadership theory in practice', *Leadership*, **3** (4), 371–395.

Boyatzis, R. (2006), 'Leadership competencies', in R. Burke and C.L. Cooper (eds), *Inspiring Leaders*, London: Routledge, pp. 119–31.

Buchanan, D.A. (2008), 'You stab my back, I'll stab yours: management experience and perceptions of organization political behaviour', *British Journal of Management*, **19**, 49–64.

Buchanan, D., and R. Badham (2008), *Power, Politics and Organizational Change: Winning the Turf Game*, 2nd edn, London: Sage.

Butcher, D., and M. Clarke (2008), *Smart Management: Using Politics in Organizations*, Basingstoke: Palgrave Macmillan.

Crick, B. (2004), 'Politics as a form of rule: politics, citizenship and democracy', in A. Leftwich (2004), *What is Politics?*, Cambridge: Polity Press.

Currie, G., and A. Lockett (2007), 'A critique of transformational leadership: moral, professional and contingent dimensions of leadership within public services organisations', *Human Relations*, **60** (2), 341–370.

Currie, G., I. Boyett and O. Suhomlinova (2005), 'Transformational leadership within secondary schools in England: a panacea for organisational ills?', *Public Administration*, **83** (2), 265–296.

Denis, J.-L., L. Lamothe and A. Langley (2001), 'The dynamics of collective leadership and strategic change in pluralistic organizations', *Academy of Management Journal*, **44** (4), 809–37.

Dickinson, H., T. Freeman, S. Robinson and E. Williams (2011), 'Resource scarcity and priority-setting: from management to leadership in the rationing of healthcare?', *Public Money and Management*, **31** (5), 363–370.

Edmonstone, J. (2009), 'Clinical leadership: the elephant in the room', *International Journal of Health Planning and Management*, **24**, 290–305.

Fletcher, C. (2008), *Appraisal, Feedback and Development: Making Performance Review Work* (4th edn), London: Routledge.

Gallop, G. (2011), 'Public leadership, public value and the public interest', *Public Money and Management*, **31** (5), 371–376.

Gardner, W., K. Lowe, T. Moss, K. Mahoney and C. Cogliser (2010), 'Scholarly leadership of the study of leadership: a review of The Leadership Quarterly's second decade, 2000–2009', *Leadership Quarterly*, **21**, 922–958.

Goleman, D., R. Boyatzis and A. McKee (2002), *Primal Leadership: Learning to Lead with Emotional Intelligence*, Boston, MA: Harvard Business School Press.

Grint, K. (2005), 'Problems, problems, problems: the social construction of "leadership"', *Human Relations*, **58**, 1467–94.

Gronn, P. (2002), 'Distributed leadership as a unit of analysis', *Leadership Quarterly*, **13** (4), 423–51.

Hartley, J., J. Alford and O. Hughes (2011), 'Leading with political astuteness: comparisons between the UK, Australian and New Zealand public sectors', Conference paper, Public Management Research Association, June, Syracuse, NY.

Hartley, J., and M. Allison (2000), 'The role of leadership in modernisation and improvement of public service', *Public Money and Management*, **20** (2), 35–40.

Hartley, J., and J. Benington (2010), *Leadership for Healthcare*, Bristol: Policy Press.

Hartley, J., and J. Benington (2011a), 'Recent trends in leadership thinking and action in the public and voluntary sectors', Report for Kings Fund Commission on Leadership and Management in the NHS, London: Kings Fund.

Hartley, J., and J. Benington (2011b), 'Political leadership', in A. Bryman, B. Jackson, K. Grint and M. Uhl-Bien, *Sage Handbook of Leadership*, London: Sage.

Hartley, J., and C. Fletcher (2008), 'Leadership with political awareness: leadership across diverse interests inside and outside the organization', in K. James and J. Collins (eds), *Leadership Perspectives: Knowledge into Action*, London: Palgrave, pp. 157–170.

Hartley, J., C. Fletcher, P. Wilton, P. Woodman and C. Ungemach (2007), *Leading with Political Awareness*, London: Chartered Management Institute.

Heifetz, R. (1994), *Leadership Without Easy Answers*, Cambridge, MA: Harvard University Press.

Heifetz, R. (2011), 'Leadership and authority', *Public Money and Management*, **31** (5), 305–308.

Huxham, C., and S. Vangen (2000), 'Leadership in the shaping and implementation of collaboration agendas: how things happen in a (not quite) joined-up world', *Academy of Management Journal*, **43** (6), 1159–1176.

Huxham, C., and S. Vangen (2005), *Managing to Collaborate: The Theory and Practice of Collaborative Advantage*, London: Routledge.

Leach, S., J. Hartley, V. Lowndes, D. Wilson and J. Downe (2005), *Local Political Leadership in England and Wales*, York: Joseph Rowntree Foundation.

Marion, R., and M. Uhl-Bien (2001), 'Leadership of complex organizations', *Leadership Quarterly*, **12** (4), 389–418.

Osborn, R., J. Hunt and L. Jauch (2002), 'Toward a contextual theory of leadership', *Leadership Quarterly*, **13**, 797–837.

Porter, L., and G. McLaughlin (2006), 'Leadership and the organizational context: like the weather?', *Leadership Quarterly*, **17**, 559–76.

Rittel, H., and M. Webber (1973), 'Dilemmas in a general theory of planning', *Policy Sciences*, **4**, 155–69.

Schneider, M., and M. Somers (2006), 'Organizations as complex adaptive systems: implications of complexity theory for leadership research', *Leadership Quarterly*, **17**, 351–365.

Selznick, P. (1957), *Leadership in Administration*, Evanston, IL: Row Peterson.

Spillane, J. (2005), 'Distributed leadership', *The Educational Forum*, **69** (2), 143–50.

Spurgeon, P., J. Clark and C. Ham (2011), *Medical Leadership: From the Dark Side to Centre Stage*, London: Kings Fund.

Stacey, R. (1995) 'The science of complexity: an alternative perspective for strategic change processes', *Strategic Management Journal*, **16**, 477–495.

Stewart, J. (2001), *Modernizing Government*, Basingstoke: Palgrave Macmillan.

Stogdill, R. (1950), 'Leadership, membership and organization', *Psychological Bulletin*, 47, 1–14.

Storey, J. (2004), *Leadership in Organizations: Current Issues and Key Trends*, London: Routledge.

Uhl-Bien, M. (2001), 'Leadership in complex organizations', *Leadership Quarterly*, **12** (4), 389–418.

Uhl-Bien, M., and R. Marion (2009), 'Complexity leadership in bureaucratic forms of organizing: a meso model', *Leadership Quarterly*, **20**, 631–50.

Vigoda-Gadot, E., and A. Drory (2006), *Handbook of Organizational Politics*, Cheltenham, UK and Northampton, MA, USA: Edward Elgar.

Waldrop, M. (1992), *Complexity: The Emerging Science at the Edge of Disorder and Chaos*, New York: Simon and Schuster.

Yukl, G. (2006), *Leadership in Organizations* (6th edn), Upper Saddle River, NJ: Pearson Prentice Hall.

Yukl, G. (2011), 'Contingency theories of effective leadership', in A. Bryman, B. Jackson, K. Grint and M. Uhl-Bien, *Sage Handbook of Leadership*, London: Sage.

PART IV

Managing staff better

13. Workforce engagement and organisational performance

Astrid M. Richardsen and Ronald J. Burke

Individuals rate health care an important priority in many countries and it is likely to be even more important as the population ages. Governments devote considerable sums of money to health care to meet these needs, health care being the largest single budget item in most countries. Nurses occupy a central role in the delivery of health care in all countries, though countries have different health care systems and methods of payment options. Unfortunately research on the nursing experience carried out in some countries has indicated high levels of job dissatisfaction, burnout and intention to leave the profession (Aiken et al., 2001). Many countries are facing nursing shortages, worsened by the fact that richer nations are luring nurses away from poorer ones, and that the nursing profession has lost popularity among younger women and men as a career option. The health care system has also undergone dramatic changes over the past decade stemming from the greater use of new technologies, off-shoring some services to developing countries, advances in medical knowledge, an aging population, more informed and critical users of the health care system and efforts by governments to further control health care expenditures.

Considerable research has been undertaken in various countries to understand the work experience of nurses, particularly as this relates to nurse work satisfaction, health and patient care. Much of this work, in keeping with trends at the time, has focused on 'what is wrong' with hospitals more generally and with nursing more particularly. It considered issues of workload, lack of resources, lack of nursing input into decision making, overtime work, tensions between doctors and nurses, staffing shortages, and increases in abuse experienced by nursing staff as these affected burnout, depression, psychosomatic symptoms, absenteeism and intent to leave the profession (Burke, 2003; Aiken et al., 2002; Aiken et al., 1994); Vahey et al., 2004; Zeytinoglu et al., 2007). Most of this work used a stressor-strain framework and has added a lot to our understanding of the experiences of nurses in their workplaces and how these experiences affect nurses themselves and the quality of patient care. These are important understandings but tell only part of the story (Bakker et al., 2008). There is an imbalance between research addressing what is wrong and how to fix it, and research dealing with developing what is right and promotes worker health (Taris et al., 2008).

The focus on these negative experiences and outcomes was guided by the emphasis over the past sixty years on pathology and illness in the field of psychology (Myers, 2000; Peterson and Seligman, 2003), and over the past forty years on dissatisfaction, withdrawal behaviors and alienation in the workplace, in the fields of organisational behavior and management (Cameron, 2003; Turner et al., 2002). But recent developments in these fields have taken a different track, with an emphasis on human flourishing and individual strengths represented by the beginnings of positive psychology (Fredrickson, 1998, 2003; Seligman and Csikszentmihalyi, 2000), and on 'what is right' in organisations, represented by positive organisational scholarship (Cameron et al., 2003) and positive organisational behavior (Luthans, 2002). Positive organisational scholarship focuses on positive outcomes such as resilience, meaning, thriving, engagement and excellence – the best of the human and work condition.

Organisations need to unleash the talents and motivations of all their employees if they are to achieve peak performance (Burke and Cooper, 2007; Katzenbach, 2000; Ulrich, 1997). There is considerable evidence that many organisations are falling short (Burke and Cooper, 2008; Sirota et al., 2005). However, recent efforts to improve organisational performance have begun to emphasise positive organisational behavior concepts and positive emotions (Cameron et al., 2003; May et al., 2004; Bakker and Schaufeli, 2008). Work engagement has emerged as the most prominent positive organisational concept, particularly among organisational consultants (Schaufeli and Salanova, 2007, 2008). In fact, practical interest in work engagement has outstripped the currently available research evidence. Issues such as what work engagement is, why it matters, how and why it benefits individuals and organisations, and if and how it can be increased, still need to be addressed (Macey and Schneider, 2008).

WORK ENGAGEMENT: DEFINITION, MEASURES AND RESEARCH EVIDENCE

Work engagement has received increasing research attention over the past ten years (Bakker and Leiter, 2010; Kahn, 1990, 1992; Leiter, 2005; Schaufeli and Bakker, 2004a; Schaufeli et al., 2003), reflecting an emphasis on positive psychology. Engaged workers are energetic, are positively connected to their work and feel they are doing their jobs effectively. It is a persistent and broad affective-cognitive state. Schaufeli et al. (2002) view it as a positive, fulfilling work related state of mind that is characterised by vigor, dedication and absorption. Vigor is characterised by high levels of energy, the willingness to invest energy in one's work and persistence in difficult times; dedication is characterised by high levels of work involvement and feelings of pride and challenge from one's work; and absorption is characterised by deep concentration in one's work, the sense that time passes quickly and one is reluctant to leave the work. Others have defined work engagement in slightly different but generally consistent ways (e.g., Harter et al., 2002; May et al., 2004; Sirota et al., 2005).

In a review of the literature on engagement at work, Simpson (2009a) identified several distinct lines of research, other than that of Schaufeli and his associates, focusing on engagement. The concept of personal engagement was introduced by Kahn (1990) and referred to the employing of oneself physically, cognitively and emotionally during work role performance. Three psychological conditions were found to impact on people's engagement and disengagement in their work, i.e., meaningfulness, safety, and availability of resources. Only two studies using this framework were found (Simpson, 2009a).

Another line of research is that of burnout and engagement proposed by Maslach and Leiter (1997), in which engagement is proposed to be the exact opposite of burnout and thus represents a continuum. Five studies of nurses have used this framework and have generally demonstrated the importance of work environment factors and the mediating role of burnout/engagement as well as the mediating role of nurse empowerment on burnout/engagement (Simpson, 2009a). Yet another research tradition is that of employee engagement, defined as the individual's involvement, satisfaction and enthusiasm for work. In a meta-analysis Harter et al. (2002) reviewed research using the Gallup Workplace Audit and provided evidence for relationships between employee engagement and several organisational and work outcomes.

Rich et al. (2010) conceptualised engagement as the investment of an individual's complete self in terms of physical, cognitive and emotional energies to work role performances, based on Kahn's (1990) description of engagement as a motivational concept. Engagement represents the simultaneous investment of cognitive, affective and physical energies into role performance (Rich et al., 2010). They developed a questionnaire to measure physical, affective and cognitive engagement. Their study of 245 firefighters indicated that engagement played a mediating role in the relationships between value congruence, perceived organisational support and core self-evaluations, and two aspects of job performance, task performance and organisational citizenship behaviour. The results provided support for the distinctiveness of engagement relative to job involvement, job satisfaction, and intrinsic motivation, and contributed to a better understanding of the degree to which the antecedents of engagement impact job performance.

The most commonly used measure of work engagement was developed by Schaufeli and his colleagues and comprises three components: vigor, dedication and absorption (Schaufeli et al., 2002). The accumulating research findings have shown that the measures of the three engagement concepts developed by Schaufeli and his colleagues (2002) are reliable, stable and valid (also see Schaufeli et al., 2006; Schaufeli and Salanova, 2007, 2008).

WORK ENGAGEMENT AND NURSES

A few studies have examined antecedents of work engagement among nurses in the hospital setting (e.g., Laschinger and Leiter, 2006; Seppala et al., 2008). Laschinger et al. (2009) compared nurses with less than two years of experience and nurses with more than two years of experience. They found that staff nurses' perceptions of structural empowerment had a direct positive effect on engagement (Laschinger et al., 2009). Engagement partially mediated the relationship between empowerment and work effectiveness, and the impact of engagement on work effectiveness was significantly stronger for nurses with more than two years of experience. For nurses, the perception of empowerment in the form of information, support, resources, formal and informal power seemed to have a strong effect on work engagement, which subsequently affected work effectiveness (Laschinger et al., 2009). Nurses who engage positively in their work, through vigor, dedication and absorption, can make a difference to the quality of nursing work life in hospital settings.

In addition, earlier work, though not using the term work engagement, has described hospital cultures that were associated with nurse job satisfaction and high quality patient care (Aiken et al., 1994; Leiter and Laschinger, 2006). These hospitals were termed 'magnet hospitals' and were characterised by hospital cultures that included lots of nursing staff access to information, nurse participation in decision making, doctor-nurse relationships characterised by trust, and low nurse turnover (Havens and Aiken, 1999; Kramer, 1990). This suggests that both resources in the work environment and work relationships are important contributors to nurse engagement.

Freeney and Tiernan (2009) collected data from focus groups of nurses in order to explore the facilitators and barriers to work engagement. They found that the concerns that were brought up by nurses centered around six areas of working life consistent with Leiter and Maslach's work life model. Interventions aimed at fostering engagement should focus on facilitating workload management, providing staff with autonomy and fostering a sense of community. Organisational practices need to ensure fair treatment and an adequate balance of efforts and rewards, and to be sensitive to potential mismatches between personal and organisational values.

Simpson (2010) also found that nursing staff with higher core work environment physical, psychological and social resources had higher levels of work engagement. Similar findings emerged from a study among 285 nurses in urban teaching hospitals (Laschinger and Finegan, 2005). Structural empowerment had a positive effect on engagement through the same six areas of working life. In other words, an empowering work place was related to perceptions of higher autonomy, manageable workloads, greater rewards and recognition, fair procedures and good working relationships. These areas of work life were in turn associated with more energy and engagement (Laschinger and Finegan, 2005).

In a study by Giallonardo et al. (2010), authentic leadership of preceptors (nurse supervisors on a one-to-one basis) was related to work engagement among new graduate nurses. Work engagement was found to partially mediate the impact of preceptor leader style on nurses' job satisfaction. The results suggest that when new graduate nurses are paired with preceptors who demonstrate high levels of authenticity, they feel more engaged and are more job satisfied (Giallonardo et al., 2010). Studies of other occupations also indicate that supervisor support is an important antecedent of work engagement (Martinussen et al., 2011).

In a descriptive cross-sectional study of 167 registered nurses, Simpson (2009b) found that the best predictors of work engagement were job satisfaction (especially professional status and interaction) and low turnover cognitions. The results suggest that hospital and nursing administration should target their efforts to enhance nurses' professional status and interaction at work.

Evidence suggests that there is a reciprocal relationship between job resources, personal resources and work engagement (Xanthopoulou et al., 2009a; Hakanen et al., 2008). In a three-year longitudinal study, Hakanen et al. (2008) found that job resources influenced future engagement, which in turn predicted organisational commitment. Job demands, on the other hand, predicted burnout over time, which in turn predicted future depression. In a study of 163 employees (Xanthopoulou et al., 2009a), it was found that job and personal resources related positively to work engagement measured 18 months later, and also that work engagement was positively related to both job and personal resources measured 18 months later. These findings indicate that the psychological processes of job resources, personal resources and work engagement are dynamic and mutually related, supporting the assumptions of Conservation of Resources (COR) theory (Hobfoll, 2002). When job resources are available, people feel more able to deal with their work goals, and when people feel self-efficacious, valuable and optimistic, they may create a resourceful work environment. In either case employees will be engaged in their work tasks (Xanthopoulou et al., 2009a).

The results of these studies are consistent with predictions of the Job Demands-Resources (JD-R) model (Schaufeli and Bakker, 2004b). The model assumes that two processes are operating regarding work behaviour. On the one hand, high job demands require employees to increase effort and mobilise active coping responses that over time may deplete or exhaust their energy, resulting in burnout. The second process is a motivational process in which job resources may reduce demands and facilitate achievement of work goals through the positive influence of work engagement. The JD-R model thus proposes that strain mediates the relationship between high job demands and negative work outcomes (health problems, reduced productivity, intention to quit), whereas engagement mediates the relationship between job resources and positive work outcomes (commitment, work performance) (Schaufeli and Bakker, 2004b).

WORK ENGAGEMENT AND PERFORMANCE

Evidence suggests that engaged workers perform better than non-engaged workers (Bakker, 2009) because they often experience positive emotions, which broaden people's thought-action repertoire (Fredrickson, 2003); and experience better psychological and physical health, which facilitates performance through enabling workers able to channel all mental and physical resources to the work. Engaged workers also have the autonomy to create their own job and personal resources, which makes people better able to deal with job demands and achieve work goals; and they transfer their engagement to others, which facilitates team effort and increased performance. The few studies that have been done on engagement and performance have indicated that engagement is positively related to both in-role and extra-role performance (Bakker et al., 2008).

Halbesleben and Wheeler (2008) found that work engagement and job embeddedness (attachment to the job) predicted both self-reported job performance and performance rated by others (supervisor and co-workers) in a sample of 587 US employees from a wide variety of industries and occupations. Harter et al. (2002) found that levels of engagement were positively correlated with business-unit performance (e.g., customer satisfaction and loyalty, unit profitability, unit productivity, turnover levels and safety) in almost 8,000 business units within 36 organisations. Engagement correlated .22 with a composite measure of performance, which increased to .38 when measurement error and restriction of range were taken into account.

Burnout has been associated with increased risk of cardiovascular disease. However, in a study of managers identified as burned out, engaged and healthy controls, Van Doornen et al. (2009) found no differences between managers in cardiac sympathetic and parasympathetic activity, or heart rate. This suggested that positive affective states such as engagement may not have more positive effects on worker health. However, in a study of 776 Japanese employees, it was found that work engagement was positively related to health and well-being as well as self-reported job performance, whereas workaholism was negatively related to these variables (Shimazu and Schaufeli, 2009).

In one of the few studies of engagement and performance in medical settings, Prins et al. (2009) found that highly engaged resident physicians made fewer errors (action/judgement, due to lack of time) than those with high burnout scores. Nevertheless, more than 50 per cent stated that they had made a mistake with negative consequences for the patient. The overwhelming majority (91 per cent) indicated that they did not have enough time for patients (Prins et al., 2010).

Evidence has also been found for the mediating role of engagement between job resources, such as autonomy and social support, and various measures of job performance. Chung and Angeline (2010) found that work engagement partially mediated the relationship between job resources (job control and social support) and both in-role and extra-role performance in 345 working adults from Malaysia. Job resources were not only directly related to employees' job performance, but also indirectly through their work engagement. The findings suggest that employees are likely to perform well if they have control over their jobs and if they receive support from supervisors and peers. Such resources would contribute to employees becoming more engaged and thus achieving their personal and organisational goals. However the study relied only on self-reported performance measures.

Ho et al. (2011) found that engagement in the form of absorption mediated the relationship between harmonious passion for work and supervisor rated work performance in a survey of 509 employees from an insurance firm. Both attention to work and absorption were correlated with work performance (although low).

In a study of how daily fluctuations in job resources (autonomy, coaching and team climate) were related to personal resources (self-efficacy, self-esteem and optimism), engagement and financial returns, Xanthopoulou et al. (2009b) found that day-level job resources had an effect on work engagement through day-level personal resources. Work engagement partially mediated the relationship between job resources and financial returns, indicating that engagement levels of individual employees may affect team performance outcomes (Xanthopoulou et al., 2009b). In particular, the role of daily coaching seemed to be important in determining performance outcomes through engagement.

Salanova and Schaufeli (2008) investigated the mediating role of work engagement among job resources and proactive behaviour at work for 338 telecom managers. The results showed that work engagement fully mediated the impact of job resources such as control, feedback and variety on employees' proactive behaviour, i.e. seeking challenging goals, problem solving behavior and showing personal iniative. This indicates that proactivity may be considered a specific work behaviour rather than a personal disposition, and that it is influenced by perceived levels of job resources. Job resources impact on proactivity, not directly but indirectly through increased levels of work engagement (Salanova and Schaufeli, 2008).

In a study of front-line service workers and their customers, Salanova et al. (2005) reported that work engagement predicted service climate, which in turn predicted employee performance and then customer loyalty. Schaufeli and Salanova (2007, 2008), based on their review of the work engagement literature, concluded that engagement is associated with positive employee attitudes, proactive job behaviors, higher levels of employee psychological well-being, and increased individual job and organisational performance.

In a study of potential antecedents and consequences of work engagement in a large sample of nurses working in hospitals in Turkey (Burke et al., 2010), the data indicated that levels of work engagement were significantly lower than in other normative groups (e.g., Seppala et al., 2008), suggesting a potential concern for their employing hospitals. The results indicated that while personal demographic and work situation characteristics were moderately related to levels of work engagement, work engagement, in turn, was found to have fairly consistent, but moderate, relationships with several work outcomes and indicators of psychological well-being. Engagement, it seems, has potentially positive consequences for both employees and their employing organisations.

In conclusion, it is important to study engagement because it is linked to positive individual and work related outcomes (Schaufeli and Salanova, 2007, 2008). While there is some consensus on the workplace antecedents of engagement (e.g., support, feedback, coaching) and consequences of work engagement (e.g., commitment, satisfaction and work performance), there is less agreement on personal characteristics (e.g., demographics and personality factors) associated with levels of work engagement. The question of who are engaged workers therefore needs additional attention. Schaufeli and Salanova (2007, 2008) found inconsistent or at best small effects due to demographic characteristics, and, among personality factors, there was some evidence that individuals high on extraversion and low on neuroticism reported higher levels of work engagement. In addition, occupation type and organisational level had some effects on engagement: managers, executives and entrepreneurs scored relatively high on engagement, while blue collar workers, police officers and home care staff scored relatively low on engagement.

The research evidence so far seems to demonstrate that work engagement is associated with positive outcomes. Work engagement has been associated with worker health and well-being, job satisfaction, commitment and performance. It also seems to have the potential to increase organisational performance (e.g., customer satisfaction, financial returns, low absenteeism and turnover) through increased team performance and both in-role and extra-role involvement. Few studies have been conducted with nurses in hospital settings. However, it is reasonable to assume that engaged nurses would contribute to improved service climate, patient satisfaction and high quality patient care. Thus, there would be considerable gains for hospitals to provide resources such as workload management, nursing input in decision making, and supervisor and organisational support in order to enhance nurse engagement and in turn, organisational performance.

INTERVENTIONS TO INCREASE ENGAGEMENT

An increasing number of organisations are concluding that they need to unleash the untapped potential of all their employees if they are to compete successfully in an increasingly demanding global market place (Burke and Cooper, 2008; Lawler, 2008). However, few research studies have looked at specific interventions to increase engagement and thereby both individual and organisational performance. One example is Kalisch et al. (2007), who tested an intervention to improve teamwork and engagement among 55 nurses and nurse assistants in a medical-oncology unit in a community hospital. The teamwork and engagement enhancement intervention was based on principles of teamwork, change management, training and staff engagement. It was carried out in several steps, including focus groups to collect data on status quo; feedback from the focus groups; sessions on values, vision and developing goals; teamwork training and creative problem solving sessions in groups; and rapid testing and implementation of ideas and changes. There was also continual communication about the project with the staff, and follow-up coaching and reinforcement of team skills were offered. Measures of patient falls, patient satisfaction, staff turnover and vacancy rates, taken before and after the intervention, indicated that patient satisfaction increased but was not statistically significant. The mean patient fall rates were significantly lower after the intervention, and there was a significant drop in both staff turnover rates and vacancy rates. Staff ratings of level of teamwork completed six months after the intervention also indicated a significant improvement in teamwork. Engaging staff and managers in teamwork training, creative idea generation, testing and implementation of ideas for change seems to have a positive effect on the quality of patient care and productivity, patient satisfaction and staff commitment to the workplace. All of these may be associated with increased productivity and potential cost savings for the health care organisation.

PRACTICAL IMPLICATIONS

The accumulating research findings on work engagement have added considerably to our understanding of implications for building more effective organisations. The research that has considered the organisational environment associated with high levels of work engagement has reported that organisational support plays a central role (Demerouti et al., 2001). Fortunately there is some understanding of the processes on mechanisms that underlie levels of support.

Rich et al. (2010) suggest that rather than spreading resources over various practices aimed at assessing and improving a variety of attitudes and motivational states, it may be worthwhile to focus resources on practices that assess and enhance employee engagement. High levels of value congruence, perceived organisational support, and core self-evaluations were associated with higher levels of employee engagement (Rich et al., 2010). This may be used in staffing practices to select employees who possess high core self-evaluations and have values that fit with the hiring organisation. Following employment, one could use various HR initiatives, e.g., mentoring, socialisation opportunities, people management practices that are aligned with organisational values, leadership training, and developmental feedback, in order to foster value congruence and perceived organisational support (Rich et al., 2010). The measure of engagement used in their study focused on the motivational nature of engagement, and the authors caution that it is unknown whether engagement conceptualised and measured largely as attitude (Harter et al., 2002) or as well-being (Schaufeli and Bakker, 2004a) would function in the same way in terms of enhancing job performance (Rich et al., 2010).

Increasing engagement with work is a challenging and complex undertaking. As the research findings show, engagement stems from the employees' contact with a work environment. Leiter (2005) offers a comprehensive look at interventions in the workplace designed to enhance engagement with work. He offers a conceptual framework to build engagement with work that considers the targets of intervention, strategies for intervention and potential consequences. Intervention targets include *energy* at work, *involvement* with one's work, and *efficacy* at work. Intervention strategies involve both individual and organisational or workplace levels. It is critical to remember that individuals have different views and values about work – which can change over time – and that employees must participate in building engagement at work.

Schaufeli and Salanova (2007, 2008) suggest a number of ways to build work engagement. These include:

- enhancing the person-job fit
- matching individual and organisational needs
- developing a meaningful psychological contract that links personal goals of individual employees with organisational resources
- surveys of employee demands and resources and their association with positive and negative outcomes
- job redesign that reduces stressors and increases resources
- leadership development that builds a positive emotional climate in the workplace
- developing training programs that are targeted at both organisational health and individual well-being.

CONCLUSION

The research reviewed here suggests that engagement at work is associated with positive work and individual well-being outcomes and that job characteristics and the work environment are major contributors to levels of employee engagement. This is consistent with the results of an increasing number of studies (Gonzalez-Roma et al., 2006; Hakanen et al., 2005;

Montgomery et al., 2003) reflecting the importance of understanding and increasing employee engagement. These findings extend our understanding of engagement in ways that have practical implications such as those proposed by Schaufeli and Salanova (2007), who suggest that selection, goal setting and the articulation of a challenging 'contract' between the individual and the organisation are ways to heighten engagement. This emphasis fits with the recognition that people and organisational culture may be the real competitive advantage held by organisations (Pfeffer, 1994, 1998; Sisodia et al., 2007). Health care organisations that are able to create empowering and high engagement work environments may have competitive advantage in terms of retaining nursing staff, thus being able to achieve positive organisational behavior and excellence in patient care.

NOTE

1. Preparation of this chapter was supported in part by BI Norwegian Business School and the Schulich School of Business, York University.

REFERENCES

Aiken, L.H., H.L. Smith and E.T. Lake (1994), 'Lower medicate mortality among a set of hospitals known for good nursing care', *Medical Care*, **32**, 771–787.

Aiken, L.H., S.P. Clarke, D.M. Sloane and J. Sochalski (2001), 'Nurses' reports on hospital care in five countries', *Health Affairs*, **20**, 343–353.

Aiken, L.H., S.P. Clarke, D.M. Sloane, J. Sochalski and J.H. Silber (2002), 'Hospital nurse staffing and patient mortality, nurse burnout and job dissatisfaction', *Journal of the American Medical Association*, 288, 1987–1993.

Bakker, A.B. (2009), 'Building engagement in the workplace', in R.J. Burke and C.L. Cooper (eds), *The Peak Performing Organization*, London: Routledge, pp. 50–72.

Bakker, A.B., and M.P. Leiter (2010), *Work Engagement*, London: Psychology Press.

Bakker, A.B., and W.B. Schaufeli (2008), 'Positive organizational behavior: engaged employees in flourishing organizations', *Journal of Organizational Behavior*, **29**, 147–154.

Bakker, A.B., W.B. Schaufeli, M.P. Leiter and T.W. Taris (2008), 'Work engagement: an emerging concept in organizational health psychology', *Work & Stress*, **22**, 187–200.

Burke, R.J. (2003), 'Length of shift, work outcomes, and psychological well-being of nursing staff', *International Journal of Public Administration*, **26**, 1637–1646.

Burke, R.J., and C.L. Cooper (2007), *Building More Effective Organizations*, Cambridge, UK: Cambridge University Press.

Burke, R.J., and C.L. Cooper (2008), *The Peak Performing Organization*, London: Routledge.

Burke, R.J., M. Koyuncu, M. Tekinkus, C. Bektas and L. Fiksenbaum (2010), 'Work engagement among nurses in Turkish hospitals: potential antecedents and consequences', unpublished manuscript.

Cameron, K.S. (2003), 'Organizational virtuousness and performance', in K.S. Cameron, J.E. Dutton and R.E. Quinn (eds), *Positive Organizational Scholarship*, San Francisco: Berrett-Koehler, pp. 48–65.

Cameron, J., J. Dutton and R.E. Quinn (2003), *Positive Organizational Scholarship*, San Francisco: Berrett-Koehler.

Chung, N.G., and T. Angeline (2010), 'Does work engagement mediate the relationship between job resources and job performance of employees?', *African Journal of Business Management*, **4**, 1837–1843.

Demerouti, E., A.B. Bakker, J. deJonge, P.P.M. Janssen and W.B. Schaufeli (2001), 'Burnout and engagement at work as a function of demands and control', *Scandinavian Journal of Work, Environment and Health*, **27**, 279–286.

Fredrickson, B.L. (1998), 'What good are positive emotions?', *Review of General Psychology*, **2**, 300–319.

Fredrickson, B.L. (2003), 'The value of positive emotions', *American Scientist*, **91**, 330–335.

Freeney, Y.M., and J. Tiernan (2009), 'Exploration of the facilitators and barriers to work engagement in nursing', *International Journal of Nursing Studies*, **46**, 1557–1565.

Giallonardo, L.M., C.A. Wong and C.L. Iwasiw (2010), 'Authentic leadership of preceptors: predictor of new graduate nurses' work engagement and job satisfaction', *Journal of Nursing Management*, **18**, 993–1003.

Gonzalez-Roma, V., W.B. Schaufeli, A.B. Bakker and S. Lloret (2006), 'Burnout and work engagement: independent factors or opposite poles?', *Journal of Vocational Behavior*, **68**, 165–174.

Hakanen, J.J., A.B. Bakker and E. Demerouti (2005), 'How dentists cope with their job demands and stay engaged: the moderating role of job resources', *European Journal of Oral Science*, **113**, 479–487.

Hakanen, J.J., W.B. Schaufeli and K. Ahola (2008), 'The Job Demands-Resources model: a three-year cross-lagged study of burnout, depression, commitment, and work engagement', *Work & Stress*, **22**, 224–241.

Halbesleben, J.R.B., and A.R. Wheeler (2008), 'The relative roles of engagement and embeddedness in predicting job performance and intention to leave', *Work & Stress*, **22**, 242–256.

Harter, J.K., F.L. Schmidt and T.L. Hayes (2002), 'Business-unit level relationship between employee satisfaction, employee engagement and business outcomes: a meta-analysis', *Journal of Applied Psychology*, **87**, 268–279.

Havens, D.S., and L.H. Aiken (1999), 'Shaping systems to promote desired outcomes: the magnet hospital model', *Journal of Nursing Administration*, **29**, 14–20.

Ho, V.T., S.S. Wong and C.H. Lee (2011), 'A tale of passion: linking job passion and cognitive engagement to employee work performance', *Journal of Management Studies*, **48**. DOI: 10.1111/j.1467-6486.2009.00878.x.

Hobfoll, S.E. (2002), 'Social and psychological resources and adaptation', *Review of General Psychology*, **6**, 307–324.

Kahn, W.A. (1990), 'Psychological conditions of personal engagement and disengagement at work', *Academy of Management Journal*, **33**, 692–724.

Kahn, W.A. (1992), 'To be fully there: psychological presence at work', *Human Relations*, **45**, 321–349.

Kalisch, B.J., M. Curley and S. Stefanov (2007), 'An intervention to enhance nursing staff teamwork and engagement', *Journal of Nursing Administration*, **37**, 77–84.

Katzenbach, J.R. (2000), *Peak Performance: Aligning the Hearts and Minds of Your Employees*, Boston: Harvard Business School Press.

Kramer, M. (1990), 'The magnet hospitals: excellence revisited', *Journal of Nursing Administration*, **20**, 25–30.

Laschinger, H.K.S., and J. Finegan (2005), 'Empowering nurses for work engagement and health in hospital settings', *Journal of Nursing Administration*, **35**, 439–449.

Laschinger, H.K.S., and M.P. Leiter (2006), 'The impact of nursing work environments on patient safety outcomes: the mediating role of burnout/engagement', *Journal of Nursing Administration*, **5**, 259–267.

Laschinger, H.K.S., P. Wilk, J. Cho and P. Greco (2009), 'Empowerment, engagement and perceived effectiveness in nursing work environments: does experience matter?', *Journal of Nursing Management*, **17**, 636–648.

Lawler, E.E. (2008), *Talent: Making People Your Competitive Advantage*, San Francisco: Jossey-Bass.

Leiter, M.P. (2005), 'Engagement with work: issues for measurement and intervention', in R.J. Burke and C.L. Cooper (eds), *The Human Resources Revolution: Why Putting People First Matters*, Oxford: Elsevier, pp. 213–230.

Leiter, M.P., and Laschinger, H.K.S. (2006), 'A work environment to support professional nursing practice: implications for burnout', *Nursing Research*, **55**, 137–146.

Luthans, F. (2002), 'Positive organizational behavior: developing and managing psychological strengths', *Academy of Management Executive*, **16**, 57–72.

Macey, W.H., and B. Schneider (2008), 'The meaning of employee engagement', *Industrial and Organizational Psychology*, **1**, 3–30.

Martinussen, M., P.C. Borgen and A.M. Richardsen (2011), 'Burnout and engagement among physiotherapists', *International Journal of Therapy and Rehabilitation*, **18**, 80–89.

Maslach, C., and M.P. Leiter (1997), *The Truth About Burnout: How Organizations Cause Personal Stress and What To Do About It*, San Fransisco, CA: Jossey-Bass Inc.

May, D.R., R.L. Gilson and L.M. Harter (2004), 'The psychological conditions of meaningfulness, safety and availability and the engagement of the human spirit at work', *Journal of Occupational and Organizational Psychology*, **77**, 11–37.

Montgomery, A.J., M.C.W. Peeters, W.B. Schaufeli and M. Den Ouden (2003), 'Work-home interference among newspaper managers: its relationship with burnout and engagement', *Anxiety, Stress & Coping: An International Journal*, **16**, 195–211.

Myers, D.G. (2000), 'The funds, friends and faith of happy people', *American Psychologist*, **55**, 56–67.

Peterson, C.M., and M.F.P. Seligman (2003), 'Positive organizational studies: lessons from positive psychology', in K.S. Cameron, J.E. Dutton and R.E. Quinn (eds), *Positive Organizational Scholarship*, San Francisco: Berrett-Koehler, pp. 14–28.

Pfeffer, J. (1994), *Competitive Advantage Through People*, Boston: Harvard Business School Press.

Pfeffer, J. (1998), *The Human Equation: Building Profits by Putting People First*, Boston: Harvard Business School Press.

Prins, J.T., F.M.M.A. van der Heijden, J.E.H.M. Hoekstra-Weebers, A.B. Bakker, H.B.M. van der Wiel, B. Jacobs and S.M. Gazendam-Donofrio (2009), 'Burnout, engagement and resident physicians' self-reported errors', *Psychology, Health & Medicine*, **14**, 654–666.

Prins, J.T., J.E.H.M. Hoekstra-Weebers, S.M. Gazendam-Donofrio, G.S. Dillingh, A.B. Bakker, M. Huisman, B. Jacobs and F.M.M.A. van der Heijden (2010), 'Burnout and engagement among resident doctors in the Netherlands: a national study', *Medical Education*, 44, 236–247.

Rich, B.L., J.A. Lepine and E.R. Crawford (2010), 'Job engagement: antecedents and effects on job performance', *Academy of Management Journal*, **53**, 617–635.

Salanova, M., and W.B. Schaufeli (2008), 'A cross-national study of work engagement as a mediator between job resources and proactive behavior', *International Journal of Human Resources Management*, **129**, 116–131.

Salanova, M., S. Agut and J.M. Peiro (2005), 'Linking organizational resources and work engagement to employee performance and customer loyalty: the mediation of service climate', *Journal of Applied Psychology*, **96**, 1217–1227.

Schaufeli, W.B. and A.B. Bakker (2004a), 'Work engagement and the measurement of a concept', *Gedrag-en-Organisatie*, **17**, 89–112.

Schaufeli, W.B. and A.B. Bakker (2004b), 'Job demands, job resources, and their relationship with burnout and engagement: a multi-sample study', *Journal of Organizational Behavior*, **25**, 293–515.

Schaufeli, W.B., and M. Salanova (2007), 'Work engagement: an emerging psychological concept and its implications for organizations', in S.W. Gilliland, W. Steiner and D.P. Skarlicki (eds), *Managing Social and Ethical Issues in Organizations*, Greenwich,CT: Information Age Publishing, pp. 135–177.

Schaufeli, W.B., and M. Salanova (2008), 'Enhancing work engagement through the management of human resources', in K. Näswall, M. Sverke and J. Hellgren (eds), *The Individual in the Changing Working Life* , Cambridge: Cambridge University Press, pp. 380–404.

Schaufeli, W.B., M. Salanova, V. Gonzalez-Roma and A.B. Bakker (2002), 'The measurement of engagement and burnout: a two simple confirmatory factor analytic approach', *Journal of Happiness Studies*, **3**, 71–92.

Schaufeli, W.B., A. Bakker and M. Salanova (2006), 'The measurement of work engagement with a short questionnaire: a cross-national study', *Educational and Psychological Measurement*, **20**, 1–16.

Schaufeli, W.B., I.M. Martinez, A. Marques-Pinto, M. Salanova and A.B. Bakker (2003), 'Burnout and engagement in university students: a cross-national study', *Journal of Cross-Cultural Psychology*, **33**, 464–481.

Seligman, M.E.P., and M. Csikszentmihalyi (2000), 'Positive psychology: an introduction', *American Psychologist*, **55**, 5–14.

Seppala, P., S. Mauno, T. Feldt, J.J. Hakanen, U. Kinnunen, A. Tolvanen and W.B. Schaufeli (2008), 'The construct validity of the Utrecht Work Engagement Scale: multi-sample and longitudinal evidence', *Journal of Happiness Studies*, **10**, 459–481.

Shimazu, A., and W.B. Schaufeli (2009), 'Is workaholism good or bad for

employee well-being? The distinctiveness of workaholism and work engagement among Japanese employees', *Industrial Health*, **47**, 495–502.
Simpson, M.R. (2009a), 'Engagement at work: a review of the literature', *International Journal of Nursing Studies*, **46**, 1012–1024.
Simpson, M.R. (2009b), 'Predictors of work engagement among medical-surgical registered nurses', *Western Journal of Nursing Research*, **31**, 44–65.
Simpson, M.R. (2010), 'Development and psychometric evaluation of the core nurse resource scale', *Journal of Nursing Management*, **18**, 1048–1059.
Sirota, D., L.A. Mischkind and M.I. Meltzer (2005), *The Enthusiastic Employee: How Companies Profit by Giving Workers What They Want*, Philadelphia, PA: Wharton School Publishing.
Sisodia, R., D.B. Wolfe and J. Sheth (2007), *Firms of Endearment: How World-Class Companies Profit from Passion and Purpose*, Philadelphia: Wharton School Publishing.
Taris, T., T. Cox and M. Tisserand (2008), 'Engagement at work: an emerging concept', *Work & Stress*, **22**, 185–186.
Turner, N., J. Barling and A. Zacharatos (2002), 'Positive psychology at work', in C. Snyder and S. Lopez (eds), *The Handbook of Positive Psychology*, Oxford: Oxford University Press, pp. 715–730.
Ulrich, D. (1997), *Human Resource Champions*, Boston: Harvard Business School Press.
Vahey, D.C., L.H. Aiken, D.M. Sloane, S.P. Clarke and D. Vargas (2004), 'Nurse burnout and patient satisfaction', *Medical Care*, **42**, 1157–1166.
Van Doornen, L.J.P., J.H. Houtveen, S. Langelaan et al. (2009), 'Burnout versus work engagement in their effects on 24-hour ambulatory monitored cardiac autonomic function', *Stress and Health*, **25**, 323–331.
Xanthopoulou, D., A.B. Bakker, E. Demerouti and W.B. Schaufeli (2009a), 'Reciprocal relationships between job resources, personal resources, and work engagement, *Journal of Vocational Behavior*, **74**, 235–244.
Xanthopoulou, D., A.B. Bakker, E. Demerouti and W.B. Schaufeli (2009b), 'Work engagement and financial returns: a diary study on the role of job and personal resources', *Journal of Occupational and Organizational Psychology*, **82**, 183–200.
Zeytinoglu, I.U., M. Denton, S. Davies, A. Baumann, J. Blythe and L. Boos (2007), 'Deteriorated external work environment, heavy workload and nurses' job satisfaction and turnover intention', *Canadian Public Policy*, **33**, S31–S47.

14. Organisational and health effects of workplace empowerment in health care settings

Heather Laschinger

INTRODUCTION

Creating empowering work environments that promote employee engagement and retention is challenging in today's fiscally constrained health care climate. Increasing workloads and patient acuity have had negative effects on nurses' workplace health and wellbeing (Stanton, 2004; Tyler and Cushway, 1992). Nurses have an illness-related absenteeism rate that is 58 per cent higher than the overall Canadian labour force (Canadian Institute for Health Information, 2007) and alarmingly high rates of job dissatisfaction (Aiken et al., 2002). These poor working conditions impede efforts to recruit and retain qualified nurses, which are critical in a time of a nursing workforce shortage. Workplace empowerment theory (Kanter, 1977, 1993; Spreitzer, 1995) offers a theory-driven approach for creating work environments that promote positive employee outcomes in health care settings (Joiner and Bartram, 2004; Laschinger et al., 2004b; Laschinger et al., 2009c).

A fundamental assumption underlying most conceptualisations of workplace empowerment relates to the idea that employees derive power from the work environment to accomplish their work in a meaningful way. In nursing, empowering workplaces have been linked to more positive employee relationships with work and better health (Laschinger and Finegan, 2005a; Laschinger et al., 2009c; Laschinger et al., 2011). Furthermore, numerous studies have found that structurally empowered employees report lower levels of burnout (Cho et al., 2006; Laschinger et al., 2010; Laschinger et al., 2011), a major antecedent of nurse job dissatisfaction and turnover (Hayes et al., 2010). Management plays an important role in creating work environments that empower nurses to provide the highest quality care for their patients, and that promote nurses' health and retention (Laschinger et al., 2003a).

THEORETICAL FRAMEWORK

A significant body of work within the general management literature has focused on the construct of workplace empowerment (Conger and Kanungo, 1988; Kanter, 1977, 1993; Kirkman and Rosen, 1999; Koberg et al., 1999; Spreitzer, 2007). Additionally empowerment has become an increasingly important paradigm within organisational practices, with over 70 per cent of organisations surveyed reporting having implemented an employee empowerment intervention over the past 15 years (Lawler et al., 2001). Two theoretical perspectives of empowerment have been described in the literature: sociocultural and psychological empowerment (Spreitzer, 2007). The sociocultural perspective views power as having access to structural conditions in the workplace that enable employees to accomplish their work in meaningful ways, such as empowering structures, policies, and practices. These structures contribute to organisational productivity and effectiveness (Kanter, 1977, 1993). Psychological empowerment is seen as a motivational construct, focusing on the growth and development of personal beliefs and cognitions about work, which reflects employees' responses to structurally empowering work conditions (Kraimer et al., 1999).

This chapter is organised around a framework that combines the structural and psychological view of empowerment into an integrated model of workplace empowerment (see Figure 14.1). Laschinger et al. (2001b) proposed a model that integrates Kanter's (1977, 1993) theory of

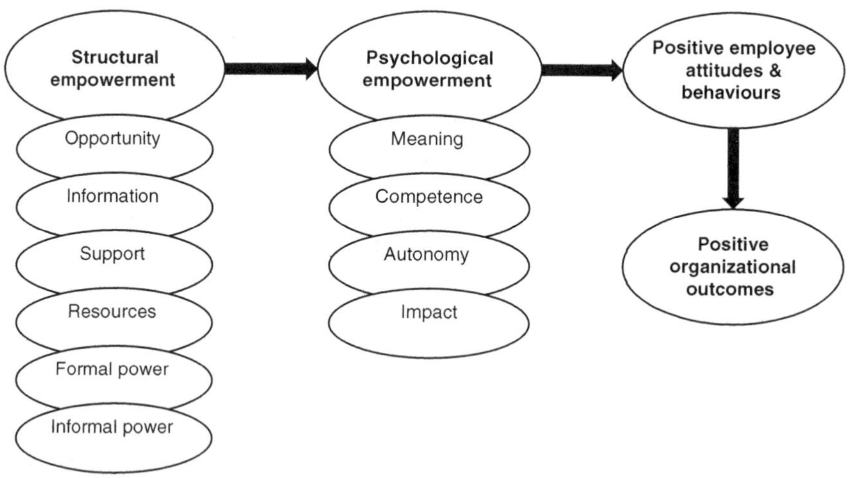

Figure 14.1 Integrated workplace empowerment model

organisational empowerment and Spreitzer's (1995) concept of psychological empowerment to provide a more comprehensive explanation of how workplace conditions influence employees' psychological response to their work and subsequently work attitudes and behaviours. In this model psychological empowerment is posited as a mediating mechanism between structural empowerment and work behaviours and outcomes (Laschinger et al., 2004a). Organisations that foster structural and psychological empowerment benefit from higher productivity and a more engaged workforce (Kanter, 1977, 1993; Spreitzer, 2007). This model has been tested extensively in health care settings (Laschinger et al., 2001b; Laschinger et al., 2009a). Components of the model are illustrated in Figure 14.1 and described in more detail in the upcoming paragraphs.

STRUCTURAL EMPOWERMENT

In her theory of structural empowerment, Kanter (1977, 1993) defines power as the ability to mobilise information, resources, and support to get things done in an organisation. Structural empowerment is defined as the extent to which employees feel they have access to these structures in their work settings. Kanter (1977, 1993) argues that formal power and informal power ensure access to two organisational structures that create an empowering workplace: (1) the structure of opportunity; and (2) the structure of power. The structure of opportunity provides individuals with the chance to advance within the organisation and to develop their knowledge and skills. Employees in high opportunity jobs are more proactive and innovative at solving challenges in their work, while those lacking opportunity are less motivated to succeed and less productive. The structure of power in the workplace comes from three main sources: (1) access to information; (2) access to support; and (3) access to the resources required for realising organisational goals.

Access to *information* refers to the knowledge that is necessary to carry out job activities in a meaningful way, which includes technical knowledge and expertise related to the core roles of employees, as well as information concerning what is going on in the larger organisation. Access to *resources* is having the ability to obtain the materials, money, and rewards necessary for achieving job demands, as well as having sufficient time to accomplish work. Access to *support* relates to sources that function in a way to maximise effectiveness, such as positive feedback from superiors in an organisation. Power is a dynamic structure that is created through formal and informal systems within the organisation. Formal power results from jobs that are visible, support discretion, and are central to organisational goal accomplishment. Informal power refers to the personal networks and alliances within the organisation, such as relationships with sponsors, peers, and other co-workers. Kanter argues that managers are vital to ensuring employee access to these structures in order to develop empowering conditions in the workplace.

Psychological empowerment Spreitzer (2007) defines psychological empowerment as a set of psychological states that are necessary for individuals to feel a sense of control in relation to their work. Spreitzer (1995) describes four components of psychological empowerment: meaning, competence, self-determination, and impact. Meaning entails congruence between job requirements and an employee's beliefs, values, and behaviours. Competence refers to confidence in one's job performance abilities. Autonomy refers to feelings of control over one's work. Impact is a sense of being able to influence important outcomes within the organisation. Spreitzer and Doneson (2005) found that managers' access to strategic information in the organisation and to information on their units' quality and cost performance were significantly related to their perceived psychological empowerment. Psychological empowerment has been studied extensively in both the nursing and management literature and found to be significantly related to numerous organisational outcomes, such as job performance (Liden et al., 2000), organisational commitment (Kraimer et al., 1999), and turnover intentions (Sparrowe, 1994). In the integrated workplace empowerment model described above, psychological empowerment is viewed as a psychological response to working in structurally empowering workplaces, as suggested by Kraimer et al. (1999).

Numerous studies have demonstrated significant positive relationships between structural and psychological empowerment in both staff nurse and nurse manager samples (Wagner et al., 2010). More recently, unit level structural empowerment has been shown to have a strong direct effect on individual staff nurse psychological empowerment, providing support for the contextual effects of empowerment (Laschinger et al., 2009a; Manojlovich and Laschinger, 2002). Numerous studies have provided empirical support for the mediating role of psychological empowerment in relation to the influence of structural empowerment on employee attitudes and behaviours, such as innovative behaviour, job strain, burnout, and job satisfaction (Knol and van Linge, 2009; Laschinger et al., 2001b; Laschinger et al., 2003b; Laschinger et al., 2004a, 2004b). Spreitzer (2007) recommends further research testing more sophisticated models linking structural and psychological empowerment to work attitudes and behaviour that take into account contextual or leadership effects.

RELATED RESEARCH

Leadership and Empowerment

Kanter (1977, 1993) contends that leadership plays a key role in creating empowering work environments by ensuring employee access to workplace empowerment structures. Numerous studies have supported this contention. Abdelrazek et al. (2010) found a link between structural empowerment and general leadership and management skills in their study of front line nurse managers. Nursing leadership, particularly at the unit level, has been shown to be a predictor of staff nurses' perceptions of structural empowerment on their units (Laschinger et al., 2009a; Laschinger et al., 2011).

A variety of leadership models have been used to study the relationship between leadership and structural empowerment. Several studies have linked structural empowerment to leadership practices described in Kouzes and Posner's (1995) transformational leadership model. This model describes five fundamental leadership practices that enable ordinary leaders to accomplish extraordinary acts within their organisations: (1) challenging the process; (2) inspiring a shared vision; (3) modeling the way; (4) enabling others to act; and (5) encouraging the heart. When nurses rated their leaders' use of these practices highly they also rated their work environment higher on structural empowerment (Laschinger, 2008; Patrick et al., 2011; Tourangeau et al., 2010). Patrick et al. (2011) found that structural empowerment significantly mediated the relationship between manager use of these five leadership practices and staff nurses' use of clinical leadership behaviours in their practice.

Structural empowerment has also been linked to the five leader empowering behaviours described in Thomas and Velthouse's (1990) leadership model (Conger and Kanungo, 1988; Greco et al., 2006; Laschinger et al., 1999). Staff nurses felt more empowered when they felt their managers enhanced the meaningfulness of their work, fostered participation in decision making, facilitated goal accomplishment, and provided autonomy and freedom from bureaucratic constraints. Staff nurse structural empowerment has also been associated with perceptions of manager emotional intelligence (Lucas et al., 2008; Young-Ritchie et al., 2009) and manager use of authentic leadership behaviours (Wong and Laschinger, 2011).

The quality of the relationship between nurses and their immediate supervisors has been found to be significantly related to staff nurses' structural empowerment. Several studies have used Leader-Member Exchange Theory (LMX) to examine this relationship (Graen and Uhl-Bien, 1995). LMX theory suggests that the nature and quality of the relationship that forms over time between the leader and the follower is an essential component in understanding employee responses to their work. LMX quality has been associated with greater organisational citizenship behaviours (Deluga, 1994), higher in-role performance (Hui et al., 1999), and job satisfaction (Janssen and Van Yperen, 2004) in the management literature. High-quality LMX relationships are associated with higher staff nurse and nurse manager structural empowerment (Laschinger et al., 2007). Furthermore structural empowerment at the nursing unit level mediates the relationship between unit level LMX quality and employee outcomes such as burnout, job satisfaction, and commitment (Laschinger et al., 2009a; Laschinger et al., 2011).

These findings suggest that leadership, regardless of how it is conceptualised, is strongly predictive of nurses' structural empowerment and that empowerment appears to be an important mediator in how leadership influences organisational outcomes. These results support Kanter's view that empowerment is an important leadership strategy for creating effective workplaces.

A related line of research has shown that employees' perceptions of their managers' power or influence in the organisation has an effect on their experiences of structural empowerment. Kanter (1977) argues that power is cyclical, in that individuals who feel empowered are more likely to share power. For instance, empowered managers are likely to empower their staff. Empowered staff tend to be more effective in their work and increase organisational productivity, thereby reinforcing their managers' power. Several studies have supported the link between staff nurses' perceptions of their managers' power and their own empowerment on their units (Haugh and Laschinger, 1996; Sabiston and Laschinger, 1995; Wilson and Laschinger, 1994). These studies support Kanter's (1977) notion that 'Power begets power' (p. 168) and reinforces the importance of ensuring that managers as well as staff are empowered to do their jobs. However, Goddard and Laschinger (1997) found evidence for the hierarchical distribution of power, such that different levels of nursing mangers reported increasingly greater access to power as they ascended in the hierarchy. This finding may suggest that more work is needed to promote sharing of power across levels in health care organisations.

Intermediate Outcomes of Workplace Empowerment

Numerous studies in the nursing research literature have identified a variety of important intermediate outcomes of structural empowerment, other than psychological empowerment, that influence organisational outcomes and worker health. Intermediate outcomes reflect employees' responses to the basic conditions in their workplaces in which they find themselves.

Structural effects

Several recent studies have found staff nurses' structural empowerment to be significantly related to the six areas of worklife described by Leiter and Maslach (2004) which influence employees' relationship with their work: manageable workloads, control over work, rewards for contribution, fair treatment, a sense of community, and congruence between personal and organisational values. Staff nurses' overall empowerment is significantly related to person-job match with all of the areas of worklife, but most strongly with rewards, fairness, and community (Cho et al., 2006; Greco et al., 2006). Nurses' overall fit with these areas of worklife is most strongly related to the support, formal and informal power components of structural empowerment, and least with access to opportunity (Cho et al., 2006; Greco et al., 2006). These authors both found that overall fit with the six areas of worklife mediated the relationship between empowerment and burnout/engagement, suggesting that empowering work environments promote a greater match with these six areas of worklife, and lower burnout.

An important retention factor in the nursing field is the extent to which nurses' work environment supports professional nursing practice (Aiken et al., 2002). Several studies have linked structural empowerment to supportive professional practice environments in hospital settings (Laschinger et al., 2003a; Manojlovich and Laschinger, 2007). Lake (2002) describes five dimensions of supportive practice environments typically associated with magnet hospitals (hospitals that attract and retain nurses): nurse participation in hospital affairs; nursing foundations for quality of care; nurse manager ability, leadership, and support of nurses; staffing and resource adequacy; and collegial nurse-physician relations. Nurses working in environments that are structurally empowering and supportive of professional practice have been shown to have higher job satisfaction (Laschinger et al., 2003a) and lower turnover intentions (Lavoie-Tremblay et al., 2011). These findings suggest that empowering work conditions may help establish supportive professional practice nursing environments, which ultimately attract and retain nurses. Thus, structural empowerment may be a critical management strategy during a time of a severe workforce shortage in the nursing profession.

Employee Attitude and Behaviour Outcomes

Employees who are empowered to accomplish their work in meaningful ways through supportive organisational structures experience attitudes and behaviours that ultimately influence performance and retention. Employee burnout and work engagement are two employee attitudes that have received a great deal of attention within the nursing and management literature.

Maslach (2004) describes burnout as 'a psychological syndrome of exhaustion, cynicism, and inefficacy which is experienced in response to chronic job stressors' (p. 93). Leiter and Maslach (2004) describe a process model of burnout, wherein employees develop a state of emotional exhaustion that, if sustained, leads to cynicism and feelings of personal inefficacy. Conversely, work engagement is characterised by feelings of vigour, dedication, and absorption at work (Schaufeli and Bakker, 2004), resulting from access to job resources. Burnout has been shown to mediate the relationship between excessive job demands and negative organisational outcomes, such as health problems, intent to leave, poor performance, and job dissatisfaction (Bakker et al., 2004; Hakanen et al., 2006; Laschinger et al., 2011; Lee and Ashforth, 1996; Schaufeli and Bakker, 2004). On the other hand engagement has been shown to mediate the relationship between job resources and positive organisational outcomes, such as greater organisational commitment, increased performance, and lower turnover intentions (Bakker et al., 2004; Hakanen et al., 2006; Laschinger et al., 2009d; Schaufeli and Bakker, 2004).

Several studies have supported the link between structural empowerment, burnout and engagement, and organisational outcomes. The six areas of worklife have consistently been shown to mediate the relationship between structural empowerment and burnout/engagement (Cho et al., 2006; Greco et al., 2006; Laschinger and Finegan, 2005a), which in turn has been shown to influence organisational commitment and physical and mental health (Cho et al., 2006; Laschinger and Finegan, 2005a). More recent studies have found that unit level empowerment significantly influences individual staff nurses' experiences of burnout which in turn negatively affected their job satisfaction (Laschinger et al., 2011). This study was the first to demonstrate unit level or contextual effects of Kanter's concept of structural empowerment on employee outcomes, supporting the validity of structural empowerment as a macro level organisational variable. Unit level structural empowerment is similar to the notion of empowerment climate described by Seibert et al. (2004). Support has also been found for the mediating role of psychological empowerment between structural empowerment and burnout, such that higher structural empowerment results in greater psychological empowerment, which in turn leads to decreased job satisfaction and physical and mental health (Laschinger et al., 2004a). Overall, the view that structural empowerment influences burnout and engagement through a variety of intermediate organisational support structures which in turn influences important organisational outcomes has been well established in the literature.

Another category of negative employee experiences that has emerged in recent studies of health care work environments relates to interpersonal conflict, including bullying (Einarsen and Hoel, 2001; Hansen et al., 2006) and incivility (Andersson and Pearson, 1999; Cortina et al., 2001). The negative outcomes of these hostile behaviours have been shown to be detrimental to employee health and productivity, and organisational goals (Dion, 2006; McKenna et al., 2003; Porath and Pearson, 2009; Quine, 2001).

Andersson and Pearson (1999) define workplace incivility as '. . . low intensity deviant behaviour with an ambiguous intent to harm the target, in violation of workplace norms for mutual respect' (p. 457). Uncivil behaviours can be subtle, such as ignoring or interrupting a colleague, or overt, such as sabotaging a project or damaging someone's reputation. Workplace incivility has been shown to have a negative effect on job satisfaction, job withdrawal, career salience, and psychological distress in non-health care settings (Cortina et al., 2001). Bullying, on the other hand, occurs when '. . . someone is subjected to social isolation or exclusion, his or her work and efforts are devalued, he or she is threatened, derogatory comments about him or her are said behind his or her back, or other negative behaviour aimed to torment, wear down, or frustrate occur' (Kivimaki et al., 2000, p. 656). Einarsen and Hoel (2001) describe three forms of workplace bullying: work-related, such as changing the work tasks or making them more difficult to perform; personal, including personal attacks through ridicule, insults and gossip; and physical, comprising both actual physical violence and threats of physical violence. Bullying has been linked to lower social support from co-workers and supervisors, and increased burnout, depression, anxiety, and negative affect (Hansen et al., 2006; Laschinger et al., 2010).

Laschinger et al. (2009c, 2010) has demonstrated relationships between structurally empowering work environments and lower rates of incivility and bullying among and between nursing colleagues and their supervisors. This makes sense because empowered work settings provide nurses with the resources, support, and information necessary to do their job, and a sense of respect for their expertise and knowledge. As a result nurses are more likely to develop respectful helping relationships and less likely to experience stress from not being able to accomplish their work, making disrespectful encounters less likely. Laschinger et al. (2009c) found that higher levels of structural empowerment and lower supervisor and co-worker incivility were significant predictors of three important nurse retention outcomes (job satisfaction, organisational commitment, and turnover intentions). In another study lower bullying experiences significantly mediated the relationship between structural empowerment and burnout of new graduate nurses (Laschinger et al., 2010). These findings demonstrate the importance of structural empowerment in mitigating the effects of negative work behaviours in health care settings.

On a more positive note, another intervening mechanism through which structural empowerment may help develop more positive collaborative relationships at work is the degree of trust and respect in the workplace. Employees will perceive that they are respected when they are given dignity, worth and self-determination (Browne, 1993). As a result, employees are more likely to identify with their group and act in their best interest (Sleebos et al., 2006). Respect is fundamental to the development of trust within an organisation (Mishra and Spreitzer, 1998). Mayer and Gavin (2005) define trust as 'the willingness to be vulnerable to another party when that party cannot be controlled or monitored . . .' (p. 874). When employees do not have access to structurally empowering conditions they may develop a sense of mistrust due to the withholding of information, inconsistent allocation of resources, and a lack of support from management.

Several studies have supported the link between structural empowerment and nurses' feelings of being respected in the workplace (DeCicco et al., 2006; Faulkner and Laschinger, 2008; Laschinger, 2004) and for respect as a mediator between empowerment and trust (Laschinger and Finegan, 2005b). Nurses' feelings of being respected and their perception of trust in management have been linked to a number of important organisational outcomes, such as perceived organisational support, work effectiveness, group loyalty, perceived quality of care, mental health, job satisfaction, organisational commitment, and retention (Finegan and Laschinger, 2001; Laschinger et al., 2001a; Laschinger, 2004; Laschinger and Finegan, 2005b; Sleebos et al., 2006). These findings highlight the importance of putting empowerment structures in place to achieve a positive workplace culture. These studies identify a variety of intermediate outcomes of workplace empowerment that influence more distal organisational outcomes, such as nurses' health, job satisfaction, organisational commitment, turnover, and nurses' health and wellbeing. In current health care settings these outcomes are key factors for ensuring high patient care quality.

Organisational outcomes

Several studies have linked structural empowerment to mental and physical health of staff nurses and nurse managers (Laschinger, 2004; Ridley et al., 2009). Structural empowerment has been related to nurses' health outcomes through a variety of mechanisms, such as job strain and burnout. In a large study of staff nurses, Laschinger and Finegan (2005a) found that structural empowerment influenced nurses' mental and physical health through positive responses to their work and lower levels of burnout. While there are no studies that we could find linking workplace empowerment to turnover through physical and mental health, the link between health and turnover has been previously supported (Spector and Jex, 1991; Williams et al., 2001).

Research efforts aimed at understanding voluntary turnover have frequently studied job satisfaction, organisational commitment, and intention to turnover as antecedents of this phenomenon (Tett and Meyer, 1993). Over two decades of research has demonstrated strong links between turnover and job dissatisfaction and low organisational commitment. Furthermore, intent to turn over consistently has been shown to be a strong precursor of actual turnover behaviour (Tett and Meyer, 1993). Job satisfaction, organisational commitment, and turnover intentions are key retention factors in the health care workforce.

Many studies using Laschinger et al.'s (2001b) integrated model of workplace empowerment have examined these three retention factors in nursing settings. Structural empowerment has been shown to be a consistently strong predictor of job satisfaction, organisational commitment, and turnover intentions in a variety of samples of staff nurses and nurse managers (Cho et al., 2006; Laschinger, 2004; Laschinger, 2008; Laschinger et al., 2009a; Laschinger et al., 2009b; Laschinger et al., 2009c, 2011; Tourangeau et al., 2010). Job satisfaction has been shown to mediate the relationship between structural empowerment and organisational commitment (Laschinger and Finegan, 2005b). Psychological empowerment has been found to mediate the relationship between structural empowerment and satisfaction and commitment (Laschinger et al., 2001b; Laschinger et al., 2007; Laschinger et al., 2009a). These studies demonstrate the importance of structurally empowering workplace conditions and the accompanying feelings of psychological empowerment, to nurse retention.

Personal Dispositional Determinants of Worklife Attitudes and Behaviours

In the past decade, organisational researchers have begun to consider the impact of personal factors in addition to situational factors on workplace behaviours and outcomes (Judge and Bono, 2001). Kanter's approach to understanding empowering work environments focuses on situational or social structures that influence employee effectiveness. This focus was based on the rationale that management can change situational factors to a greater extent than personality or personal characteristics. However, researchers have identified modifiable personal factors, such as core self-evaluation (CSE), that should be taken into consideration by management as they try to build healthy work environments (Judge and Bono, 2001). CSE is composed of four personality characteristics that affect how people interpret and respond to their environments: self-esteem, general self-efficacy, locus of control, and emotional stability (Judge and Bono, 2001). Recent studies have shown that CSE has shown explained additional variance beyond nurses' perceptions of structural empowerment (Laschinger et al., 2007; Laschinger et al., 2009a). These findings suggest that when exposed to similarly empowering working conditions, individuals with higher self-evaluation may be more likely to perceive their work environment as empowering than those with lower CSE. Given the relative stability of personal dispositional traits such as CSE, it is generally more fruitful to design strategies based on situational factors such as workplace empowerment that are more amenable to change. However, social learning theory suggests ways of increasing self-efficacy by exposing individuals to various sources of efficacy information through positive role modeling, verbal encouragement, and realistic learning experiences (Bandura, 2001). Thus, further research is needed to explore the impact of personal dispositional factors beyond situational factors on important organisational outcomes.

LIMITATIONS

Despite an extensive body of work testing Kanter's original empowerment theory and the expanded integrated model in health care settings, much of the work has used cross-sectional designs. Few have used a longitudinal or experimental design, which precludes our ability to make strong inferences of cause and effect (Pedhazur and Schmelkin, 1991); therefore the results must be interpreted with caution. However, consistent support for a priori theory-driven models and replication of similar relationships across studies offset these concerns somewhat. An additional issue is the possibility of common method variance in self-report survey data, although Spector (2006) has argued that this problem may be overstated when well established validated questionnaires have been used.

CONCLUSIONS

A large body of research has demonstrated the relevance of workplace empowerment (both structural and psychological) to important organisational outcomes. Structural empowerment theory offers an actionable approach to creating healthy work environments that lead to positive employee experiences and organisational outcomes. Nurses represent the largest group of health care professionals in hospital settings (Bureau of Labor Statistics, 2000; Canadian Institute for Health Information, 2010), and every effort must be made to ensure that health care work environments support a healthy engaged workforce. The profession is facing a severe workforce shortage, as a large cohort of nurses near retirement and not enough nurses are entering the profession to replace them (Pyper, 2004). Workplace empowerment is a promising management strategy that has been shown to be related to important characteristics of high quality workplaces in the health care sector.

REFERENCES

Abdelrazek, F., B. Skytt, M. Aly, M.A. El-Sabour, N. Ibrahim and M. Engstrom (2010), 'Leadership and management skills of first-line managers of elderly care and their work environment', *Journal of Nursing Management*, **18** (6), 736–745.

Aiken, L.H., S.P. Clarke, D.M. Sloane, J. Sochalski and J.H. Silber (2002), 'Hospital nurse staffing and patient mortality, nurse burnout, and job dissatisfaction', *Journal of American Medical Association*, **288** (16), 1987–1993. doi:10.1001/jama.288.16.1987

Andersson, L.M., and C.M. Pearson (1999), 'Tit for tat? The spiraling effect of incivility in the workplace', *The Academy of Management Review*, **24** (3), 452–471.

Bakker, A.B., E. Demerouti and W. Verbeke (2004), 'Using the job demands-resources model to predict burnout and performance', *Human Resource Management*, **43** (1), 83–104.

Bandura, A. (2001), 'Social cognitive theory of mass communications', in J. Bryant and D. Zillman (eds), *Media Effects: Advances in Theory and Research* (2nd edn), Hillsdale, NJ: Lawrence Erlbaum, pp. 121–153.

Browne, A. (1993), 'A conceptual clarification of respect', *Journal of Advanced Nursing*, **18** (2), 211–217.

Bureau of Labor Statistics (2000), 'US Bureau of the Census current population survey', Technical Paper: Design and Methodology No. 63.

Canadian Institute for Health Information (2007), *Absenteeism of nurses—what do we know . . . how do they compare?*

Canadian Institute for Health Information (2010), *Regulated nurses: Canadian trends, 2005 to 2009.*

Cho, J., H.K.S. Laschinger and C. Wong (2006), 'Workplace empowerment, work engagement and organizational commitment of new graduate nurses', *Nursing Leadership*, **19** (3), 43–60.

Conger, J.A., and R.N. Kanungo (1988), 'The empowerment process: integrating theory and practice', *The Academy of Management Review*, **13** (3), 471–482.

Cortina, L.M., V.J. Magley, J.H. Williams and R.D. Langhout (2001), 'Incivility in the workplace: incidence and impact', *Journal of Occupational Health Psychology*, **6** (1), 64–80.

DeCicco, J., H.K.S. Laschinger and M. Kerr (2006), 'Perceptions of empowerment and respect', *Journal of Gerontological Nursing*, **32** (5), 49–56.

Deluga, R.J. (1994), 'Supervisor trust building, leader-member exchange and organizational citizenship behavior', *Journal of Occupational and Organizational Psychology*, **67** (4), 315–326.

Dion, M.J. (2006), 'The impact of workplace incivility and occupational stress on the job satisfaction and turnover intention of acute care nurses', Unpublished PhD, University of Connecticut. Retrieved from http://digitalcommons.uconn.edu/dissertations/AAI3221535 (AAI3221535)

Einarsen, S., and H. Hoel (2001), 'The negative acts questionnaire: development, validation and revision of a measure of bullying at work', Prague: Paper presented at the 10th European Congress on Work and Organizational Psychology.

Faulkner, J., and H.K.S. Laschinger (2008), 'The effects of structural and psychological empowerment on perceived respect in acute care nurses', *Journal of Nursing Management*, **16**, 214–221.

Finegan, J., and H.K.S. Laschinger (2001), 'The antecedents and consequences of empowerment', *Journal of Nursing Administration*, **31** (10), 489–497.

Goddard, P., and H.K.S. Laschinger (1997), 'Nurse managers' perceptions of power and opportunity', *Canadian Journal of Nursing Administration*, **10** (2), 40–66.

Graen, G.B., and M. Uhl-Bien (1995), 'Relationship-based approach to leadership: development of leader-member exchange (LMX) theory of leadership over 25 years: applying a multi-level multi-domain perspective', *The Leadership Quarterly*, **6** (2), 219–247.

Greco, P., H.J.S. Laschinger and C. Wong (2006), 'Leader empowering behaviours, staff work empowerment and work engagement/burnout', *Nursing Leadership*, **19** (4), 41–56.

Hakanen, J. J., A.B. Bakker and W.B. Schaufeli (2006), 'Burnout and work engagement among teachers', *Journal of School Psychology*, **43**, 495–513.

Hansen, A.M., A. Hogh, R. Persson, B. Karlson, A.H. Garde and P. Orbaek (2006), 'Bullying at work, health outcomes, and physiological stress response', *Journal of Psychosomatic Research*, **60** (1), 63–72.

Haugh, E., and H.K.S. Laschinger (1996), 'Power and opportunity in public health nursing work environments', *Public Health Nursing*, **13** (1), 42–49.

Hayes, B., A. Bonner and J. Pryor (2010), 'Factors contributing to nurse job satisfaction in the acute hospital setting: a review of recent literature', *Journal of Nursing Management*, **18**, 804–814.

Hui, C., K.S. Law and Z.X. Chen (1999), 'A structural equation model of the effects of negative affectivity, leader-member exchange, and perceived job mobility on in-role and extra-role performance: a Chinese case', *Organizational Behavior and Human Decision Processes*, **77** (1), 3–21.

Janssen, O., and N.W. Van Yperen (2004), 'Employees' goal orientations, the quality of leader-member exchange and the outcomes of job performance and job satisfaction', *Academy of Management Journal*, **47** (3), 368–384.

Joiner, T.A., and T. Bartram (2004), 'How empowerment and social support affect Australian nurses' work stressors', *Australian Health Review*, **28** (1), 56–64.

Judge, T. A., and J.E. Bono (2001), 'Relationship of core self-evaluation traits – self-esteem, generalized self-efficacy, locus of control, and emotional stability – with job satisfaction and job performance: a meta-analysis, *Journal of Applied Psychology*, **86** (1), 80–92.

Kanter, R.M. (1977), *Men and Women of the Corporation*, New York: Basic Books.
Kanter, R. M. (1993), *Men and Women of the Corporation* (2nd edn), New York: Basic Books.
Kirkman, B.L., and B. Rosen (1999), 'Beyond self-management: antecedents and consequences of team empowerment', *The Academy of Management Journal*, **42** (1), 58–74.
Kivimaki, M., M. Elovainio and J. Vahtera (2000), 'Workplace bullying and sickness absence in hospital staff', *Occupational and Environmental*, **57**, 656–660.
Knol, J., and R. van Linge (2009), 'Innovative behaviour: the effect of structural and psychological empowerment on nurses', *Journal of Advanced Nursing*, **65** (2), 359–370.
Koberg, C., R. Boos, J. Senjem and E. Goodman (1999), 'Antecedents and outcomes of empowerment: empirical evidence from the health care industry', *Group and Organization Management*, **24** (1), 71–91.
Kouzes, J.M., and B.Z. Posner (1995), *The Leadership Challenge: How to Keep Getting Extraordinary Things Done in Organizations*, San Francisco, CA: Jossey-Bass.
Kraimer, M., S. Seibert and R. Liden (1999), 'Psychological empowerment as a multidimensional construct: a test of construct validity', *Educational and Psychological Measurement*, **59** (1), 127–142.
Lake, E.T. (2002), 'Development of the practice environment scale of the nursing work index', *Research in Nursing and Health*, **25** (3), 176–188.
Laschinger, H.K.S. (2004), 'Hospital nurses' perceptions of respect and organizational justice', *Journal of Nursing Administration*, **34** (7/8), 354–364.
Laschinger, H.K.S. (2008), 'Effect of empowerment on professional practice environments, work satisfaction, and patient care', *Journal of Nursing Care Quality*, **23** (4), 322–330.
Laschinger, H.K.S., and J. Finegan (2005a), 'Empowering nurses for work engagement and health in hospital settings', *Journal of Nursing Administration*, **35** (10), 439–449.
Laschinger, H.K.S., and J. Finegan (2005b), 'Using empowerment to build trust and respect in the workplace: a strategy for addressing the nursing shortage', *Nursing Economics*, **23** (1), 6–13.
Laschinger, H.K.S., C. Wong, L. McMahon and C. Kaufmann (1999), 'Leader behaviour impact on staff nurse empowerment, job tension and work effectiveness', *Journal of Nursing Administration*, **29** (5), 28–39.
Laschinger, H.K.S., J. Finegan and J.Shamian (2001a), 'The impact of workplace empowerment, organizational trust on staff nurses' work satisfaction and organizational commitment', *Health Care Management Review*, **26** (3), 7–23.
Laschinger, H.K.S., J. Finegan, J. Shamian and P. Wilk (2001b), 'Impact of structural and psychological empowerment on job strain in nursing work settings', *Journal of Nursing Administration*, **31** (5), 260–272.
Laschinger, H.K.S., J. Almost and D. Tuer-Hodes (2003a), 'Workplace empowerment and magnet hospital characteristics', *Journal of Nursing Administration*, **7** (8), 410–422.
Laschinger, H.K.S., J. Finegan and P. Wilk (2003b), 'Workplace empowerment as a predictor of nurse burnout in restructured healthcare settings', *Longwoods Review*, **1** (3), 2–11.
Laschinger, H.K.S., J. Almost, N. Purdy and J. Kim (2004a), 'Predictors of

nurse managers' health in Canadian restructured healthcare settings', *Nursing Leadership*, **17** (4), 88–105.

Laschinger, H.K.S., J.E. Finegan, J. Shamian and P. Wilk (2004b), 'A longitudinal analysis of the impact of workplace empowerment on work satisfaction', *Journal of Organizational Behaviour*, **25**, 527–545.

Laschinger, H.K.S., N. Purdy and J. Almost (2007), 'The impact of leader-member exchange quality, empowerment, and core self evaluation on nurse managers' job satisfaction', *Journal of Nursing Administration*, **37** (5), 221–229.

Laschinger, H.K.S., J. Finegan and P. Wilk (2009a), 'The impact of unit leadership and empowerment on nurses' organizational commitment', *Journal of Nursing Administration*, **39** (5), 228–235.

Laschinger, H.K.S., J. Finegan and P. Wilk (2009b), 'New graduate burnout: the impact of professional practice environment, workplace civility, and empowerment', *Nursing Economics*, **27** (6), 377–383.

Laschinger, H.K.S., M. Leiter, A. Day and D. Gilin (2009c), 'Workplace empowerment, incivility, and burnout: impact on staff nurse recruitment and retention outcomes', *Journal of Nursing Management*, **17**, 302–311.

Laschinger, H.K.S., P. Wilk, J. Cho and P. Greco (2009d), 'Empowerment, engagement and perceived effectiveness in nursing work environments: does experience matter?', *Journal of Nursing Management*, **17** (5), 636–646.

Laschinger, H.K.S., A.L. Grau, J. Finegan and P. Wilk (2010), 'New graduate nurses' experiences of bullying and burnout in hospital settings', *Journal of Advanced Nursing*, **66** (12), 2732–2742.

Laschinger, H.K.S., J. Finegan and P. Wilk (2011), 'Situational and dispositional influences on nurses' workplace well-being', *Nursing Research*, **60** (2), 124–131.

Lavoie-Tremblay, M., M. Paquet, C. Marchionni and U. Drevniok (2011), 'Turnover intention among new nurses: a generational perspective', *Journal for Nurses in Staff Development*, **27** (1), 39–45.

Lawler, E.E.I., S. Mohrman and G. Benson (2001), *Organizing for High Performance: Employee Involvement, TQM, Reengineering, and Knowledge Management in the Fortune 1000*, San Francisco: Jossey-Bass.

Lee, R.T., and B.E. Ashforth (1996), 'A meta-analytic exmaination of the correlates of the three dimensions of job burnout', *Journal of Applied Psychology*, **81** (2), 123–133.

Leiter, M.P., and C. Maslach (2004), 'Areas of worklife: a structured approach to organizational predictors of job burnout', in P. Perrewe and D.C. Ganster (eds), *Research in Occupational Stress and Well Being: Vol. 3. Emotional and Physiological Processes and Positive Intervention Strategies*, Oxford, UK: JAI Press/Elsevier, pp. 91–134.

Liden, R., S.J. Wayne and R.T. Sparrowe (2000), 'An examination of the mediating role of psychological empowerment on the relations between the job, interpersonal relationships, and work outcomes', *Journal of Applied Psychology*, **85** (3), 407–416.

Lucas, V., H.K.S. Laschinger and C.A. Wong (2008), 'The impact of emotional intelligent leadership on staff nurse empowerment: the moderating effect of span of control', *Journal of Nursing Management*, **16** (8), 964–973.

Manojlovich, M., and H.K.S. Laschinger (2002), 'The relationship of empowerment and selected personality characteristics to nursing job satisfaction', *Journal of Nursing Administration*, **32** (11), 586–595.

Manojlovich, M., and H.K.S. Laschinger (2007), 'The nursing worklife model:

extending and refining a new theory', *Journal of Nursing Management*, **15**, 256–263.

Maslach, C. (2004), 'Different perspectives on job burnout', *Contemporary Psychology: APA Review of Books*, **49** (2), 168–170.

Mayer, R.C., and M.B. Gavin (2005), 'Trust in management and performance: who minds the shop while the employees watch the boss?', *The Academy of Management Journal*, **48** (5), 874–888.

McKenna, B.G., N.A. Smith and J.H. Coverdale (2003), 'Horizontal violence: experiences of registered nurses in their first year of practice', *Journal of Advanced Nursing*, **42** (1), 90–96.

Mishra, A.K., and G.M. Spreitzer (1998), 'Explaining how survivors respond to downsizing: the roles of trust, empowerment, justice, and work redesign', *Academy of Management Review*, **23** (3), 567–588.

Patrick, A., H.K.S. Laschinger, C. Wong and J. Finegan (2011), 'Developing and testing a new measure of staff nurse clinical leadership: the clinical leadership survey', *Journal of Nursing Management*, **19** (4), 449–460.

Pedhazur, E.J., and L.P. Schmelkin (1991), *Measurement, Design, and Analysis: An Integrated Approach*, Hillsdale, NJ: Erlbaum.

Porath, C., and C.M. Pearson (2009), 'How toxic colleagues corrode performance', *Harvard Business Review*, **87** (4), 24.

Pyper, W. (2004), *Employment Trends in Nursing*, Statistics Canada: Perspectives No. 75-001-XPE.

Quine, L. (2001), 'Workplace bullying in nurses', *Journal of Health Psychology*, **6** (1), 73–84.

Ridley, J., B. Wilson, L. Harwood and H.K.S. Laschinger (2009), 'Work environment, health outcomes and magnet hospital traits in the Canadian nephrology nursing scene', *Canadian Association of Nephrology Nurses and Technologists Journal*, **19** (10), 28–35.

Sabiston, J.A., and H.K.S. Laschinger (1995), 'Staff nurse work empowerment and perceived autonomy. Testing Kantor's theory of structural power in organizations', *Journal of Nursing Administration*, **22** (9), 42–50.

Schaufeli, W.B., and A.B. Bakker (2004), 'Job demands, job resources, and their relationship with burnout and engagement: a multi-sample study', *Journal of Organizational Behaviour*, **25**, 293–315.

Seibert, S., S.R. Silver and W.A. Randolph (2004), 'Taking empowerment to the next level: a multiple-level model of empowerment, performance, and satisfaction', *The Academy of Management Journal*, **47** (3), 332–349.

Sleebos, E., N. Ellemers and D. de Gilder (2006), 'The carrot and the stick: affective commitment and acceptance anxiety as motives for discretionary group efforts by respected and disrespected group members', *Personality and Social Psychology Bulletin*, **32** (2), 244–255.

Sparrowe, R.T. (1994), 'Empowerment in the hospitality industry: an exploration of antecedents and outcomes', *Journal of Hospitality and Tourism Research*, **17** (3), 51–73.

Spector, P.E. (2006), 'Method variance in organizational research: truth or urban legend?', *Organizational Research Methods*, **9** (2), 221–232.

Spector, P.E., and S.M. Jex (1991), 'Relations of job characteristics from multiple data sources with employee affect, absence, turnover intentions, and health', *Journal of Applied Psychology*, **76** (1), 46–53.

Spreitzer, G.M. (1995), 'Psychological empowerment in the workplace: dimensions, measurement, and validation', *The Academy of Management Journal*, **38** (5), 1442–1465.

Spreitzer, G.M. (2007), 'Giving peace a chance: organizational leadership, empowerment, and peace', *Journal of Organizational Behaviour*, **28**, 1077–1095.

Spreitzer, G.M., and D. Doneson (2005), 'Musings on the past and future of employee empowerment', in T. Cumming (ed.), *Handbook of Organizational Development*, Thousand Oaks: Sage, pp. 311–324.

Stanton, M.W. (2004), 'Hospital nurse staffing and quality of care', Agency for Healthcare Research and Quality: Research in Action No. 04-0029.

Tett, R.P., and J.P. Meyer (1993), 'Job satisfaction, organizational commitment, turnover intention, and turnover: path analyses based on meta-analytic findings', *Personnel Psychology*, **46** (2), 259–293.

Thomas, K.W., and B.A. Velthouse (1990), 'Cognitive elements of empowerment', *Academy of Management Review*, **15**, 666–681.

Tourangeau, A., L. Cranley, H.K.S. Laschinger and J. Pachis (2010), 'Relationships among leadership practices, work environments, staff communication and outcomes in long-term care', *Journal of Nursing Management*, **18** (1060), 1072.

Tyler, P., and D. Cushway (1992), 'Stress, coping and mental well-being in hospital nurses', *Stress and Health*, **8** (2), 91–98. doi:10.1002/smi.2460080206.

Wagner, J.I.J., G. Cummings, D.L. Smith, J. Olson, L. Anderson and S. Warren (2010), 'The relationship between structural empowerment and psychological empowerment for nurses: a systematic review', *Journal of Nursing Management*, **18** (4), 448–462.

Williams, E.S., T.R. Konrad, W.E. Scheckler, D.E. Pathman, M. Linzer, J. McMurray, M. Schwartz (2001), 'Understanding physicians' intentions to withdraw from practice: the role of job satisfaction, job stress, mental and physical health', *Health Care Management Review*, **26** (1), 7–19.

Wilson, B., and H.K.S. Laschinger (1994), 'Staff nurse perception of job empowerment and organisational commitment', *Journal of Nursing Administration*, **24** (4S), 39–47.

Wong, C.A., and H.K.S. Laschinger (2011), 'Authentic leadership, performance and job satisfaction: the mediating role of empowerment'.

Young-Ritchie, C., H.K.S. Laschinger and C. Wong (2009), 'The effects of emotionally intelligent leadership behaviour on emergency staff nurses' workplace empowerment and organizational commitment', *Canadian Journal of Nursing Research*, **22** (1), 70–85.

15. Stress amongst health care professionals and what can be done

Cary L. Cooper

INTRODUCTION: THE COSTS OF WORKPLACE STRESS

There have been numerous studies over the years on doctors (e.g. Rout et al., 1996), junior hospital doctors (Antoniou et al., 2003), nurses (e.g. McElfatrick et al., 2000), the ambulance service (e.g. Young and Cooper, 1999), anaesthetists (e.g. Cooper et al., 1999) and many more professionals allied to medicine. The evidence is overwhelming that many of these health care professionals suffer, from different sources and from varying degrees, stress-related outcomes ranging from burnout to mental ill health to physical manifestations linked to the emotional labour of their job. The sources of stress may be different, but the demands of patients, the management of staff, the organisation of the health care facility, the hours of work and many more underlying problem areas are plain to see in the literature.

We also know that not only is this costly to the individual and his/her family in terms of the ill health consequences, but also to the organisation as well. In a paper by Cooper and Dewe (2008) it was found in the UK, as assessed by the Chartered Institute of Personnel Development (CIPD, which is the professional body for HR professionals), that sickness absence accounted for 175 million lost working days, and the biggest proportion of this was due to the common mental disorders of depression, anxiety and stress, roughly 40 per cent of the total. In terms of incapacity benefit, which costs the UK something in the order of £12bn per annum, roughly £5bn is accounted for by mental ill health and stress at work. The Sainsbury Centre for Mental Health (Cooper and Dewe, 2008) estimated that the total cost, without factoring in the enormous cost of treatment, of workplace stress and mental ill health in 2008, was £25.9bn per annum in terms of sickness absence, presenteeism (which is when people turn up to work but are so stressed they deliver very little added-value to their job) and labour turnover. Indeed, they found that presenteeism due to stress was twice the cost of sickness absence. In Germany in 1989, the leading cause of early retirement from work was musculoskeletal disease but by 2004 it was 'stress and mental ill health', which now represents 40 per cent of all early retirements (German Federal Health Monitoring, 2007). Indeed, Sobocki et al. (2006) found that the total direct cost of depression alone in the European Union was 41bn euros, with 77bn euros in terms of productivity losses to all the economies.

These are the gross national costs, but the costs for an individual employer, like the National Health System, can be penal. The Confederation of British Industry in their annual absence report with AXA calculated the direct cost of absence at £537 per employee per year, with indirect costs estimated at an additional £270 (CBI, 2007). In addition, the CIPD (2007) estimated the costs of employee turnover at approximately £7750 per employee, with the indirect negative effects of declining morale. These costs would have escalated drastically since the recession and must put a major financial burden on employers, particularly health care providers.

And in a major study of more than 26 different occupational groups, Johnson et al. (2005) found that those working in the health care field were high up the league table of physical and psychological ill health outcome measures, using the most established psychometric measure of stress and wellbeing, ASSET (Faragher et al. 2004), as well as in terms of job dissatisfaction. Ambulance personnel were top of the physical ill health league table, with nurses, doctors, dentists and allied health professionals significantly above the norm but in the middle of the high range scale. When it came to lack of psychological wellbeing, once again all health care professionals were in the top half of the distribution. But what was worrying is that all these professionals were in the top quartile of the job dissatisfaction scale, which is counter-intuitive because the stereotype of them is that they self-select into the health sector and should therefore be relatively content. But in the end, it is how they are managed, and the pressures on them from unrealistic patient expectations, constant government interventions, the state of investment into health care, and the resources available to them which will determine levels of job satisfaction.

MANAGING WORKPLACE STRESS

So what should organisations do to manage the downsides of stress and enhance wellbeing (Cartwright and Cooper, 2011). How should organisations manage the pressures currently experienced by their employees in a changing workplace culture? Cartwright and Cooper (1994) suggest a three-pronged strategy for stress management in organisations. For the prevention and management of stress at work, the following three approaches could provide a comprehensive strategic framework: primary (e.g. stress reduction), secondary (e.g. stress management) and tertiary prevention (e.g. employee assistance programmes/workplace counselling).

Primary prevention is concerned with taking action to modify or eliminate sources of stress inherent in the work environment, so reducing their negative impact on the individual. The focus of primary interventions is in adapting the environment to 'fit' the individual.

Possible strategies to reduce workplace stress factors include:

- Redesigning the task
- Redesigning the working environment
- Establishing flexible work schedules
- Encouraging participative management
- Including the employee in career development
- Analysing work roles and establishing goals
- Providing social support and response
- Building cohesive teams
- Establishing fair employment policies
- Sharing rewards

Primary intervention strategies are often a vehicle for culture change. The type of action required by an organisation will vary according to the kind of stress factors operating. Any intervention, therefore, needs to be guided by prior diagnosis or a stress audit or risk assessment, to identify the specific factors responsible for employee stress. A number of case studies of successful auditing of workplace stress, and their impact, can be found in Robertson and Cooper (2011).

Secondary prevention is concerned with the prompt detection and management of experienced stress. This can be done by increasing awareness and improving the stress management skills of the individual through training and educative activities. Individual factors can alter or modify the way employees, exposed to workplace stress, perceive and react to their environment. Each individual has his or her own personal stress threshold, which is why some people thrive in a certain setting and others suffer.

Awareness activities and skills training programmes, designed to improve relations techniques, cognitive coping skills and work/lifestyle modification skills (e.g. time management courses or assertiveness training), have an important part to play in extending the individual's physical and psychological resources. The role of secondary prevention is, however, one of damage limitation. Often the consequences, rather than the sources, of stress, which may be inherent in the organisation's structure or culture, are being dealt with. They are concerned with improving the 'adaptability' of the individual to the environment. Consequently, this type of intervention is often described as the 'sticking plaster' approach. The implicit assumption is that the organisation will not change but will continue to be stressful; therefore the individual has to develop and strengthen his or her resistance to that stress.

Tertiary prevention is concerned with the treatment, rehabilitation and recovery process of individuals who have suffered, or are suffering, from serious ill health as a result of stress (Palmer and Cooper, 2012).

Intervention at the tertiary level typically involves provision of counselling services for employee problems in the work or personal domain. Such services are provided either by in-house counsellors or by outside agencies (EAPs), which provide counselling, information and/or referral to appropriate treatment and support services. There is evidence to suggest that counselling is effective in improving the psychological wellbeing of employees, and has considerable cost benefits.

Counselling can be particularly effective in helping employees deal with workplace stress that cannot be changed. It can also help non-work related stress (e.g. bereavement, marital breakdown etc.), which tends to spill over into work life.

ORGANISATIONAL POLICIES ON STRESS MANAGEMENT

The UK Government Office for Science, in their Foresight project on Mental Health and Wellbeing explored policies and interventions on enhancing mental wellbeing (Cooper et al., 2009). In the Foresight 'work and wellbeing' stream of work, they came up with some general conclusions.

One of the recommendations that came from their stakeholders, and based on the science reviews (Cooper et al., 2009), was that doing a stress or wellbeing audit of employees, and then intervening to reduce the stress identified, produces not only positive health and productivity outcomes, but also has beneficial cost-benefit consequences. It was felt, therefore, that key performance indicators (KPIs) should be created by organisations in their annual reports, and in appraisals for managers at all levels, on wellbeing factors such as levels of job satisfaction, sickness absence reductions, average working hours, etc.

Another aspect of work covered was how to mitigate the adverse effects of work on homelife. The evidence is clear that a long-hours culture damages health, with flexible working a policy option for employers to minimise these negative outcomes. In policy terms, the idea was to explore the 'right to request' flexible working, not only for employees with children, but for those without children. The cost-benefit analysis suggested that employers would benefit significantly more from allowing the 'right to request flexible working' for all employees, rather than just for those with children.

A third policy arena was in the training and development of managers. Evidence suggested that poor managers damage people's health. The evidence from the Foresight report suggested that social skill and interpersonal training for managers was essential for effective people management. It was felt that incentives were needed to encourage organisations to do this training, so the recommendation was for government to put up half the funding for this training and employers the other half.

Another policy idea was the creation of a Workplace Commission for the small and medium sized businesses, and public sector bodies (e.g. Primary Care Trusts), who don't have the infrastructure to do some of the important health and wellbeing interventions the larger organisations have. This Commission would provide support and advice for reducing stress and enhancing wellbeing, with employers who are too small to fund this activity themselves. The SME sector and smaller public sector organisations employ nearly two out of every three workers in the UK; their need is great and their knowledge limited in improving the health and wellbeing of their employees. They need a national body to help them with some of the basic workplace wellness activities, given their importance to the economy as a whole. This would apply to most countries.

CONCLUSION

As we have seen, the wellbeing of our working populations is an important bottom-line health and productivity issue for health care providers, which needs our urgent attention. It is safe to say that we have, at this point in time, all the ingredients of workplace stress: an ever increasing workload with a decreasing workforce in a climate of rapid change and Government cutbacks. The end result is that there are fewer people performing more work, in more job insecure environments. And the pressures on all of us are likely to get worse. There is a real 'health imperative' to devise policies to enhance wellbeing in the workplace. It is not just GDP that is important but our Gross National Wellbeing as well. As Robert Kennedy said in a campaign speech at the University of Kansas in 1968:

> Too much and for too long, we seemed to have surrendered personal excellence and community values in the mere accumulation of material things. Our Gross National Product now is over 800 billion dollars a year, but that Gross National Product – if we judge the United States of America by that – that Gross National Product counts air pollution and cigarette advertising, and ambulances to clear our highways of carnage. It counts special locks for our doors and the jails for the people who break them. It counts the destruction of the redwood and the loss of our natural wonder in chaotic sprawl. It counts napalm and counts nuclear warheads and armoured cars for the police to fight the riots in our cities. It counts Whitman's rifle and Speck's knife, and the television programs that glorify violence in order to sell toys to our children. Yet the gross national product does not allow for the health of our children, the quality of their education or the joy of their play. It does not include the beauty of our poetry or the strength of our marriages, the intelligence of our public debate or the integrity of our public officials. It measures neither our wit nor our courage, neither our wisdom nor our learning, neither our compassion nor our devotion to our country, it measures everything in short, except that which makes life worthwhile.

REFERENCES

Antoniou, A., M. Davidson and C.L. Cooper (2003), 'Occupational stress, job satisfaction and health in male and female junior hospital doctors in Greece', *Stress and Health*, **18**, 592–621.

Cartwright, S., and C.L. Cooper (1994), 'Healthy mind, healthy organizations', *Human Relations*, **47**, 455–471.

Cartwright, S., and C.L. Cooper (2011), *Innovations in Stress and Health*, London: Palgrave Macmillan.

CBI (2007), *Attending to Absence: Absence and Labour Turnover Survey 2007*, London: Confederation of British Industry.

CIPD (2007), *Recruitment, Retention and Turnover*, London: Chartered Institute of Personnel and Development.

Cooper, C.L. (ed.) (2008), *New Directions in Organizational Behavior*, London: Sage.

Cooper, C.L., and P. Dewe (2008), 'Wellbeing – absenteeism, presenteeism, costs and challenges', *Occupational Medicine*, **58**, 522–524.

Cooper, C.L., S. Clarke and A. Rowbottom (1999), 'Occupational stress, job satisfaction and wellbeing in anaesthetists', *Stress Medicine*, **15**, 115–126.

Cooper, C.L., J. Field, U. Goswami, R. Jenkins and B. Sahakin (2009), *Mental Capital and Wellbeing*, Oxford: Wiley-Blackwell.

Faragher, E.B., et al. (2004), 'A shortened stress evaluation tool (ASSET)', *Stress and Health*, **20**, 189–201.

German Federal Health Monitoring (2007), 'Trends in causes of early retirement'. http://wwwgber.bund.de/

Johnson, S., et al. (2005), 'The experience of work-related stress across occupations', *Journal of Managerial Psychology*, **20**, 178–187.

McElfatrick, S., et al. (2000), 'Assessing coping skills in mental health nurses', *Personality and Individual Differences*, **28**, 965–976.

Palmer, S., and C.L. Cooper (2012), *How to Deal with Stress*, London: Kogan Page.

Robertson, I., and C.L. Cooper (2011), *Wellbeing: Productivity and Happiness at Work*, London: Palgrave Macmillan.
Rout, U., C.L. Cooper and J. Rout (1996), 'Job stress amongst British GPs: predictors of job dissatisfaction and mental health', *Stress Medicine*, **12**, 155–166.
Sobocki, P., et al. (2006), 'Cost of depression in Europe', *Journal of Mental Health Policy and Economics*, **9**, 87–98.
Young, K., and C.L. Cooper (1999), 'Change in stress outcomes following industrial dispute in the ambulance service', *Health Services Management Research*, **12**, 51–62.

16. A safer clinical systems approach

Matthew Cooke, Steve Cross and Peter Spurgeon

INTRODUCTION

The various patient safety initiatives in health systems around the world quite properly are motivated by trying to prevent harm and distress (and potential tragedy) to the individual patient. Most obviously this clinical focus is sometimes linked to organisational performance by the cost of legal claims against the system for any negative impact upon the patient.

Patient safety though goes further than this in terms of organisational implications. The delivery of patient care is the basic business of the health care industry and if this is provided poorly or inadequately it is an underlying deficiency in the functioning of the organisation. In addition to potential costs from legal challenge, organisations risk additional costs from having to provide remedial care for patients adversely affected, potential re-admission, longer stay in hospital etc., not to mention the breakdown in reputation and trust in the provider role. Poor care is inefficient care and in this chapter we describe a system based approach to enhancing patient safety and thereby improve the effectiveness of the overall organisation.

SAFER CLINICAL SYSTEMS

There is an increasing realisation that patient safety is a whole system issue. The way in which a system operates is a major determinant of the risk in that system. In the past the focus has been on investigating adverse events and making recommendations to ensure they are not repeated. The recommendations may only apply to the very specific circumstances of the individual event but many of the factors contributing to the causation are common to other adverse events. A common solution is to look at the individual members of staff and determine whether they need more training or advice. At organisational level recommendations often focus on developing new policies and on informing staff of what they should be doing.

Other sectors favour an approach that proactively searches for risks in the system rather than dwelling on harm. In this chapter we describe an emerging new approach that follows this methodology, which shifts the balance far more towards the organisation and the environment, and away from the individual.

Safer Clinical Systems, a patient safety programme introduced by the Health Foundation in 2009, enters its second phase of development in 2011 at eight acute provider sites in the United Kingdom. In this chapter, we describe the need for new approaches to building patient safety, some findings from phase one of the Safer Clinical Systems programme, and outline our methodological approach.

PATIENT SAFETY IS A CONTINUING PROBLEM

Despite many initiatives in developing better safety for patients in hospitals, being admitted and treated is still is a hazardous process. Some patients – perhaps about 10 per cent – receive care that isn't merely of a poor standard, but is actually harmful (Box 16.1).

The studies cited in Box 16.1 have all taken place since 2001 during a decade which has seen an unprecedented and rising interest in patient safety. Documents highlighting the problem (Kohn et al. 2000; 'An organisation with a memory' 2000) and setting out goals for public health care providers were followed by safety and quality initiatives in many countries. The USA saw the 100,000 lives campaign (Berwick et al. 2006) managed by the influential Institute for Healthcare Improvement; the UK saw the foundation of the National Patient Safety Agency and the Safer

BOX 16.1 INCIDENCE OF PATIENT HARM ACROSS A WIDE RANGE OF COUNTRIES

Systematic review: 9.2% (De Vries 2008)
Latin America: 10.5% (Aranaz-Andrés, 2011)
Canada after discharge: 23% (Forster 2004)
New Zealand: 11.2% (Davis, 2002)
Sweden: 12.3% (Soop 2009)
USA Harvard: 3.5% (Brennan 2004)
Denmark 9% (Schiøler, 2001)
England 10.8% (Vincent 2001)

Patients Initiative, sponsored by the Health Foundation, to name some of the higher-profile initiatives amongst many, both local and national.

Asking the legitimate question, 'Has patient safety improved?' results in surprisingly ambiguous responses. In some areas – hospital-acquired infections, for example – it does seem as if patients are less at risk from MRSA and Clostridium Difficile than they were during the 1990s. For most other indicators, though, the picture isn't clear. Vincent (2011) provides a summary of these data and concludes, rather worryingly, that while there is some evidence of overall mortality in hospitals, of nine other patient safety indicators, seven showed an increase, indicating falling levels of patient safety.

Two recent studies provide more information. Landrigan and colleagues (Landrigan et al. 2010) conducted a retrospective review of a range of safety indicators included in the IHI Global Trigger tool over a five-year period in ten US hospitals. They found little evidence of improvement: there were no significant changes in the level of harm per 1000 patient days, or in the rate of preventable harms to patients. In the UK, a thorough evaluation of the Safer Patients Initiative in UK hospitals found that the introduction of the programme was associated with only a few indicators in specific areas, such as the monitoring of vital signs, but found no evidence of more significant or widespread organisational change (Benning et al. 2011).

SYSTEMS THINKING

Systems thinking is a way of understanding how individual elements in a greater whole influence each other. It is a process of understanding the inter-relatedness of system components and seeing all those components as part of a common process with a particular common purpose. In practical terms, it recognises that reacting merely to a specific, often small, part of a problem not only frequently fails to solve the problem but also brings the danger of unintended consequences.Systems thinking is probably best understood as a conceptual framework, a body of knowledge and a toolkit that has been developed to try to make larger patterns clearer and to help researchers and improvement teams to determine how to change them most effectively.

All things exist in systems. In health care, individual system components include the patient, the clinicians, the equipment and the environment in which the care takes place. Systems thinking in general is a process of understanding the interrelatedness of the system components as part of a common process with a common purpose. In several public services there has been a growing recognition that improvements in quality and safety need to occur at a so-called 'systems' level in order to be widespread and sustainable. In health care this requires focusing not only on the clinical care of the patient but also on the many systems that support and enable clinical care.

The systems approach in health care was perhaps most visibly introduced following the inquiry into infant cardiac surgery at the Bristol Royal Infirmary (Walshe and Offen 2001). In this inquiry, though individual errors or lapses in performance were identified, there was an attempt to see them as the product of systems that failed to work properly. The inquiry adopted an approach that effectively began with an examination of the organisational context and practices before considering the performance of individual events and clinicians. This approach can therefore be described as a 'systems-based' approach to medical safety and contrasted with the 'person-based approach'.We describe these models in more detail below.

SYSTEMS THINKING IN PATIENT SAFETY

Thinking in terms of systems factors when things go wrong for a patient, especially when there seem to be failings in professional competence or vigilance, for example, can be difficult. In many industries we have often tended to assign personal blame to those actually in the critical situation – the 'last person to touch the controls'; or, in the case of health care, perhaps the last person to treat the patient. In the sections below, we explore the key differences between what might be called a 'person-based' approach and a more mature 'systems-based' approach.

The Person-Based Approach

When an accident, adverse event or lapse in quality occurs it is natural to try and trace the cause and ask why and how it happened. In general, this has two aims: to learn where in the process the error occurred, and to judge whether any individuals were responsible and should be blamed. In this context, by far the most common allocation of cause is 'human error'. Implicit in this concept is the assumption that of many causal factors in what is sometimes a long chain of events, the action or inaction of a small number of human beings is of crucial significance.

What generally follows is a focus on punishment or reward, the reduction of the role of humans in systems as far as may be possible, and an increase in 'command and control'. Blame, which seems a natural consequence of the identification of human error, seems always to follow.

The Systems Approach

Health care systems are highly complex and can interact in unexpected ways. Our understanding of health care systems in recent years has moved from a person-centred approach towards a view that recognises that errors are more often consequences rather than causes. Performance is shaped by local circumstances, by the nature of the task and the tools, equipment and environment in which the activity is carried out. In this model, the human being is only one factor amongst many and the final outcome is a product of the interaction of many factors.

The systems approach therefore views causality in a different way. It demands a more nuanced explanation, in which the goal is to understand why an event occurs through building up knowledge of how errors are affected by elements of the system.

The Model of Organisational Accidents

Person-centred views of safety or quality events often reflect the so-called 'domino theory', whereby human error triggers a following error, and then a subsequent error and so on until the event occurs: a row of dominos falling down, fully determined and with an easily identifiable initiating step in the chain.

In place of the domino metaphor, the dominant image in systems thinking in health care has become the 'Swiss cheese' model (Reason 1997), introduced by James Reason to illustrate his 'model of organisational accidents'. This describes a system as possessing a series of layers of defence that prevent error. In an ideal world none of these defences would be breached; in reality the defences might resemble slices of Swiss cheese and have many 'holes' or routes through which failures may propagate. Part of this model is the distinction between active failures, which may be thought of as unsafe acts committed by people directly in contact with the patient, and latent failures which arise from organisational states resulting ultimately from decisions made by procedure writers, designers, administrators and management.

The Swiss cheese model, which has become widely accepted in health care, was developed because the very basic approach of the domino model did not allow the identification of wider systems factors which, when modified or improved, could be expected to allow better performance across the wider organisation.

Other Systems Approaches

The Swiss cheese model, which has been accepted for many years, is usually regarded as a linear model (Hollnagel 2004) that assumes that a latent error is a constant condition and therefore accessible to change. It assumes, for example, that if only enough information were available we would be able to predict accurately how all the different factors within the system would interact, and thus we would be able to manage quality and safety effectively. In practice, however, systems factors vary constantly: the level of resource may be sufficient at times and at other times not – even varying within a day, a shift or an hour. Levels of training may be excellent or up-to-date in one ward and have only begun in another. In addition, factors that may be perfectly safe in isolation may become unsafe in combination with other variables within the system. Adverse events in this model are therefore seen as the result of a conjunction of a number of different factors: it was a lack of adequate supervision, combined with the violation of procedure, combined with the desire to deliver a care package, combined with the lack of reliable communication and checking which allowed the intrathecal administration of an incorrect drug in the best-known of medical adverse events, the Vincristine incident (Toft 2001).

In this way, adverse events can be viewed as emergent, nonlinear and difficult to predict. This represents a move from a deterministic view of organisations to a probabilistic view that raises significant questions with regard to top-down control mechanisms and other traditional methods used in improvement (Hollnagel 2009).

Whatever the issues may be around predictability or the management of organisational risk factors, in health care the application of the system approach is sadly lagging behind its recognition. Though systems factors such as training, team management, task design and communication have been clearly implicated in adverse events or poor quality of care, the factors have not yet been subject to systematic measurement or widely applied improvement programmes.

WHAT ARE 'CLINICAL SYSTEMS'?

An understanding of a systems approach in health care might begin with *Crossing The Quality Chasm* (2001). Following a systems approach to safety pursued in other safety-critical industries, this document identified the 'clinical microsystem' as the front line interface between the patient and the immediate health care individual or team where care is delivered. The practices within a clinical microsystem determine the quality of the

BOX 16.2 FRAMEWORK FOR ANALYSING RISK AND SAFETY IN CLINICAL PRACTICE

The 'London Protocol' (Vincent 2011) for the analysis of clinical incidents, which is based on Vincent et al.'s framework (1998), includes a set of contextual or influencing systems factors that an investigator is urged to consider when trying to understand how things went wrong for a patient.

patient experience but themselves sit within an organisational context. The organisational system in turn resides in a wider political and economic environment and this hierarchy of systems determines through its many interactions how care is provided to the service users.

The links between the organisational system, however, and the clinical microsystem are not well understood. How do organisational systems actually affect clinical care? What are the routes through which this takes place? What factors would need attention and management in order to assure quality and safety? We do not believe that health care has arrived at a clear answer to these questions. When talking about systems, for example, NHS staff often think exclusively in terms of policies, procedures or protocols rather than in terms of the factors that make up the context of the event. Retrospective analyses of why things go wrong frequently ask the question 'Were the appropriate systems in place?' as if preventing recurring events were a simple matter of identifying failing protocols or policies. We believe that this is an insufficiently nuanced view of clinical systems. A more comprehensive appraisal should encompass all the variables that make up the workplace and influence performance. These include tangible factors like procedures, equipment, task support, working conditions and resources but also should include less concrete factors such as team or organisational culture and the explicit or implicit messages communicated throughout the organisation. The most complete approach to understanding these systems factors has been developed by extending Reason's model of organisational accidents. In classifying conditions that would tend to increase error in clinical practice (Vincent et al. 1998), or 'contributory factors', Charles Vincent's 'London Protocol' (Box 16.2) reflects systemic issues that may well go beyond the local area in which a patient safety incident occurred, and therefore highlight areas for change or improvement.

This methodology is not intended, we believe, to address all systems factors that influence care delivery, but to direct the investigator to those factors with a known effect at the point of care (Dean et al. 2002). The factors themselves – such as communication, teamwork and task design – may have their origin in financial policies, information technology or in corporate services more generally, as well as in less tangible factors such as leadership and clinical engagement. Many of these factors are pervasive, in that they extend throughout the organisation, so that identifying them through incident analysis points us to factors that may influence care delivery in many other situations. Identifying these factors and interactions retrospectively, however, does not always lead to systems changes. Interventions following a safety incident are usually local rather than organisational, and findings from many investigations can be difficult to aggregate into meaningful organisational learning.

In fact, the underlying approach to safety management in the NHS is essentially reactive. There is an expectation that Trusts will generate high levels of incident reporting and incident analyses, which should inform managers regarding systems factors and lead to systems changes that cross boundaries and have positive effects on many areas at once. This process becomes difficult in practice for a number of reasons (Nicolini et al. 2011), most cogently because of the persistence of a culture of blame depressing reporting levels and because of difficulties in aggregating findings from many incidents and hence forming a mature view of organisational failings and opportunities.

A SYSTEMS APPROACH TO PATIENT SAFETY

Proactivity

We believe that a systems approach to patient safety must begin by being proactive – that is to say, not waiting until something has already gone wrong for a patient but taking a prospective approach to managing risk. There are a number of techniques routinely used in other safety-critical industries that support this process – the most common ones, used sometimes in health care, being process mapping and failure mode and effect analysis (FMEA). More detailed approaches less commonly used are task-based analyses such as hierarchical task analysis, management of performance influencing factors and other techniques, many of which have emerged from the hybrid discipline of Human Factors.

Human Factors

This discipline falls into two broad approaches, based either on the understanding of the role of the human and his or her tasks in the system

('system-based human factors'), or on key non-technical skills such as communication and teamwork ('person-based human factors'). In both approaches, there is a recognition that the role of humans as both a source of error and a source of safety is crucial and must be understood in advance and in the context of a system. Human error or human factors have been heavily implicated in safety incidents in all industries. Its management can only really be accomplished by building an understanding of the system and the role of human agency proactively, through designing out error traps and waste, supporting error-prone tasks and so on. Human factors accepts that error is inevitable, but also that it can be managed by designing the system to fit with the person rather than the person with the system – to make it easy to do the 'right thing'.

Risk and Reliability

A systems approach to safety would seek to apply these proactive approaches more fully and to use them to begin to unpick the relationships between, for example, microsystems and the larger organisation. In conducting analyses of this nature, there will be a strong focus on identifying and managing risk (the probability of harm) proactively, and on understanding the level of reliability (the probability that a system works according to its specification for a given amount of time) in patient care. Proactive knowledge of risk allows us to review the design of the system; knowledge of the reliability of safety- or quality-critical steps should allow us to design interventions aimed at increasing the reliability of care.

Safety Culture

Safety culture is a quality of the wider organisation describing how individuals, teams and systems understand and manage safety. It is based on individual attitudes, beliefs and behaviours. Most workers believe that safety culture has a material effect on human performance and that it is a critical element in the context of practice. A safe clinical system would therefore exist in a cultural environment that supports safety through openness and fairness, and has a shared understanding of such factors as risk, reliability and error.

BUILDING SAFER CLINICAL SYSTEMS – PHASE 1

'Safer Clinical Systems' is a safety improvement programme introduced and supported by the Health Foundation (2012) in the United Kingdom. Phase 1 of the programme ran across four NHS acute Trusts or Health Boards from 2008 to 2010; phase 2 began in eight Trusts and Boards in 2011.

Phase 1 of the programme supported several safety interventions, all targeted, however, at trying to understand the systems in which the intervention was occurring and how these factors influenced risk to patients and their eventual quality and safety in care. Site teams, supported by a Technical Support Team based at Warwick Medical School, worked to improve pathways of care for vulnerable patients, the availability of clinical information at point of care, handovers in neurology and Hospital at Night and prescribing errors in pharmacies. Site teams were usually a mixture of front-line clinicians and improvement specialists, and the technical support team included practitioners in Lean methodologies, service improvement and human factors specialists.

In this exploratory stage, Safer Clinical Systems sought to understand the utility of the various tools and techniques brought to the sites, their usability as seen by site teams, and the degree to which they informed proactive risk management, safety management and reliability. Learning from phase 1 was captured by the support team and used to design a more closely specified approach for phase 2. During the second phase of Safer Clinical Systems, the programme will focus on two key safety concerns – handovers and prescribing – and use those tools and techniques found most useful during phase 1.

BUILDING SAFER CLINICAL SYSTEMS – PHASE 2

In Phase 1, we used an iterative approach to explore and validate the safer clinical systems concept. It highlighted some key methodologies and measurement processes, and also the wider issues of establishing a sustainable safety culture, at both team and organisational level. It also illustrated the importance of understanding factors that can influence a micro-system that may be common to other micro-systems. In order to understand these influencing factors it was found that a 'zoom-in zoom-out' approach was needed (looking at the microsystem and then the whole system being studied).

The experience of the various projects carried out in phase 1 of Safer Clinical Systems has led to a working definition of Safer Clinical Systems:

> Safer Clinical Systems is a systems approach to building safe and reliable patient care through:
>
> - proactively searching for and managing risk,
> - ensuring feedback to create continuous learning, engagement and sustainable solutions.

> A safer clinical system is a clinical system that delivers high quality care to the patient, is demonstrably free from unacceptable levels of risk and has the resilience to withstand normal and unexpected variations and fluctuations.

To build and measure a safer clinical system will be significantly influenced in its detail by the specific patient pathway under consideration, but there seem to be some common factors in approach that are required. We describe some of these below, together with the methodological approach from phase 2 of the programme. One thing was clear to all involved in Safer Clinical Systems phase 1, and that was that there are no one-line solutions in patient safety, no silver bullet that will solve our problems at a stroke. Health care is complex and takes place in complex systems; there will be many interlinked approaches and interventions for us to understand and validate as the programme unfolds. We begin, however, with a need to understand the organisational context and how this varies between phase 2 award holder sites.

Understanding the Organisational Context

Many safety or quality improvement initiatives fail. Imposed 'solutions' developed from outside the clinical microsystem often fail to engage clinical staff and lack sustainability as a result. Interventions that look perfectly sensible at the outset can be difficult to implement if the wider organisational context doesn't support them, or if the prevailing culture is unwilling to embrace the changes. We believe that understanding the organisational context and factoring this into the design of safety interventions is essential to building sustainable change, and the Safer Clinical Systems programme seeks to address this through beginning the programme with a contextual assessment. In part, this involves a familiarisation phase to ensure that all staff along the chosen patient pathway understand and support the objectives and approach of the project. A more formal appreciation of safety culture and organisational attributes as seen from the perspective of those involved in the site projects is built through two additional processes: the Manchester Patient Safety Framework (MaPSaF) (Parker 2009) and the Safety Culture Index (Spurgeon et al. 2011) – a comprehensive survey tool developed from the Medical Engagement Scale – which assesses norms in key attributes of organisational culture. Taken together, these data provide the site team and the technical support team with a triangulated perspective on context. It includes qualitative views of safety and safety management from key personnel and also a quantitative measure of perceptions of effectiveness, contribution, accountability and development – terms that describe major elements of organisational safety culture. The objective realities that these terms go some way towards measuring are likely to have significant effects on safety interventions, both positive and negative, and need to be understood at each site. Any changes in cultural attributes that result from Safer Clinical Systems may also be detected through these instruments.

Phase 2 Approach and Objectives

The key to the approach that we will use in phase 2 is that it is a structured approach. The teams will apply a systems thinking process that diagnoses safety issues along a patient pathway and attempts to build an understanding of the various factors that influence that pathway. It is undertaken in four steps with peer review and assistance at various stages, to ensure that the interventions undertaken are the most appropriate for that pathway.

Overall objectives for this phase are to:

- Continue to test and develop a new approach to improving patient safety via improving system reliability.
- Design and implement measures demonstrating impact of approach on patient safety.
- Develop a cadre of experts to support others in the UK to improve clinical systems for patient safety and in doing so build internal improvement capability within the NHS.
- Develop a UK-wide evidence base for the application of clinical systems improvement to improve patient safety.

Programme Outline

In Safer Clinical Systems phase 2 we will be working on two topic areas – building safe and reliable prescribing in the patient pathway, and building safe and reliable handovers along the patient pathway (including transfer of clinical information, primary responsibility and authority). These topics have been selected on the basis of successful initiatives in phase 1 of the programme (Box 16.3), though we expect that the methodology could be applied to any clinical area or clinical pathway.

The essential methodology rests heavily on a detailed preliminary diagnostic phase, in contrast to the rapid dive into continuous improvement cycles or waste elimination that characterise most safety initiatives within the NHS. The reason for this lies in the recognition that the safety improvements needed depend not only on efficiencies in local areas, but on the larger system that they reside in – and also on interventions that require dedicated safety input and human factors knowledge. Without

BOX 16.3 SYSTEMS CHANGES AND HUMAN FACTORS IN HOSPITAL AT NIGHT

A senior clinician working on Safer Clinical Systems phase 1 had the responsibility to ensure patient safety in three acute sites. There was considerable organisational resistance to change. Detailed human factors-based task and risk analysis across all sites showed very variable systems, with one site's practices placing patients at an unacceptable level of risk. The use of a structured, consensus-based systems analysis helped to build support for a radical system redesign at the critical site, building in reliable handovers and redundant checks for at-risk patients.

This redesign was based on eliminating risks identified through human factors analysis, taking into account task design and support, risk analysis and ranking, and the effect of performance influencing factors at front line care. Once a reliable design was established across all three sites, the clinician judged that further interventions were needed, again on a human factors basis, to ensure that the handovers themselves were reliably identifying and managing patients most at risk. This involved training in person-based human factors or 'non-technical skills' to help support good leadership, communication and decision-making in the hospital at night teams.

In this case, which was typical of phase 1 work in Safer Clinical Systems, the elements were a knowledge of systems design and systems risk, the involvement and input from staff at all levels, and the application of human factors knowledge.

understanding how these elements interact, we believe that a sustainable solution cannot be developed.

Including a preliminary assessment of context and culture, Safer Clinical Systems has four programme steps:

1. *Pathway definition and context* Scoping the pathway to be developed and its boundaries; qualitative and quantitative assessment of organisational and safety culture; analysis of issues from existing sources including reports, audits and incident analyses.
2. *System diagnosis* High-level mapping of the pathway and its linkages to wider systems; identification of hazards; detailed human factors analysis of critical steps, risk factors and performance

influencing factors; setting reliability measures and targets for outcomes and key processes.

3. *Option planning and appraisal* Define patient safety improvement objectives in risk reduction and reliability improvement; design interventions to be enacted through redesigning 'hard' systems (the things we do to care for patients) and 'soft' systems (the way we interact with patients and each other, and the way we use the hard systems).
4. *System improvement cycles* Carry out and evaluate system improvement cycles; work with site teams to carry out initial system redesign followed by continuous improvement cycles; reassess hazards and risk using the same techniques employed in the diagnostic phase.

These steps are supported by a series of 'gates' whereby diagnostics and option planning are reviewed by the support team. An underlying principle in the working approach will require sites alternately and continuously to 'zoom in' on the problem area and then 'zoom out' to understand the wider system context and influencing factors within which the microsystem is contained.

Tools

Each site will use a core toolkit during each programme step – a toolkit intended not to restrict award holders but to ensure that a common approach can be adopted and evaluated. The tools and techniques initially focus on context (using MapSaf and the Safety Culture Index, for example) before moving on to system diagnosis through using process mapping, failure mode and effect analysis (FMEA) and human factors analysis. All are targeted at the proactive management of risk and patient harm along the pathway, rather than the reaction to adverse events.

During the option planning phase, prospective analyses of the effect of system changes will be carried out – in part using the same toolkit as for diagnostics. We believe that safety and traditional 'efficiency' can sometimes be found in conflict, and therefore improvement cycles will employ both systems redesign and the management of human factors through continuous improvement cycles supplemented by expert input on patient safety.

ASSESSMENT – THE SAFETY CASE

Assessing the safety of a system is at the heart of the Safer Clinical Systems programme. To be comprehensive, an assessment must go beyond reliability measures – though these must be a critical component of an assessment – and evaluate those performance influencing factors which determine human activity in creating safety and process reliability. To be a true assessment, it must be proactive in that it identifies risk within the system and is able to demonstrate that it has been controlled.

Such an assessment can be found in other safety-critical industries and is frequently required by their regulators before operations can be begun. It is called a 'safety case' and will contain information about the system and its boundaries, the assumptions on which the analysis is based, a systematic identification of risk, including that having its origins in human performance, and a combination of rational argument and evidence demonstrating that risk is 'as low as reasonably practicable'.

In health care, there is no direct equivalent to a safety case – and in any event, it is rare that a completely new system is introduced from scratch, where such an approach might be taken. However, we have begun to incorporate this thinking in developing a Systems Safety Appraisal for Safer Clinical Systems as our primary assessment tool. Unlike a true safety case, this assessment must change over time as the system develops. A Safety Case will be written by each award holder at the conclusion of the diagnostic step of the programme to describe how the targeted system sits within the wider organisational context, where the hazards and their associated risks are located, how human factors affect performance, and the baseline reliability measures in outcome and process. Some of this, such as the reliability measures, will be in standard numerical form. Some, however, will be in the form of narrative description and some in the form of system mapping and risk profiling. All will be subject to change as the programme unfolds, so that the Safety Case will be revised at points throughout the programme. The aim will be to demonstrate that the risk profile changes positively, that reliability improves and that patients are cared for safely and effectively. At each iteration, the Safety Case provides a mature assessment of safety, beyond heavily boundaried point measures of safety.

CONCLUSION

By following this approach we hope that in future adverse events the questions will be focused on 'How did the system fail to prevent the individual from making this error?', and 'How did our safety management systems fail to mitigate against this series of events?'

ACKNOWLEDGEMENTS

In preparing this chapter we would like to thank the Health Foundation for their sponsorship of the Safer Clinical Systems programme and other colleagues on the Support Team as well as participating sites.

REFERENCES

'An organisation with a memory. Report of an expert group on learning from adverse events in the NHS' (2000), The Stationery Office.

Aranaz-Andrés, J.M., et al. (2011), 'Prevalence of adverse events in the hospitals of five Latin American countries: results of the "Iberoamerican study of adverse events" (IBEAS)', *BMJ Quality & Safety*, 10.1136/bmjqs.2011.051284.

Benning et al. (2011), 'Large scale organisational intervention to improve patient safety in four UK hospitals: mixed method evaluation', *BMJ*, 342 10.1136/bmj.d195.

Berwick, D.R., C. Calkins, J. McCannon and A.D. Hackbarth (2006), 'The 100 000 lives campaign: setting a goal and a deadline for improving health care quality', JAMA, **295** (3), 324–327.

Brennan T., L. Leape, N. Laird, L. Hebert, A. Localio, A. Lawthers et al. (2004), 'Incidence of adverse events and negligence in hospitalized patients: results of the Harvard Medical Practice Study I', *Quality and Safety in Health Care*, **13**, 145–52.

Crossing the Quality Chasm: A New Health System for the 21st Century (2001), Committee on Quality Health Care in America, Institute of Medicine, Washington: National Academy Press.

Davis, P., R. Lay-Yee, R. Briant, W. Ali, A. Scott and S. Schug (2002), 'Adverse events in New Zealand public hospitals I: occurrence and impact', *New Zealand Medical Journal*, **115** (1167): U271.

de Vries, E., M. Ramrattan, S. Smorenburg, D. Gouma and M. Boermeester (2008), 'The incidence and nature of in-hospital adverse events: a systematic review', *Quality and Safety in Health Care*, **17** (3), 216–23.

Dean, B., M. Schachter, C. Vincent and N. Barber (2002), 'Causes of prescribing errors in hospital inpatients: a prospective study', *Lancet*, **359** (9315), 1373–1378.

Forster, A.J., H. Clark, A. Menard, N. Dupuis, R. Chernish, N. Chandok et al. (2004), 'Adverse events among medical patients after discharge from hospital', *Canadian Medical Association Journal*, **170** (3), 345–49.

Health Foundation (2012), *Safer Clinical Systems*. http://www.health.org.uk/areas-of-work/programmes/safer-clinical-systems/.

Hollnagel, E. (2004), *Barriers and Accident Prevention*, Ashgate.

Hollnagel, E. (2009), *An Application of the Functional Resonance Analysis Method (FRAM) to Risk Assessment of Organisational Change*, Stockholm, Sweden: Swedish Nuclear Inspectorate.

Kohn, L., J. Corrigan and M.S. Donaldson (2000), *To Err Is Human: Building a Safer Health System*, National Research Council, Washington, DC: The National Academies Press.

Landrigan, C.P., G.J. Parry, C.B. Bones, A.D. Hackbarth, D.A. Goldmann and P.J. Sharek et al. (2010), 'Temporal trends in rates of patient harm resulting from medical care', *NEJM*, **363**, 22, November.

Nicolini, D., J. Waring and J. Mengis (2011), 'The challenges of undertaking root cause analysis in health care: a qualitative study', *Journal of Health Services Research and Policy*, **16**, 34–41.

Parker, D. (2009), 'Managing risk in healthcare: understanding your safety culture using the Manchester Patient Safety Framework (MaPSaF)', *Journal of Nursing Management*, **17** (2), 218–222.

Reason, J. (1997), *Managing the Risks of Organisational Accidents*, Aldershot: Ashgate.

Schiøler, T., H. Lipczak, B.L. Pedersen, T.S. Mogensen, K.B. Bech, A. Stockmarr et al. (2001) [Incidence of adverse events in hospitals. A retrospective study of medical records], *Ugeskr Laeger*, **163** (39), 5370–8.

Soop, M., U. Fryksmark, M. Köster and B. Haglund (2009), 'The incidence of adverse events in Swedish hospitals: a retrospective medical record review study', *International Journal for Quality in Health Care*, 1 August, **21** (4), 285–91.

Spurgeon, P., J. Clark, C. Ham and B. Keogh (2011), *Medical Leadership: From the Dark Side to Centre Stage*, Radcliffe.

Toft, B. (2001), 'External Inquiry into the adverse incident that occurred at Queen's Medical Centre, Nottingham, 4th January 2001', London: Department of Health.

Vincent, C. (2011), *Patient Safety*, 2nd Edition, Wiley-Blackwell.

Vincent, C., S. Taylor Adams and N. Stanhope (1998), 'Framework for analysing risk and safety in clinical medicine', *BMJ*, 316 doi: 10.1136/bmj.316.7138.1154.

Vincent, C., G. Neale and M. Woloshynowych (2001), 'Adverse events in British hospitals: preliminary retrospective record review', *British Medical Journal*, **322** (7285) 517–9.

Walshe, K., and N. Offen (2001), 'A very public failure: lessons for quality improvement in healthcare organisations from the Bristol Royal Infirmary',*Quality and Safety in Health Care*, **10** (4), 250–256.

PART V

Concluding comments

17. Concluding comments

Peter Spurgeon, Ronald J. Burke and Cary L. Cooper

Each reader will take from each chapter in this text whatever resonates with them and whatever he/she sees as meaningful to their own context and way of thinking. These final comments represent only what we consider to be important by abstraction from the range of topics and disciplines covered here. Our aim was to consider how the virtually universal challenge of financial constraint upon health systems could be met whilst maintaining (or improving) the quality of service provision and meeting the steadily rising demands and expectations. Health care delivery is heavily dependent upon its staff/employees and so the human resources function, in its widest sense, should be making an important contribution to meeting the challenge.

Perhaps a particular challenge identified was that of providing much more evidence of the link between the use of good HR techniques and organisational performance. A few examples exist in the literature (Ferlie and Shortell 2001; Harris et al. 2007) but the value of HR as a mediator of performance has not yet become mainstream thinking in the health sector. Under pressure organisations are much more likely to turn to their finance department than their OD specialist. Yet flexible and new ways of utilising the skills in the workforce aligned to changing work practices via modern technology may well be a much more effective way of producing large-scale savings.

Our sense is that it could, in that we (as represented by authors here) have relevant and valuable concepts and processes to offer. However, we also sense a degree of frustration in that despite knowing some of the strands of thinking that would help, we (as health systems) struggle with the process of delivery and implementation. There appears to be a reluctance to learn from the past and to incorporate learning into our whole system. Rather there seems a preference for current fashion, for ideas that are a re-working of older ones and, perhaps most debilitating of all, a focus on short term solutions.

Bohmer (2010) rather harshly ascribes much of this frustration and failure to enact to poor management practice. Given the current financial turmoil attributable in part at least to the banking crisis and the number of household name companies contracting or folding, it is perhaps a little too easy to attribute the problems of the health sector to poor management. Market based health systems certainly do not compare well with tax based systems in terms of efficiency. Perhaps a more reasonable challenge is that of McAlearney (2006) who points to the relative lack of focus on leadership development in the health sector. This is perhaps especially true of clinician leadership where these broader non-clinical skills have not typically been part of the educational basis of clinical training. Spurgeon et al. (2011) confirm this position in the UK but also go on to describe a systematic innovation in medical education that is beginning to address the issue. The different perspectives of clinician and manager can certainly be a difficulty in taking forward radical change.

Authors write to the challenge of implementation and sustaining change. Yet the literature, not just academic but based on organisational experience, on creating and supporting change is vast. It is clear that organisations perform better and sustain this level of performance if they function in an open culture that engenders trust and engagement. Leadership styles that facilitate the emergence of such cultures are reasonably well documented. It seems then that at some level we know what to do but for a variety of reasons we just don't do it.

Is this due to a failure of leadership or more specifically of leadership training? Creating the right culture, appropriate environments for positive comment and engagement from the workforce is repeatedly described as key. Yet cases of bullying by health system managers are increasing, staff in the health sector have very high levels of stress, and many are demotivated by continual criticism and the highlighting of deficiencies in performance.

Health systems present a challenging work context, especially today in the face of the well documented challenges. It is unsurprising that under such pressure managers revert to more hierarchical and directive behaviours in an attempt to hit targets and save resources. The need for creativity and innovation in the way services are shaped and provided has never been greater. But innovation does not just happen and is unlikely to be fostered by hectoring or exhortation. Rather it requires (yet again) a conducive environment and this in itself needs sustained support and encouragement to emerge.

As Williams (2011) concludes, in a review of the current literature on how organisations innovate, the process requires 'a multi-determinant and multi-layer approach'. He talks of ensuring that organisational strategies, including incentives to support adoption of new ideas, are in place. These will involve leadership at all levels, boundaries between working groups being permeable and hierarchical groupings being replaced with open, multifunctional networks.

Even when good practice is identified there is a difficulty in its widescale uptake and also sustainability. Perhaps one very clear message here is that change must become embedded in the system. If it is isolated then however good it is the gradual inertia of maintenance and work pressures will see it eroded.

Perhaps the two most powerful concepts to emerge from the arguments in this text as to how HR processes may contribute to a radical and sustained improvement in health systems are:

1. A need for much more holistic systems thinking rather than well-meaning but often fragmented and inconsistent change initiatives.
2. Individual and organisational leadership processes that foster environments where the potential of the workforce can be harnessed.

Both elements are possible, both will take time to be successful but unless we commit to this direction health systems will battle on buffeted by political and financial storms lacking the internal resilience to transform quality to the highest standards of care possible.

Many examples of good HR practice exist – Erwin (2009) linking executive leadership to hospital financial performance; Mowles et al. (2010) linking complexity theory to service improvement; and Baker et al. (2010) documenting significant improvements in the delivery of day-care across four countries. There are certainly others and some are documented here in this text. But the great challenges are to build these isolated initiatives into a coherent body of knowledge and practice in the HR/health sector and to ensure that they move from being 'good projects' to sustainable service delivery.

REFERENCES

Baker, G.R., J.L. Denis, M.P. Pomey and A. MacIntosh-Murray (2010), 'Designing effective governance for quality and safety in Canadian healthcare', *Healthcare Quarterly*, **13**, 38–45.

Bohmer, R.M.J.C. (2010), 'Fixing health care on the front lines', *Harvard Business Review*, April, 62–69.

Erwin, D. (2009), 'Changing organisational performance: examining the change process', *Hospital Topics. Research and Perspectives on Healthcare*, **87**, 28–40.

Ferlie, F., and S.M. Shortell (2001), 'Improving the quality of health care in the

United Kingdom and the United States: a framework for change', *The Millbank Quarterly*, **79**, 281.
Harris, C., P. Cortvriend and P. Hyde (2007), 'Human resource management and performance in healthcare organisations', *Journal of Health Organisation and Management*, **21**, 448–459.
McAlearney, A.S. (2006), 'Leadership development in health care: a qualitative study', *Journal of Organisational Behaviour*, **217**, 967–982.
Mowles, C., A. Van Der Gaag and J. Fox (2010), 'The practice of complexity: review, change and service improvement in an NHS department', *Journal of Health Organisation and Management*, **21**, 1127–1134.
Spurgeon, P., J. Clark and C. Ham (2011), 'Medical leadership: from the dark side to centre stage', Oxford: Radcliffe.
Williams, I. (2011), 'Organisational readiness for innovation in health care: some lessons from the recent literature', *Health Services Management Research*, **24**, 213–218.--

Index